WALKING THE GREAT NORTH LINE

*From Stonehenge to Lindisfarne to
Discover the Mysteries of
Our Ancient Past*

ROBERT TWIGGER

WEIDENFELD & NICOLSON

First published in Great Britain in 2020 by Weidenfeld & Nicolson
an imprint of The Orion Publishing Group Ltd
Carmelite House, 50 Victoria Embankment
London EC4Y 0DZ

An Hachette UK Company

1 3 5 7 9 10 8 6 4 2

A CIP catalogue record for this book is available
from the British Library.

ISBN (Hardback): 978 1 4746 0905 0
ISBN (eBook): 978 1 4746 0907 4

Typeset by Input Data Services Ltd, Somerset

Printed and bound in Great Britain by Clays Ltd, Elcograf S.p.A.

MIX
Paper from
responsible sources
FSC® C104740

www.weidenfeldandnicolson.co.uk
www.orionbooks.co.uk

WALKING
THE GREAT
NORTH LINE

'He who only England knows, knows not England'

RUDYARD KIPLING

To Samia

CONTENTS

SO ARE WE TALKING LEY LINES HERE? NOT REALLY. LEY LINES ARE THE 1920s INVENTION OF ALFRED WATKINS. LEY LINES ARE OBSER--VABLE ALIGNMENTS OF CHURCHES, HILLS, WELLS AND STANDING STONES, BUT THEY DON'T ALIGN WITH NORTH, SOUTH, EAST OR WEST.

ALFRED J. WATKINS PHOTOGRAPHING LEY LINES.

SACRED WELLS AND SPRINGS ABOUND.

IN THE SAME WAY THAT CHURCHES WERE BUILT ON ANCIENT SITES, WELLS AND SPRINGS OF PAGAN SIGNIFICANCE WERE RECONSECRATED AS HOLY WELLS.

WHAT I HAD BEGUN TO CALL THE GREAT NORTH LINE RAN REMARKABLY CLOSE TO THE EAST-WEST WATER--SHED DIVIDING LINE. IT WAS WHERE MANY STREAMS AND RIVERS STARTED. MOVING WATER CHANGES AND CHARGES WITH SUBTLY DIFFERENT ENERGY ALL SUCH PLACES, ALL SOURCES.

GREAT NORTH LINE (1° 50' WEST)

---- = DIVIDE LINE FOR WATER FLOWING EAST OR WEST.

1

FALSE STARTS AND REAL STARTS

'To convince someone of what is true, it is not enough to state it; we must find the road from error to truth.'

Ludwig Wittgenstein*

It was quite typical of the enterprise that I didn't even start at the beginning.

I had been buggering about for a while now, threatening to start, visiting Christchurch in Dorset where the Line starts but then crying off, telling my wife the weather was wrong or on one occasion that the trains were cancelled so I couldn't be sure of arriving before nightfall. I was all mixed up, in the wrong headspace, in a right funk, a suitably *Boy's Own* word for a *Boy's Own* adventure. Except this was only a stroll, a walk in the park. Well, not only.

The Great North Line was what it was mostly about. From Christchurch to Old Sarum to Stonehenge, to Avebury, to Notgrove barrow, to Meon Hill, to Thor's Cave, to Arbor Low stone circle, to Mam Tor, to Ilkley and its three stone circles and the Swastika Stone, to several forts and camps in Northumberland, to Lindisfarne (plus about thirty more sites en route). A single dead straight line following 1 degree 50 West through Britain – and I meant to walk it. If I could ever start.

I had found the Great North Line by accident, extending the known north–south orientation of Stonehenge and Avebury and Old Sarum upwards and downwards. The palpable pleasure and shock at discovering the Line ended at Lindisfarne, a place of mystery I had

* Ludwig Wittgenstein (trans. A. C. Miles and R. Rhees), *Remarks on Frazer's Golden Bough* (Byrnmill, 1979).

long wanted to see, convinced me then and there that I had to do this.

But then I got nervous. Wasn't this all cognitive bias? Finding proof because it supported my point of view? In a scientific frame of mind, I drew arrow-straight north–south lines up the OS Map of ancient sites in Britain. The lines (oriented to true north) were roughly twenty miles apart. One, the line through the Uffington White Horse and the Rollright Stones, was promising: both lie on the same north–south line. But then it peters out in Lincolnshire. No other lines come close to the forty-two ancient sites of note on the Great North Line. I had some proof.

Actually I had a correlation. Nothing more. Well, I had a suggestive coincidence, in the parlance of scepticism. Could I make it bear any more weight than this? I thought I could. I was fondly hoping to develop ideas about England's 'primitive' past and to point out that ancient man was just as intelligent as we are. Indeed as the philosopher Ludwig Wittgenstein writes of James Frazer, author of *The Golden Bough*, 'Frazer is much more savage than most of his savages, for these savages will not be so far from any understanding of spiritual matters as an Englishman of the twentieth century. His explanations of the primitive observances are much cruder than the sense of the observances themselves.'*

At this point in the story, if I'm telling someone new, they usually butt in with: 'Is it a ley line?' As if knowing the right label will help. No, don't get me wrong, I'm not a scoffer. I have a soft spot for strange earth energies and power places and other sundry interesting things, it's just that even the ley line people can't agree what a ley line is, beyond being a fairly short alignment of significant ancient sites, hills and churches. Just calling the Line a ley line doesn't really get us anywhere.

A coincidence, a piece of anecdotal evidence if you like. But the mulch of hard science is anecdotal evidence. It was the folk cure of chewing willow tree bark that lead researchers to salicylic acid, the active ingredient in aspirin.

What headache was I going to cure? My own for a start.

---

* Wittgenstein, *Remarks*.

*

To develop that earlier thought about not starting at the beginning, there should be a word for the instinct to start things in a half-arsed fashion (Farsing? Harsing?), as if starting properly will jinx the enterprise, set it up on too high and unachievable a pedestal. The instinct to start in a half-arsed way for fear you'll never start at all.

A couple of weeks earlier I had been down at the real start, at Hengistbury Head, fully loaded with my gear. This was another dry run where I was 'testing' my umbrella – I mean how can you test an umbrella, really? The umbrella as a backpacking essential was a new departure for me, brought up as I was in 1980s cagoules. Various people and a trip to the Himalayas had convinced me that a brolly, lightweight with a sawn-off handle, was a very useful aide; but we'd see. It was OK on my walk into town, but what about on a breezy mountainside somewhere up north? I'd nearly been blown off a cliff while wearing a poncho that inconveniently turned into a giant hang glider (or one of those suits that resemble a flying squirrel) when an onshore wind suddenly switched 180 degrees; wouldn't an umbrella be a similar liability? Another piece of kit that might need to be curtailed in high wind was one I was particularly fond of: the rain kilt. Made of super lightweight and 100 per cent waterproof Cuben Fiber (developed for racing sails and probably hang gliders too), it hung around the waist like an untucked shirt. When it rained you dragged it down to make it into a kilt that didn't look *too* bad. You could always roll it up again going into shops and pubs. If you remembered.

Why was Hengistbury Head the real start? Because it was where Christchurch (the southernmost town on the Line) hit the sea. Walk a short distance from the beachside of the Head and you are in the town, the home to an ancient priory, and a perfect Norman motte-and-bailey castle.

The Head strangely mimics Lindisfarne, which is three hundred or more miles away at the opposite end of the Line. Both are peninsulas reached by a causeway, which is tidal in the case of Lindisfarne (making it an island for half the day). Both show signs of inhabitation since the earliest times. There are Palaeolithic remains on

Hengistbury Head that predate the end of the last Ice Age by a few thousand years. Then, the English Channel was the outflow of a great river fed by the Rhine and the Thames, and was 120 metres lower than it is today. The Head, with its modest sandy peak, would have been one of the first landmarks you'd see approaching England on foot, or later, by boat.

Hengistbury Head also has the most expensive real estate, per square foot, anywhere in England. But not houses – beach huts. Hengistbury huts sell for hundreds of thousands. Five went in 2015 for a million pounds. This is for something you'd normally store garden tools in. But, then, as ancient man knew, Hengistbury Head is special.

There is an impressive double dyke protecting the bulk of the promontory from attackers. And numerous Bronze Age burial mounds have been detected. Now the place is favoured by long-boarders as the windy paths that curve gently downhill make for easy skateboarding fun.

My parents agreed to drive me to Christchurch railway station, which I had designated as the new start point, being two kilometres from the real start etc. etc. My 79-year-old parents. Me in the back, a fifty-something cuckoo in a rather comfy nest; on-board Wi-Fi and GPS. Sign of the times: modern man seeks adventure while remaining an eternal child cossetted by Ma and Pa. Here at the station I would meet two other modern men: Nigel and Joe, who had both been on an earlier trip with me, crossing Canada in a birchbark canoe some years before.

Snug in the back of the Nissan Note, I was reminded of other camping adventures in which my parents had kindly involved themselves long after what would have been considered normal by the more conventionally minded. Quite a few starts and a few ignominious rescues too; they never held my failures to finish the Cleveland Way, the South Downs Way or even the nearby Ridgeway against me. Always there with a smile and a car that didn't need MOT-ing.

Joe and Nigel were on time and fully loaded with their own gear. Gear is always a big deal at the beginning of an expedition, even a modest one like this. The whole trip threatens to pivot on single bits of kit that you'll probably chuck away much later or completely disregard. Things like special waterproof towels, mosquito head nets or spare mess tins. And of course you'll completely overlook some piece of kit that is of crucial importance. There is a certain kind of walking book that revels in *not* mentioning kit or blisters or other workaday aspects of hiking – all of which play a *huge* part in the first days of a walk. If you're averagely fortunate, you gradually solve the physical problem of moving forward under your own steam and you start to think about other things. So by the time you write the book you've forgotten the hardship and pain and the gear you put so much pathetic hope in. Well, in this book the pain will not be forgotten.

You can get very close to certain key items of kit. One of the most moving passages in Reinhold Messner's book about climbing Everest solo without oxygen is when he realises he's lost his old friend his rucksack, and then, to make matters even more tragic, his ice axe. He breaks down and cries, not because he can't climb any more – he can – it's the emotional loss that sears his hypoxic soul.

I had lots of gimmicks and gizmos including a new very fancy sleeping bag (which I suspected was too small, had slept indoors with, had asked for a refund, been refused, so hoped wasn't) and a very lightweight and also new tent – but tried and tested boots (or were they too old?). Nigel had new footwear but was borrowing my old sleeping mat as his son was using his. Joe lived in Canada and had scavenged some rather ratty old stuff from UK-based friends. He never got blisters, and I suspected it had something to do with his high-arched walk, almost on tip toes.

Neither was coming for the entire walk, which would take several months; they were just coming for as long as they could stand it, or me.

I had seen neither of them for several years. There was an air of reunion about the car park, and my parents didn't hang about; they had never cramped my style, even now, when I wouldn't have minded them doing so. We laughed and shook hands and cracked jokes and set off with big rucksacks for the River Avon valley, tramping down empty suburban alleyways well signposted with anti-dog-fouling signs and new roads through industrial estates; there is something quite thrilling in such a mundane start. Of course you feel a tad over-dressed when you have to lumber off the pavement for a mum, her pushchair and the kids coming home from school, but, like an astro-naut in his reflecting helmet and clumpy boots, you feel elevated, different, alien, a privileged visitor and not just another poor sod living in the *real world*.

We left Christchurch at lunchtime and by the afternoon we had reached Ringwood. Walking too fast (I didn't want to hold up the group . . . yet) past St Catherine's Hill, I noted the odd fort-like con-struction deemed now to be a Stone Age animal pound. Such con-structions that mimic the design of forts and camps and henges yet seem too small (or even too large) would become a common sight as I went up the Line. But I had nothing really to judge this first one by: a ditch, a circular bank, not much to look at, move on. I was able to tick off the first ancient site on the Line but it left me a little troubled about the way the adventure would unfold. Would the shamanistic heritage of such places infect our journey in a useful way, maybe driving us all a little crazy but in a good way, or would each element of the walk remain aloof and separate and fail to connect up? Well, you plod on, ever hopeful.

And then, in a development that would surely have cheered Jack Kerouac, who was always suffering from poor footwear, after only eight miles of walking I already had the hot foot prickle of new blis-ters. I had show-off stridden through the flooded fields either side of the Avon. Nigel had prevaricated, angling for a dry path; looking about with his head tipped back and prominent Adam's apple, he looked like a heron scouting for prey. Then he and Joe had tiptoed their way through the lush grass floating wave-like in the water. In these flooded meadows there was birdsong, even if I couldn't see the birds. 'Peewit,' said Nigel, staking out his role as team ornithologist (every group has to have one). 'Curlew.' Not only did he look like a bird, he loved to see and hear them, drawing some kind of solace from their very existence, but at the same time demonstrating that oddly solipsistic effect I've noticed with other bird watchers who somehow convey that a perfect world would be just birds ... and bird watchers. No one else allowed. And why didn't I know he was such an expert already? I couldn't remember him knowing much about wildlife before. With old friends you assume they are in aspic or suspended animation until you meet again. They aren't supposed to change even if you do. Meeting them can be a rude awakening, like those pop-up messages that demand valuable time to update a computer program you were quite happy with before and want to use *right now*. The old one worked, wasn't it good enough?

And how had Joe changed? I would find out soon enough. Both lads were just as fit as they used to be; I probably wasn't but that didn't really matter. Joe, I was especially careful with. Two previous expeditions with him had been riven by strife and discord, so now I was friendly, maybe too friendly, but cautious. The discord had been before I had children of my own, and dealing with Joe had been a little like dealing with a teenager prone to tantrums. Anyway, I was a little more aware of what causes kids to get stroppy – transitions, for example, which is something you never suspect when you start out as a parent.

But the first incredible revelation was that Joe, now thirty-eight, had four kids ... by three different mothers. Nigel and I (both fifty-four), both on a standard issue two-apiece from one mum, were both moderately gobsmacked. It was the kind of news I wasn't used to hearing in my rather sheltered life. Last we heard, Joe was the reluctant father of one ... That said, I should describe Joe a little more fully. Born in the UK to a Canadian mother and an English father, Joe had been a child acting star at seventeen, a Magnum photography trainee at nineteen, and had been offered a lead role in a feature film when he was twenty (which he turned down). But Joe had a dark side and whenever success came too easily he ran away from it. Finally he had settled down in Toronto as a tree surgeon and was highly successful, with several trucks and a team of employees. I remembered him as a confused 25-year-old tree planter – and here he was, sorting accountancy problems out on his phone deep in the Hampshire countryside. Wow – Joe could do stuff I couldn't!

And the second revelation was that Nigel was depressed. He was on medication and in therapy. I had an intimation of this, suspected things weren't quite right. Over the preceding months, I'd learnt to recognise the signs in others: another friend had told me he was on medication for anxiety; a third had tried to commit suicide, failed, tried again but was now stable. He was also on meds and in group therapy.

The world, my little part of it, could no longer be assumed to be rising, on the up and up. Part of it was going down. For a long time I'd thought the mental health crisis was 'out there', affecting others, not people I knew. Encouraged by Nigel's revelation, Joe, too, told us he had been through depression a few years back. He'd taken these meds that allowed him to drink as much as he liked without getting drunk, plus causing the dangerous side-effect that he thought he was invincible. It was during this upsurge of invincibility that one of his children had been conceived in the US – and not Canada, where he lived, which made it even more inconvenient.

I hoped without saying as much that this walk would be a cure of sorts for Nigel. He told me he'd taken time off for it from his therapy (which he said he needed very much), managing a cheery smile you couldn't help examining for signs of strain. None seemed that apparent in the car park in Ringwood, where I gamely offered to fill up our water bottles in the public loos.

The loo was modern, even high-tech; it had a hot water tap that extended out of a tank above the basin. I couldn't find the cold water. Hot water would be fine. When the bottle was half full, I thought gosh this water has some kind of natural fizziness, maybe a local mineral water supply – but oh no, I had filled it with soap.

How could I have made such a mistake? Some sort of performance anxiety? Intent on 'being helpful', my brain had skidded over what was right in front of my eyes. Now I had to scrub out and clean the soapy bottle. And no matter how many times I did this (loads, having found the water button was activated by holding the bottle in the right place), the taste of soap lasted for at least a week afterwards.

I didn't tell Joe that I had part-filled his bottle with soap too. Not as much as mine, not by a long chalk. I didn't want to upset him. Joe had that effect on you.

Wittgenstein wrote: '[T]oo little is made of the fact that we include the words "soul" and "spirit" in our own civilised vocabulary. Compared with this, the fact that we do not believe our soul eats and drinks is a minor detail.' Never mind the ups and downs of the walk, this was just as powerful a motivation: nothing more than an exploration of the England that used to believe in souls that ate and drank. But not a bookish exploration, not another perusal of the library shelf; the evidence I was after would be intuitive, fleeting, known because of a sharpened sense of knowing, sharpened by the walk itself. The intellectual case for this strengthened every year. Evidence had been mounting slowly in the last two decades, through the work of such archaeologists as David Lewis-Williams, David Pearce and Jean Clottes, that the roots of knowledge in prehistoric man lay not in random superstition but in working shamanism. Earlier writers such as Mircea Eliade had hinted at this, but the new writers were more academically respectable and mainstream.

By unpicking the experience of modern shamans still operating with indigenous peoples from Siberia to South America, Lewis-Williams presents a case that explains the truly bizarre rock art, monuments and artefacts of ancient man. And he explains it in a way that has no recourse to those tired old chestnuts 'fertility doll', 'fetish' or 'ritual sacrifice'. In other words, for the first time, ancient man is made believable and understandable – because he, or she, is no longer presumed to be a child. He or she is assumed to be just as intelligent and several yards wiser than we are.

The Line was an alignment of ancient sites. Alignment is a key aspect of shamanism. It refers to the need to be in accordance with nature, your environment, your future and your past. I increasingly saw people who had all kinds of symptoms as basically misaligned. I know I was. Walking up England, my land, was about finding the wisdom of this place, wisdom buried by the ancients when they built the Line . . .

AND NOW THE PRACTICAL STUFF: SAVING WEIGHT IS **KEY!**

SUPERLIGHT SLEEPING BAG

RAIN PONCHO THAT BECOMES

A TENT!

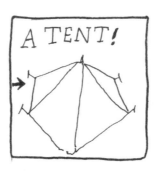

ERGONOMIC WALKING POLE THAT BECOMES

A TENT POLE!

STAINLESS STEEL MESS TIN FOR COOKING

AND EATING.

DETACHABLE VEST + SLEEVES

MAKES JACKET FOR ALL CLIMES.

SWISS ARMY KNIFE AND A SINGLE SPOON.

LONG JOHNS AND WOOL VEST ARE YOUR ONLY SPARE CLOTHES.

2

FIRE AND WATER

It should be easy finding water in a damp place like England. There's water everywhere. Too much, half the time, what with flood plains being built over and run-off with nowhere to go. Yet, funnily enough, finding water *is* a problem when walking through England, sometimes more so than dryer but remoter places. The problem is societal rather than geological. In the past, every village and town had water troughs for draft animals and water fountains, pumps and springs for the populace. In the last fifty years these have all but dried up. Privatised water companies put the final nail in the coffin: where's the money in maintaining a communal water supply? Bastards!

Paranoia about chemical run-off, liver fluke, bovine tuberculosis and other nasty stuff puts you off taking a long cool slug of river water unless it's treated in some way. But filtration is fiddly and Puritabs don't work if there is floating matter in the water. Boiling is usually your best option, but again you need to be sure nothing is floating around in your water.

Asking farmers for water used to be what walkers did. I often obtained water and even milk as a boy walking across Derbyshire and the Lake District. But the spread of rural crime in the last few decades and the increase in the trendiness of walking has changed things a little. Though most farmers remain friendly, there is a greater separation between farm folk and town folk, and all walkers are assumed to be townies now. It's like the weird distinction in North America between rednecks and urbanites. Two tribes.

I feel I belong to both. My grandfather was a farmer. My mother started driving a tractor during harvest when she was twelve. I grew up spending my holidays on a farm, one that oddly enough lies on the Line, yet when I walk across a stranger's farm and see the growing number of 'private' and 'keep out' signs, and the farmer zooms by on his quad without a greeting, just a beady-eyed look in my direction, I can't help feeling a little out of place. Increasingly I like to tell myself that long before there were farmers and landowners, England was full of communal agricultural land. It is our land by right, even if quadbike man is making a profit out of it. Land is a funny thing: it's a constantly growing store of monetary value, and that adds another wrinkle – walking across it is like sightseeing in someone else's bank vault. But you can't take it with you and, after all, as Tolstoy's famous story puts it: how much land does a man really need?[1]

So this increasingly complicated relationship between landowners and those who walk across it makes asking for water a bit of a pain. Not that I imagine you'd be turned down, but the possibility of it happening means you explore easier avenues first.

Like buying the stuff in big plastic polluting bottles. Unless you own a Sawyer bag-filter. A water filtration system with no moving parts, it works by squeezing a super-strong bag to force the water through a filter that takes out everything you need be worried about. I've used the Sawyer everywhere from Himalayan villages to dodgy hotels to even taking water from a puddle. No problems. At all.

But it does take a little time (fifteen minutes a litre with all the mucking about) and it does look weird. So, again, something that's easier in remote spots than built-up ones. Until, like all truly acclimatised street people, you lose your inhibitions about performing domestic tasks in full view.

First water, then fire. You can't go camping without a fire. And this walk, past all those old stones, those ancient sites, needed the elemental, so the element of fire should not be excluded.

You bond better round a fire. Slinking off after a gas-cooked ready meal just isn't the same. The fire can be small, even symbolic. I've sat with Bedouin late into the night round embers that are barely glowing. Beside the Zambesi river, a hollow scooped into the sand with three large candles protected from the breeze sufficed as a true campfire; I don't think any of the canoeing group noticed the difference. But tonight we wanted a real fire, I think, reminiscent of our Canadian trip when we burnt poplar logs, the gnawed-off remains washed down from countless beaver dams, heaped high to make great bonfires on the beaches of the rivers of Alberta and British Columbia. A nostalgic fire.

And sitting round a fire is an act of nostalgia. It connects you to the past, to all fires you've ever experienced, all fires you have ever seen, and the most ancient and primordial fires of our ancestors. To deny the camper and backpacker fire is a little mean to say the least . . . As for all those forest fires, well very often it turns out that arson and arsing about with petrol and lighters are the cause – not a sensible backwoods campfire. The solution, as I see it, is a fire-making course for all school children, preferably involving flint and steel or a hand drill, to teach them a real skill rather than the laptop lunacy of desperate teachers: introductory MS Office or GarageBand . . . I jest, but only just.

In the wonderfully titled *The Psychoanalysis of Fire*, Gaston Bachelard writes persuasively about the impossibility of being objective about fire. The way we have studied it and conceptualised it, our experiential attitude to it, is conditioned by our time in the cave. Which is most of the human story. His mockery of early science is fun too, though, I understand, riddled with errors; *tant pis*: Bachelard is an author who liberates the sense of the poetic from the musty-scented confines of Emily Dickinson's stocking drawer, out into the fire-scorched, water-drenched, windblown reality of living.

Now we were on the fine uphill section to the plateau of the New Forest it was growing closer to dusk. We toiled up a long bracken slope close to the village of Mockbeggar, then up Summerlug Hill and past the Pillow Mounds, burial barrows shaped like big lumpy pillows. That barrows are omnipresent in our landscape, thousands of years after they were made, is extraordinary in itself. It's hard to go on a walk through the English countryside without seeing evidence of our distant but direct ancestors. Walking through America or Canada isn't the same. Anything ancient there belongs to an entirely different group of people, maybe native folk we have abused in the past. Archaeology is always mixed with shame in conquered lands. All that is too far in the past here. And, cosy irrelevance though it is,

I *am* a native. As an aide to empathy, and a counterbalance perhaps to inflated ideas of self, knowing you share DNA with the people in those ancient graves is a help.

Mockbeggar and Summerlug: old English words that convey their meaning without further research. You can know too much, it can get in the way. On this walk I'd be speaking the poetry of the names, not looking them up on Google. And now we are on the darkening moor, beside the New Forest but not, in a strict legal sense (checking the map here), in it; the nasty *no fire* rules don't apply to us. In only a few yards, the common we are upon feels instantly wild and ancient, in the way that happens all the time in England. One minute you're on a manicured road of houses backing on to a golf course, or an A-road avoiding the steady stream of slick campervans and shiny Mercs; and the next minute, stepping over a drystone wall, across a boggy field, dodging a few cowpats and over another stile and you are here: seemingly pristine wilderness. There are no house lights on the horizon, the forest reveals itself in the distance as successive layers of dark, like subtly graded flats in a theatre. It certainly feels wild.

As if to confirm this, a large herd of fallow deer (the wilderness being defined by profligate quantities of wildlife in groups, herds, swoops, murders, batches, troons, zardars) spreads out on an opposing bracken hill, cheekily close to us – in fact unafraid either through over exposure to walkers or because they are protected and have never been fired on in anger.

'That's a white hind,' said Nige, always the first to notice things. I couldn't see it myself, then did. Joe too.

'A white hind,' we repeated dutifully, hoping by this archaic locution for some of the obvious magic and symbolism to rub off on us. And indeed, despite their constant movement, the others in the group by some sort of self-organising instinct surround this animal, like ancient Japanese bodyguards with an utterly precise instinct for *maai*, distance and space, so there was always an aesthetically correct number of brown deer encircling the majestic white hind.

'It's almost as if they're protecting it,' said Nige, and because we said nothing it was obvious that we all agreed – and this was a good omen with regard to the forthcoming camp.

Though, to be honest, nowhere looked promising. We'd left Enid Blyton land somewhere back on the common and now were in a work by Tolkien, darker and more mysterious. As if to confirm this, a sparrowhawk flew overhead. Nige saw it first of course, just as he had spotted the red kite earlier prompting the usual red-kite diatribe – spreading everywhere, those red kites. As the light grew dimmer, and not being in a pub but perhaps wishing we were, we bandied more pubtalk about the ethics of releasing birds of prey.

'They crowd out other species,' I said.

'Kites eat songbirds,' said Nigel.

'But they also eat roadkill,' said Joe, and we all laughed with warm nostalgia because on our Canadian trip we'd been asked if we ate roadkill by some tourists we met and Nigel had honestly answered, 'Where we've been, there aren't any roads.' But after laughing now all we wanted was a fire and a place to put up tents.

In the gloom up ahead was a stand of pine trees, elderly and with good gaps between them. No paths, but no path was needed. We blundered into the middle of the wood and found a pile of dry branches left by a group of would-be survivalists or kids building leaf shelters. Old branch and twig shelters are great firewood. There were even logs to park our tired butts on. It was perfect.

But before we could build a fire we heard voices, carrying clear in the still twilight and then the creaking of pedals and the ticking of gears, as a group of mountain bikers laboured up the slope and stood in black silhouette on the edge of our wood. We looked out and they looked in. But after a moment's wait they went on their way without seeing us, we knew. Then came some children, invisible although we heard their laughter in the leaves, quite a gang of them. It was like being in some Dennis Potter play where the adults play children, and vice versa; then they too were gone and everything was silent except for the hooting of owls.

I lit the fire quickly with birch bark off a rotten trunk; the bark, saturated in resin, lasts much longer than the wood, and the resin is what causes the fire to catch so easily. Breathing in the oily black smoky flame, I shoved the burning scrap of silvery bark into the pyr-amid of twiglets and – *fluff-pfoof* – we had fire.

The flames were soon double burning. Down in the embers and then about two feet above, a secondary ignition of gases released by the lower heat; this is when the fire becomes a work of art in which extravagant changing faces appear in the isolated licks and squiggles of flame, floating above the fire like the genie released from the bottle. Ghouls and shape shifters – all are there in the flames, all hovering in a quite separate magic above the embers and lower parts of the fire. And so Nigel began to tell his tale. It started with something I knew already – he had cheated on his wife once too often. But now she'd reacted, told him to leave. They shared a business; that was dissolved. They shared a house; that was sold. Two sons, grown up, one still trying to get them back together. It was heartbreaking just to hear it, never mind live it.

The harsh would say it was all his fault. Why couldn't he have been faithful? I looked into the fire which promised answers, especially as we had now broached the rum. (Alcohol + fire, that double-edged sword, promising enlightenment but also accounting for an astonishing 70 per cent of all accidents in the wild.) I drank on. Marvelling again at how quick a bottle can go down when you pass it round, swig, swig, swig and back again. At first it seemed simple but now Nigel's problem seemed very complicated. Normally I'd have been looking for ways to decide once and for all. Now all the subtleties of the situation started to take over. The fire offered up connections I would not usually make; the fire created a backdrop of nuance and empathy. Nige was not at fault; no one was, the world was, but not this world, where we were right now, but the world out there, the one we were avoiding.

Unequal to all the alone time, the down time, all the time in the world in a room he rented off a man he knew from the squash club, Nige had gone from being married with a home and business to being a lodger in someone's house, a couple who thought they were doing him a favour though he was paying them good money. Not surprisingly Nige began to spiral down. Antidepressants helped him battle the dark thoughts and therapy gave him a structure of sorts, got him out of bed.

Joe and Nigel then had a quick and knowledgeable discussion about antidepressants. Some were good with booze, but, speaking personally said Nige, alcohol had not helped. Joe told us about the antidepressant that had allowed him to drink without any hangover: 'I was Mr Party. I was out of control. It hurt my business. Messed up my life. I thought I could do anything.' I secretly liked the sound of this particular pill. Perhaps one now and then wouldn't hurt. Maybe on a significant birthday. But a moment's reflection on the chaos it had brought to Joe's life diminished its attraction considerably.

As the firelight, our only light, played across our faces and the night wore on, it's true, I learnt a few new and interesting things, but most of the time I was studying the fire in its infinite variety of commentary and nuance. Everything looks different, everything sounds different when the visuals are altered and given subtle life by fire. Writers like Huysmans, who insist that they must write by the light of two ecclesiastical tallow candles, know a thing or two. I might even try it myself. When that thought, or one like it, ended I would stare back into the fire for more inspiration. We all looked into the fire at the same time, from time to time, all three of us synchronising our looking, which left a poignant question mark hanging over the whole proceedings. This subtle rhythm of matching silence with fire, focusing on the penumbra of ever-changing light, suggesting lives more changeable than suspected; we looked into our lives and listened to what was reflected back, which surely had in its own right a therapeutic effect.

Some fires keep a good warm glow along the diminishing darkening path to emberhood. Others don't. Fires made with hardwoods and resinous pines are usually better than softwoods; aspens and sycamore are fairly crap. If you're picky about choosing fine hardwoods and good pine then I speculate you'll be rewarded. But almost every fire I've had in the wild has been a scavenged affair, pot luck with the fallen boughs and branches. Now that we had burnt much of the shelter, we scrounged off into the dark to get more wood, any that we could find. I was somewhat drunk now and blundering into face-lashing brambles and trippy-uppy withies that can never be slashed away with a knife without it being way more effort than it's worth. I gave up wood collecting after a while and took a long leisurely piss illuminated by my head torch – this pleasure was diminished by realising my batteries were fading. But not before I was reminded for a moment of a water feature at a pool party long ago, at night, abroad. Long ago. And so, finally, to bed.

Backing out of the tent in the cumbersome fashion you do after a chilly night of moderate to extreme discomfort, I forced myself to stop obsessing over the fact that a too small sleeping bag is crap, however fancy and expensive it may be. I fumble-fingered the 'pac-a-bac' on. It was raining. A little like a poncho with arms, the pac-a-bac had a huge bulge that went over the rucksack and kept it dry. Something of a specialist item, it made you look a bit like a Mutant Ninja Turtle. I loved it. It was big and airy enough to stop the tight little build-ups of steam that cause so much distress when walking; sweat and condensation are your enemy here more than rain. It was also properly waterproof, unlike many 'breathable' garments I had worn over the years.

I also put up the umbrella and instantly re-evaluated its stunning ordinariness as a great discovery. The slow build-up of damp as you potter about camp in the pouring rain, always gets into crevices and cracks over time; it's there that it annoys the most and causes the most discomfort. With a brolly you are dry with no leaks at all.

My final bit of kit in the war against wet was my Buffalo Special Forces top made of Pertex nylon and pile fibre, a design unchanged since the 1980s for a very good reason: it was superbly efficient. The Buffalo worked on the brilliant principle of dynamic rather than static waterproofing. Most of the time we are not standing still in pissing rain, we are walking. And generating heat. So why not use this to evaporate moisture out of the garment we are wearing? This is what happens with the Buffalo, which also retains warmth even when wet. By attacking a fundamentally different problem – how to stay warm rather than the related but different problem of how to stay dry – Buffalo had invented a great garment that is not 'waterproof' unless you are doing something in it, which of course you are, most of the time. When I wasn't I could hide under the pac-a-bac, which also made a handy ground sheet.

In such wet, slightly hungover conditions, the WindBurner stove came into its own. If I sound like I am advertising this stuff, I am not – other stoves work, but I find them to be slightly more hassle what with their draft excluders and need for priming. The WindBurner also appealed on an aesthetic level. Though ontologically a gas stove, it seemed to me to owe something to the design of the V2 rocket, the cutaway one I remembered on display at the Science Museum; made from titanium, with heating and cooling fins and a sort of heat pad instead of a flame, noisy as a V2 on take-off with a built-in pot, it was high-tech but in a good way: it worked. Even in a gusty wind, it brewed our coffee in minutes.

Rather than make porridge, we dunked French bread in our coffee like disgruntled German soldiers contemplating another difficult day in the last retreat through the Ardennes. Talking was at a minimum: too much had been done the night before. Yet when later we walked through a town with an off-licence, Joe sprang inside for another bottle of rum; evidently there was more talking to be done. But not now, not at 7 a.m. Packing up the camp took ages, as it always does on the first few days. We all moped about picking up saturated tents and leaving them in forlorn bundles and wandering back again and finally screwing them up in the kind of haste designed to help you forget that they will never dry out miraculously in your pack. The others be-hooded and with dribbly foreheads, me wanly smug and snug under the brolly. The fire long out, damp black water running away between sodden lumps of charcoal; the giant log we sat on, shiny with wet. There was a trace of melancholy, always there when parting, assuaged by a last pointless hunt for tent pegs and water bottles you know you've already packed. The rituals of parting; the terrors of transition.

Walking through drizzly mist. First shit off-piste, surrounded by tick-harbouring bracken, getting used to it, burning the paper – very satisfying and eco-friendly too. The others keep going in diplomatic haste. I have to run after them when all buttoned up again; *kerplonk*, *kerplunk* goes my rucksack as I hoof along.

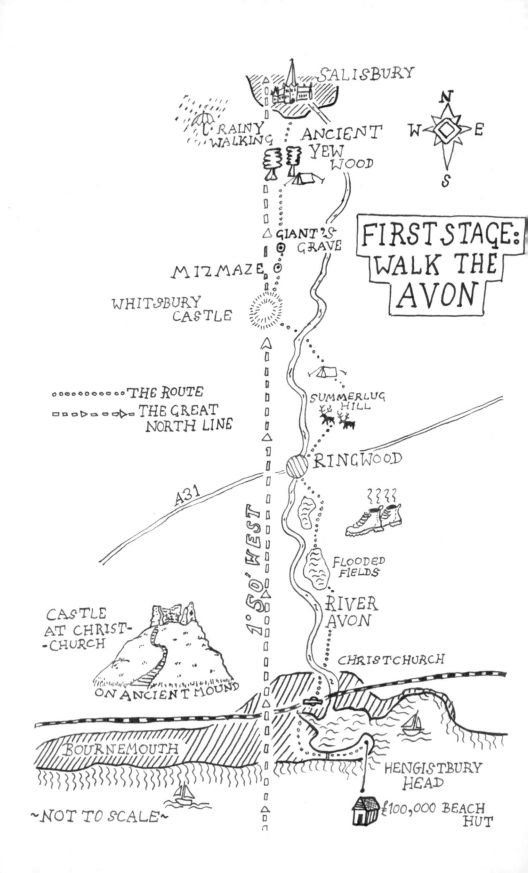

3

TO THE MIZMAZE AND A CIRCLE OF YEWS

First rule of blisters: you mustn't ignore them. The blister – a bubble of liquid caused by cramped damp feet (one will cause the other, softening the skin and causing dermal separation) – exacerbates thirst and tiredness. That tiny, ever-growing bubble right on the sole (blisters elsewhere are much more bearable) can threaten everything. It's like walking on tacks, on heated tacks. In fact your feet are on fire but when the bubble bursts, as it does sometimes, the fire is quenched by the water in the blister. Momentary relief – for about a second – and then the fire returns, redoubles . . . You rack your brains as to the cause, but experience has finally taught me there is but one cause for the mega blister on the sole of the foot: shoes that are normal sized.

I knew this yet I had ignored it.

Normal-sized boots and shoes are fine for walking without a pack and for distances of no more than five or ten miles. Beyond that your feet swell, and adding a pack makes them squash out and swell even more. Super-walker Ray Jardine, who has walked the Pacific Crest Trail five times, not to mention the Appalachian Trail and the Continental Divide Trail (all several thousand miles long), is convinced that trail shoes should be one-and-a-half if not two sizes too big. He's right. Already my sorry little flappers had swollen and filled my size ten boots. And getting my feet wet had just speeded up the process.

Over the years I had tried many different cures for blisters. Each method (even the plainly ludicrous and barbarous one of slicing off the blister with a razor blade and slapping a dressing directly on the red rawness below) has its passionate advocates. Surely they can't all be right? Many sojourns in the land of the blister have taught me that as long as you do *something*, the blister tends to get better rather than worse – even if just owing to the placebo effect. But do nothing, pretend it's not there and there'll be hell to pay.

On the long downhill stretch into Fordingbridge I did just that. The fiery bubble under my sole gave rise to the blister sufferer's first line of defence – a crabbed way of walking. Then, seeing ruts filled with water, I splashed through them, real folly, soaking the feet to try to cool the pain down; it only makes things worse in the long term. I needed the ultimate solution in blister terms, I needed the Foreign Legion technique.

I'd learnt it from an ex-legionnaire called Fred (an Italian) many years before when we had both worked as van couriers in London (there were lengthy periods of standing around, waiting for jobs, in which a number of interesting topics such as 'What do legionnaires do when they get blisters in the desert?' came up quite naturally). And once learnt, I realised that this was indeed the gold standard of blister control and cure. The desert is a harsh place for walking: each step is the same, your feet sweat and sand gets everywhere. Sand and sweat and swollen feet lead to terrible blisters; but the legion, with plenty of time spent in the most blistery place on the planet, had solved the problem. First use a needle to puncture the blister but make sure it is threaded with thin cotton. When the blister is punctured, leave the thread dangling either side. This acts to wick out any future build-up of moisture. A few days later, when the blister has hardened up you can finally remove the thread.

In my haste to get packed before my lift with my parents, I had left behind my army issue 'housewife', a mending kit which had talismanic value in that it had been on every trip I had made since 1989. I had bought the little roll-out wallet of camo cloth with needles and thread and buttons inside when I was much younger and still a keen patron of W. S. Surplus Supplies, an army surplus shop that used to exist in George Street in Oxford. There were always immensely attractive cheap things for sale there: civil defence armbands, mess tins, commando cap comforters (never quite the same as those worn in *The Heroes of Telemark*, but close) and army housewives.

In Fordingbridge, I found a pound store and bought about twenty needles with tiny spools of cotton. They were crap needles with tiny eyes but they did the job as I darned my puckered, pulsating feet in a steamed-up coffee shop. I ignored the other patrons daintily sipping their tea. Nige and Joe, too, evinced no interest as they chowed down on full English breakfasts. Outside, it poured down.

As we went to pay for our food, the quick, highly tattooed girl at the till took an interest in Joe. When one member of your group excites interest, especially from the opposite sex, things lighten up, even if it's raining. He told her our plan to walk the Line and she mentioned the mizmaze. I would have missed it, even though it is bang on the Line. Too focused on stones, even though the Breamore Mizmaze is right next to a long barrow we had planned on looking at in an ancient yew wood. This was especially exciting to Joe, whose life revolved around trees and wood. And Joe has the admirable ability to communicate his enthusiasms.

Mizmazes are really labyrinths: there are no dead ends, unlike a conventional maze. Breamore is cut into turf, one of only eight turf mazes in the UK; two of them are mizmazes. Oddly enough the other one is on another St Catherine's Hill, this one being near Winchester.

A turf maze rises up plumply from the earth but not a huge amount. The mounded rounded turf is cut down to chalk below. Sometimes the chalk is the path and sometimes, confusingly, the risen-up turf is the path.

Walking a labyrinth was seen as a mystical way to complete a pilgrimage without having to go to Jerusalem, and the mizmaze pattern mimics the labyrinth at Chartres Cathedral, which, suggestively, was known as 'Jerusalem'. The Breamore Mizmaze was first written about in 1783 though it must predate that in construction. Speculation then and since puts its creation as being either medieval or Bronze Age – a massive disparity but not unusual in the murky world of ancient monuments. It is right next to a burial mound and surrounded by yew trees. Really ancient yew trees, such as these, left to their own devices, grow long branches that dip into the ground and root again, producing outlier trees in a circle around the original. Sometimes the original is dead, leaving a pit in the centre. A pit you could easily bury someone in. Fairy circles of mushrooms and other fungi display the same ever-widening circular nature; natural models perhaps for the stone circle. Shamanic thinking is either hyper-connective or poetic, depending on your point of view, seeing links between things based on dreamlike rather than 'real' similarities: yew circles, mushroom circles, stone circles. And a potted pilgrimage in the form of a labyrinth.

We approached the yew wood through hot damp fields; fluff and spores stuck to our wet legs. My trousers were soaked below the knee by wading through grass drenched in unevaporated dew, all steaming in the sudden hot sun under black clouds. Then, without warning, a burst of rain, enough to get the lads back into rain-proofs. Walk a few sweating yards and then sun again. English weather; I was glad of my brolly.

We left the path deliberately and broke into the wood through undergrowth. Looking for official entrances to places like a magical wood seems slightly wrong. Such places can never be owned by anyone; they can only be looked after. It has always seemed absurd to me that an ancient monument can be owned. That the land it is on can be private.

These yews were old, not like the younger ones you tend to see in churchyards – bushy and dense. These had had time to spread out (and avoid the topiarist's clippers). Joe was excited in his brisk, man-on-a-mission way. As a tree surgeon and wood sculptor, he's always on the prowl for strange pieces with interesting grain, growths, burrs and stubby suggestive branches. There were lots here. He darted around, like a happy kid on an Easter egg hunt.

Nigel spotted the rabbit-proof fence circling which indicated the mizmaze ahead. Although such mazes were used as a substitute for a pilgrimage in the Middle Ages, the usual explanation is that when medieval piety started to give way to Reformation freedoms, turf mazes became a popular form of entertainment, a place of games.

But a more sophisticated reading is that religion was not the po-faced version we have today – it co-existed happily with children's games. With the increasingly 'written' and left-brain textualisation of religion, the games disappeared along with the earlier more mystical take on religion. Even by Shakespeare's day there was a nostalgia for these games. In *A Midsummer Night's Dream* (Act 1, scene 2), he writes:

> *The nine men's morris is fill'd up with mud,*
> *And the quaint mazes in the wanton green,*
> *For lack of tread are indistinguishable.*

Turf mazes were created for fairs and festivals all over Britain, but the gradual loss of awareness of their shamanic origins meant that these were simply empty ritualised games – good for entertainment but stripped of any more significant meaning.

Today, the mizmaze looked rather uncared for. The sign was dilapidated, and green showed among the chalk carved lines. I wondered how long it took for the turf to bulk up and create the look of bouncy hair on either side of a dandruffy parting. The only new things were odd twists of cloth tied into the yew trees by neo-pagans. I had come across similar votive offerings at Wayland's Smithy on the Ridgeway. What are they for? A way of showing respect, of showing you've been present – like adding a stone to a cairn. Also a way of symbolising prayer; of showing others this is not just a tourist site.

It's not so unusual to find cloth and paper messages tied into trees around ancient sites. Dolls too, and various burnt offerings standing in melted candle wax. It's part of a low-key, rain-soaked kind of paganism. Once I found a plastic Virgin Mary in a niche in the rock wall of a Dorset holloway, where it was attended by flickering night lights. It had just been set up. Near dusk, I scanned the area for a . . . well, not a pagan . . . but no one was to be seen. But next time I went, the niche was bare of the Virgin and the lights.

The Breamore Mizmaze has its own vibe for sure. There is

something expectant, a stillness, a waiting, a recently prepped UFO landing site, or irreverently something out of *Dr Who and the Auton Invasion*. We dried our tents and sleeping bags on the rabbit-proof fence in another brief burst of hot steaming sunshine. When we left, Joe's pack was laden with stubby branches he'd cut with his folding saw.

The labyrinth as a metaphor for the twists and turns, perils and pitfalls of a seeker's life is an ancient one.[2] Christianity embraced it from ancient sources as far apart as Greece and Scandinavia. That a metaphor could replace something substantially experiential – a bona fide pilgrimage – is interesting. Perhaps that's the very definition of a powerful idea. Certainly the right story, the right metaphor, even the right comment at a suitable time and place can change your entire life. I know mine had been changed in just that way. And the person delivering the comment or story can be a complete stranger, or even someone you don't even like that much.

That I was on a pilgrimage was obvious to others; it was usually the second or third question they asked me (after, 'Are you camping?'). When you announce you're walking from Christchurch in Dorset to Lindisfarne in Northumberland, people like the girl in the café who told us about the mizmaze ask, 'What happened?' A modern pilgrimage is rightly assumed to be a form of therapy.

The labyrinth bears a resemblance to the twisting shapes of the brain's surface; and certainly the mind's inner workings – known as Satan's intestines in some Eastern languages. The labyrinth as mind, involuted and confused, can only be solved by straightening it out through walking in a single straight line. The Afghan thinker Idries Shah wrote: 'A man on a straight path never got lost.'

It had been a good day for ancient sites. Earlier we had seen the site of the huge hillfort at Whitsbury Castle Ditches, as well as Giant's Grave, a 67-metre-long barrow about half a mile from the Breamore Mizmaze.

The sagging central ridge of Giant's Grave suggests excavation, though none has been recorded. There are the remains of a ditch around the place – why? Because ditching puts a ring around something and one thing is clear: ancient man liked to ring things off. Though now the ditch is mostly ploughed up under damp heavy soil.

More circles form Whitsbury Castle Ditches, mainly two large raised rings with a wide ditch in between them, wide enough for a Land Rover to pass through. Other outer ditches add more circles, as does a third ridge on the northern side. Circles within circles. The two doughnuts of the raised ridges are six metres high and there in the middle stands a big house, almost a stately home, part of a stud farm. You can't help wondering when humans first began dwelling here; probably once started it never ceased. There have been Mesolithic finds that predate the Iron Age dates for this site's use as a fort; Roman and medieval finds too.

There was mown grass, a drive that cut through the ditch walls as if they were not ancient at all, and fine racing horses in paddocks, the satin black sheen of their coats dully reflecting the sun, which was again peeping through the humid-heavy rain clouds. Like over-protected daughters of the rich, the skittish racehorses were easy to scare and mock as we passed their paddocks, us the envious yokels, humpbacked under the weight of our ungainly rucksacks.

The Line had delivered today, but where would we sleep? Larks guided us along brambly footpaths. We were going north as the Line dictated – and that was all – with a couple of hours to go until nightfall. We had left behind the gorse and pine of the New Forest, its peaty streams and friendly moorland, for the cornfields of the unfolding downs that rise and fall from here until the escarpment of the Cotswolds.

I would notice many times how walking up England was about surmounting waves; each ridge you climbed laid out another wide valley or plateau to cross that subtly changed the landscape, a change in terrain that signified other changes – accent, people, wildlife, weather even; sometimes small changes, sometimes large ones. In these wide valleys and wider plateaus England can alter abruptly in less than ten miles . . .

The dark dull green of corn, high but not yet ripe, still damp from the rain, our trousers again wet and flapping as we walked the edge of it. Gaiters would have saved me but mine were too deep in the pack. I could dry my trousers later by the fire; we knew we would have to have another fire.

The fields were a long stretch of patchwork separated by wide tracks and given a modicum of interest by the remnants of barns and angular-shaped copses and, in these parts, yew groves. In the seventeenth century, John Aubrey wrote: 'Yew trees naturally grow in chalkie country. The greatest plenty of them in the West of England is at Nunton Ewetrees.'

I wondered at the odd spelling of the name, drawing a connection between the trees and the sheep that grazed the 'chalkie country'. The village of Nunton was near Odstock, which appropriately has a Yew Tree Inn; both places lay only a few miles from the groves we were looking at now.

Almost at random, I picked the largest yew grove named on the map and sought it out on the horizon. 'Let's camp there.'

The wood had 'private' written all over it as we approached. Huge tree trunks had been rolled into place to protect gateways from car and mountain bike access. We sat on the logs, legs stretched out, a good place to pause for thought.

'What do you think?'

'Looks private. Probably a pheasant shoot.'

'Let's just have a gander.'

'OK, you two go.'

Nervous, I waited while Nigel and Joe sloped off into the darkness of the wood. They took an age before returning.

Nige said, 'I saw a bloke. He looked our way but we didn't move. He had a dog but it didn't seem interested. If he saw us he's ignoring us.'

So either we'd been seen or we hadn't – and even if we had, it didn't matter.

'OK,' I said. 'Let's go in.'

The wood quickly opened out under the vast spreading yews. There were almost too many of them, their knobbly branches like knotted hands overhead blocking out light. Even more than beeches, yews leave very little undergrowth once they mature, which made the wood easy to walk around in. No leaves underfoot as they are evergreen; sometimes just the bare chalky ground here and there deep holed by a badger sett.

It was easy to see the bowl-shaped depressions left by rotting former trees and the ring of younger trees encircling them. Or were they burial holes that the trees had been planted around?

One rather convincing but prosaic explanation for yew's prominence in Celtic and other European mythologies is its toxicity.[3] Animals and humans find the leaves potentially fatal. So it makes an ideal protective hedge for a burial ground. But do horses, cows and other grazers really dig up bodies? Surely it is the scavengers – dogs, wolves, foxes and badgers? Well, we'd seen the badgers' homes, they loved a yew wood it seemed. The bone white tailings of the sett spewed across a clearing. There was the musty, murky smell of earth-dwelling creatures.

The smell of yew contributed to another place where yew trees once proliferated: the communal jakes. The odour of yew wood masks the high pong of urine and excrement. It would be a huge irony if every church was actually built on the village shitter.

Yew may be poisonous but the wood is useful; and the tree is very long lived. There is evidence that yews were planted as parish and, earlier, communal boundary lines. Perhaps they shared that duty with standing stones. Yew makes for a good longbow, though Italian and Spanish yew were later preferred for the bows that fought at Agincourt. English wood is too knotty.

Here, the separate groves of yew were interconnected, sometimes through a kind of arch of thick twisted branches. Each zone was subtly different but all had some trees with exploded trunks, like a book opened backwards until its spine splits. On one tree there was a rope swing fixed in place with a chain, I wondered where the children came from who played here; we were miles from a village or town.

Dark, but not yet dark enough. My tent, which had a curious luminosity, seemed designed to attract attention. The Cuben Fiber was a patchwork of bright green sheets, but with a crumpled-tissue texture that only flattened out after serious pegging. I didn't wait any longer and put the thing up. To hell with it. We'd heard no more of the man and his dog.

Gathering wood for the fire, I wondered how well yew would burn. All right was the answer. Joe unscrewed the top of the new bottle of rum and, with typical North American forthrightness, turned his full attention on helping Nigel out of his depression. Nigel rallied somewhat under the intensity of Joe's interest, and I joined in by supporting Joe when he urged Nigel to go on an extended trip to India. But Nigel said he had already 'done the hippy thing'. I realised that issuing instructions from above, so to speak, looking down on Nigel, somewhat fearful eyed and alone in his hole, was useless, because only Nigel could bunk himself up and out of that hole. We would have done better to have got down there with him and let him stand on our backs, heads, shoulders . . .

We all stared into the fire and drank the bottle dry, but it wasn't quite as good as the night before, despite the magical wood we were in.

Even late at night, light reflected off the chalk granules in the wood's floor, giving the tent a ghostly glow. I felt cheered that no one had driven us away despite this quite obviously being a private wood (though mercifully short on nasty signage).

Before sleeping, I looked through the flint finds I had made. In such an ancient place, I hoped to find at least some knives or flint cores. In the Sahara and along native trails in British Columbia, I had found flint tools easily. I still had with me the notched spoke-shave I had found at Hengistbury Head and another notched tool I'd found at Whitsbury Castle Ditches. It often surprises people how roughly made some Mesolithic flint knives and scrapers are, but even knowing that, I found nothing in the wood except some chips that maybe, just maybe, had been left over from work on a bigger piece of flint.

4

METEORITES AND ALTARS

We came down into Salisbury from the yew wood, not knowing that two days earlier there had been a biological warfare attack by the Russians. The town was not busy, but people were about. The cathedral had a healthy queue of visitors, so healthy that I decided to not go inside. Been before, anyway. I was discovering that places can get used up by tourism, whatever your high hopes of them. Even if they lay on the Line, some were not that important, except maybe as signposts. And the cathedral spire was certainly good for that: we had navigated our way for miles by aiming for that landmark.

We said goodbye to Joe, who was heading back to Canada. It had been good having him and his love of trees with us. But now it was just me and Nige, heading up to the next major site on the Line: Old Sarum. The line from Sarum to Stonehenge to Avebury was noted by antiquarians in the eighteenth century. In more recent times, it has been the template for a 47-mile walk called the Great Stones Way, though the guidebook showed that detours were needed from the official path to visit both Avebury and Stonehenge! No doubt hampered by rights-of-way issues, the authors of the walk had to concoct a suboptimal route. No such concerns bothered us . . .

Even if you stripped out the other thirty-five or more sites, the fact that Sarum, Stonehenge, Avebury and Lindisfarne all fell on the same line was quite remarkable. Many people struggled to believe it when I told them, although I didn't know why; but now I was getting a glimmer. Because if it were true, it meant ancient man was smarter than most of us; I mean the smartest ancient man was *smarter than the average guy*.[4] The average modern person couldn't plot a straight line from somewhere thirty miles away, let alone three hundred . . .

Old Sarum is reached up a road of fine family dwellings in the north of town. The kind of homes that make you reflect uneasily on your own vagabond status. Not too huge to engender a 'fuck the rich' bravado but not so modest either; large enough to disturb complacency in the envious minded and to unsettle complacent thoughts about one's own position in the status malarkey. Only a week earlier, my daughter had told me we weren't middle-class because we 'didn't go to church, didn't have ski holidays and didn't send our kids to private school'. Apparently you only had to do one of the above to qualify. I said I didn't do the class thing: I identify with nomads rather than settlers. Which is an answer she'd heard too many times before.

Does anyone really identify with settlers by preference? I never have, yet my nomad-friendly feelings were under attack as I sweated past the big houses. Nigel and I examined the ditches, and the odd strange tree growing out of the ditch walls at Sarum, but felt no need to pay and enter and do the tourist thing. I was beginning to think ancient sites should have a device like the 'shutter count' on a digital camera – after X amount of visits the place is closed, covered over, left to lie fallow . . .

So we moved on, and it was raining again as we tramped around the complex ancient circles of the nearby but much less visited Ogbury Camp. Found at Ogbury by excavators: Iron Age pottery and a Neolithic scraper; thousands of years apart, they give a typically confusing timeline. What becomes apparent with *all* ancient sites is that they get used for very long periods of time.

Ogbury is considered by some to be an animal enclosure, because it would be hard to defend as a fort; but think about it for a moment: why build an eight-foot rampart (that's just its height in the twenty-first century, so add another eight feet to account for the soil lost over two thousand years of erosion) and a great ditch – all for a field the size of twenty football pitches? If you didn't want all the grass to be eaten, you'd need to circulate the cattle, leaving parts of it fallow (and there are signs of dividing walls within). But a little thought compels more: when there is no outside feed available, it is usual to calculate five acres of pasture per cow per year. Those fifty acres would be good for ten beasts. All right, say it's a compound for keeping beasts before they are slaughtered, but again, why make it so hefty? The one argument is that wolves and bears preyed on domestic cattle and this was the only way to protect them. But if that were the case, knowing the spread of population was already wide by Neolithic times (as many tracks linking hamlets and villages date from those times), surely we should expect far more 'farms' like this, not just a few, situated on my mythical Line?

It would actually make more sense to say it *was* a football stadium than a place for keeping animals. Camps, henges, forts, circles within circles; already I was beginning to suspect things weren't as simple as the official position claimed.

Sting obviously knew what he was doing: like that other pop star antiquarian Julian Cope (who lived in Avebury for years), he had picked his house wisely – bang on The Line. Lake House had in the past been home to those famed eighteenth-century antiquarians the Duke family. On the steps of Lake House for two hundred years before Sting bought the place in 1991, lay a 90kg meteorite; a giant chondrite dated to over thirty thousand years old, certainly one of the oldest and largest meteorites ever to fall in the UK. (It is now in Salisbury Museum after a long stint at the Natural History Museum.) What is more interesting is where Edward Duke (1779–1852) unearthed it: almost certainly during one of his excavations of the barrows in the area.

We can speculate, so here goes . . . Inuit were known to worship meteorites in ancient times; later they used them as a source of metal, there being none available on the tundra ice. (It is quite probable the working of metal started with iron-rich meteorites, and then moved on to native rock of lesser and lesser purity.) The dastardly explorer Robert Peary (1856–1920) famously stole three of the largest Inuit meteorites and put them in the Smithsonian – an act of incredible colonial insensitivity, the cultural equivalent of stealing the Black Stone set in the walls of the Kaaba in Mecca. Out on the retreating ice of the last glaciers to cover Britain, meteorites would have been easy to spot. Or perhaps this one fell on the tundra that was southern England during the last Ice Age. Could it have been, like the Inuit meteorites, a religious object, a reason for pilgrimage to this area around Stonehenge? When Edward Duke unearthed it, was it already an historical remnant buried alongside a Bronze Age lord?

In short, did the former owner of Sting's luxury pad accidentally discover the real reason for all that religious-inspired building activity centred on Stonehenge and Avebury? I'd like to think he did. Oddly enough, before science told us otherwise, people who dared to suggest that meteorites came from outer space were deemed credulous fools . . .

The Elizabethan Lake House is unpretentious but rather beautiful, not especially tall but with a discrete tower in one corner. From one angle, it looks like a row of houses rather than a single building. It is made mainly of the same stone as Salisbury Cathedral.

We looked enviously for Sting, maybe in the garden doing yoga or practising his golf drive, but the place seemed empty when we passed. No flag flying. No tagged Range Rover in the drive. Mind you, the sensible chap has quite a few other houses . . .

We were moving fast, almost too fast it seemed, into the densely barrowed terrain of Stonehenge. This area, Normanton Down, is perhaps the most important barrow cemetery in England. Everywhere you looked, there was some kind of mound, ditch or rampart; odd bulges in the landscape that dot the hills as they flatten out in preparation for Stonehenge and Salisbury Plain. It is not a particularly beautiful or picturesque part of Britain, but it does have an impressively broad sweep, a sort of grandeur. And the skies seem wider, more open, the wide horizons excellent for star gazing. For seeing the Pole Star.

But from whatever direction you approach Stonehenge, you

cannot avoid the growing indications that it is popular, very popular. The footpaths go from being brambly and neglected to well-signed with warnings to NEVER leave the path. Drystone walls are backed with double rungs of barbed wire like WW1 defences. Rabbit-proof fences are tipped with more barbed wire, some of it ingeniously angled so as to tear your nuts off if you were so foolish as to attempt ingress. Even fields with no obvious entrance are signed 'Private'.

My usual hatred of such signage was mitigated by the knowledge that every year thousands of mad people try to camp here for all sorts of strange reasons. I'd even attended an illegal festival myself, back in 1984, the last one held at Stonehenge before the Battle of the Beanfield in June 1985 stopped the festivals there for twenty or more years. I felt for those farmers in a way I didn't for others. Stonehenge attracts more tourists than any other site in the UK apart from the Tower of London. And nutters and campers and nutty campers make up a fair percentage of them . . .

'What about over there?' said Nige, pointing to a copse across a wide ploughed field as a place to pitch camp. It was within earshot of the busy A303, close to Stonehenge.

'What about her?' I muttered as an elderly but active lady came into sight with a dog straining at its lead. She looked like a landowner and as we were about to head up a private track, I expected a reprimand. None came as Nigel petted her dog.

'You out walking?' she said in homely tones.

'We are. Great day for it.'

'Oh, it is. I love to get out here as much as I can.'

'Looks like it'll be nice tomorrow too.'

'I hope so. Now you have a lovely time!'

Emboldened by this friendliness, we waited till she was out of sight before we skipped across the ploughed field to the copse. Less than a mile away the toy-like impertinence of Stonehenge caught the setting sun. Nigel and I both stopped and stared. The evening light made the stones sing.

After haltingly climbing a nasty, snaggy fence we got to the edge of the wood. Signs: 'Keep Out – Private Property', and then a hastily painted afterthought, 'Natural habitat – do not disturb'; and if that didn't work, another sign low to the ground: 'Danger of Lyme disease.'

'Oh, that's a good one,' said Nige sarcastically. 'Haven't seen that before.'

Secretly thankful for my tick-proof trousers, I entered the wood intent on finding the disc barrow we knew to be at its centre. Again it was the un-ownable quality of ancient sites that emboldened us. Perhaps one sign would have put us off but so many just looked amateurish.

The trees were not very tall but they were old and covered in grey-green lichen like hairy peeling paint, perhaps a semi luminous kind as the lichen glowed in the reduced light of the wood. Rotten trunks lay everywhere, the sign of a wild and untouched woodland; they were easily crushed under foot, the frail bark held together by lichen and the inner wood rotted away completely. I wasn't even sure what kind of trees they were at first, so entwined were they with lichen and ivy, as if the parasites were taking over, the trees sapped of their strength. Closer, I saw they were mainly birch trees with some hazels, like a wood closer to the Arctic Circle. The hazels had been coppiced at some point and sprouted straight branches, ideal for making hurdles and chair legs and fishing poles. The place felt like a remnant from the Ice Age, a bit creepy and mysterious.

At the north end of the copse lay a bowl barrow, in addition to the disc barrow in the wood's centre. It had been excavated to reveal two bodies along with a bronze dagger in a wooden scabbard, a Beaker-style pot and some deer antlers. A tripod of poles was also found. Most of these barrows had been excavated in the heyday of antiquarianism from the mid eighteenth to the early nineteenth century, the finds including gold pins, bronze knives, faience and amber traded from as far away as Turkey.

When we got to the central barrow, it was surrounded by a ring of hazel hurdles to keep people out. Fair enough. As we peered over the fence, I noticed a small moss-covered platform made of concrete blocks. On it was a jar, a shallow candle holder and a lantern made of cheap metal and glass. This seemed a cute sort of altar until I noticed the fox skull on the ground. I climbed over the hurdle and put the skull on the altar next to the lantern, because it seemed to belong there.

When Nige joined me, I said to him, 'Watch your head.'

'Why?'

'There's a pentangle hanging over it.'

'Where? Oh – weird!'

Indeed it was. Right above his head and the altar hung a wooden pentangle about the size of something you could make with wire coat hangers – except this was nicely made of hazel withies bound with string. It dangled in the breeze, turning slightly, witness to whatever goings on the wood's other visitors provided.

Without a fire the place would have been too depressing, so as soon as it was decently dark we started one. Nigel's account of being depressed and his lowered mood since Joe had left us were having an effect on me. I was beginning to feel sorry for myself too, volatile, jumpy and resentful of Nigel being 'down', since my being 'up' was no longer a pleasurable and easy duty, but hard work. It was hard, man! Two down men walking the downs with their down sleeping bags (mine very obviously too small, but which had been refused a return by the fancy sleeping bag makers, the bastards!). In the rain. Actually whenever it rained, I felt better because then I could show Nige my superior brolly/rain kilt kit system which was evidently superior to his Gore-Tex drowned rat alternative. Such are the nasty ramifications of co-dependency.

Oh yes, we got a fire going in the creepy wood. The hazel and birch burnt all too quickly and I stumped off in search of timber with my new head torch bought in Salisbury. Head torches are now complex and I had forgotten the instructions, so mine was stuck on a single laser-like beam. The utter brightness of it was as captivating as it was narrow. With this pencil-wide beam, I could identify fallen branches and good timber. The laser would seek them out.

I focused the beam onto a stick, bent forward to pick it up – and rammed my head into a thicket of thorns that had been above laser height. They were nasty thorns, the sort that aren't supposed to grow in England. Thorns with an inward angled bite like the teeth of a python, engineered by natural selection to grip harder the more you pull away. Thorns like this should not be allowed, I thought as felt my face for thorn-torn flesh.

I was angry. First, rejected by that smug sleeping bag company (PHD if you are interested) who, in addition to refusing to exchange my too-small sleeping bag for a bigger one (I only slept in it once for goodness sake!), took great pleasure in announcing on their website their ongoing sponsorship of Ben Fogle, TV adventurer (almost a dyslexic anagram of that other one, Bear Grylls), who I naturally hated even though I knew nothing about him. And second, ripped by thorns in a wet wood in Wiltshire. The taste of blood was coppery and bitter but strangely the thought of scarring cheered me up. A good superficial scar like those of sabre-wielding students duelling in Heidelberg might earn me some respect, the respect that PHD, a bunch of duvet-making, celebrity-loving bastards, had so recently denied me. Respect on the street, fear even. A homeless git with a scar.

Yep, those thorns should have been a lesson. Turn the fucking laser off and find the wide beam. But I stubbornly didn't. I carried on lasering around the creepy wood, banging into trees and snagging my tear-proof top on more thorns; while struggling with feeble anagrams of ben fogle such as *gnob feel* and *beef ogln*.

'Took a while getting that wood,' said Nige. (If he didn't exactly say this, he implied it.)

'Lot of thickets out there.' (I didn't say thorns, as that sounded incompetent: only the foolish stumble into thorn bushes.)

'Looks fairly open from here,' said Nigel.

'Well, beyond the visual range, out there, near the altar and the pentangle, it's tougher going, a lot more thickets and, er, thickets.'

'Oh, OK.'

We piled up the fire with my meagre offerings. It flared up for a while and we were both transfixed. But we'd not got any booze left and had very little to say. It was a sad indictment of us both. Struck dumb by the fire. Soon after that we both turned in for the night.

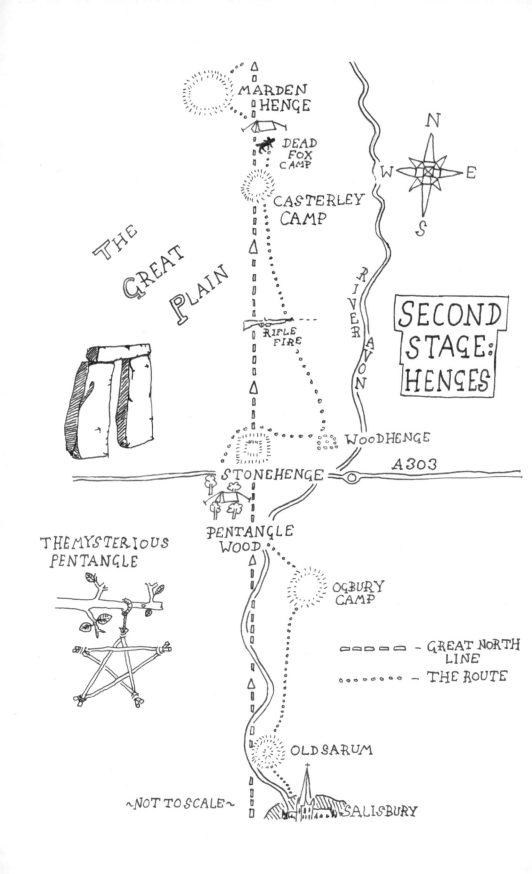

5

STONEDHENGE

A shuffling, a scuffling, pre-dawn light at 5.30 a.m. Too uncomfortable to lie still and make the most of the over-warm and yet too tight and somehow supremely irritating sleeping bag. Goddam PHD. I had turned that bag inside out and sniffed very carefully and there was *no* foot smell; well, none that I could detect. Naturally, I didn't put this in my squirmy, matey email where I implied that me and Ben were equals in the world of adventure. But no deal, so now that PHD was never going to take back my bag, I decided to fart long and loud into its soft interior. I decided to fart as much as possible into that bag, a pre-dawn, pre-rise fart of no small pretension . . . The appropriately named WindBurner was to hand and in cramped be-bagged style, I brewed a cup of coffee from the comfort of my revenge fart-inflated sleeping bag.

'Stonehenge, eh?' I said to Nige, mouth full of coffee-dipped pitta, which had replaced sloppy sweet porridge as the morning meal.

'Yep.'

'Nice day for it.'

Nige craned his heron neck skyward. 'Might rain later.'

'Maybe.'

Ah, the quality of conversation at dawn in the dripping woods.

Stonehenge. What can you sensibly say about Stonehenge? I certainly don't want to regurgitate the subtly shifting dates and facts that Wikipedia peddles. Go there for an update if you will. My intention now was to attempt something harder – to make a useful connection to the place, to its place on the Line. I wouldn't be credulous yet I wouldn't be insensitive and cynical; I would try to listen to the sort of intuitions you get when no emotion is involved, the quiet kind for which you need a bit of inner silence.

From a distance, across two fields and a road, now that we had emerged from the wood, the henge was in shadow. The evening before, it had glowed gold in the sunset, like some crazy monument made of caramel; something the Wispa Gold team at Cadburys might have dreamed up, or a video producer for a bar of that ilk; but now there were just black faraway shapes. Some complain that Stonehenge always looks 'smaller than you think' – maybe true from a speeding car on the A303, but not now.

The stones are not, however, like the pyramids, though they were built at a roughly similar time (started earlier, finished later). The pyramids look far bigger than you think they will, positively looming out of the smoggy traffic as you round the low cliffs of the Giza escarpment. My kids (who were spoilt by seeing the pyramids first) joked that if the 'fundies' managed to blow them up, as they have promised to do on several occasions, the result would look like . . . Stonehenge.

Unlike my kids, I saw Stonehenge long before I travelled abroad. It loomed big in my childhood imagination, along with the Pennine Way and Ben Nevis; places that I desperately wanted to visit but were somehow looked down on for their popular appeal. So, as soon as I could hitch, I found my way to the henge in a German hippy's VW van. He bought me and my pal Pete ice creams and we checked out the vibes of the stones. I didn't really think there were actual vibrations I could feel, but in a Herman Hesse-induced state of radical openness, I went along with the general consensus that there was something going on here. And there was, but not anything I could usefully talk about – except perhaps as a kind of mirror of a desire for calm and connectedness.

This time, Nige is out in front, he usually is. We scamper across the busy A303. Now we're walking down a wide track with wild unruly camper vans, some with flags and washing hanging out, all waking up in the early morning sun. Tinny recorded music, something Indian. Nige even spots an Indian flag flying from one aerial. These are the real aficionados of the stones.

A thin man in a sheepskin flying hat is walking his dog, and stops to tell us, 'They can't shut us down. Look around you! These are the Stones!'

'Do you ever get raided?'

'Oh, they'd love to do that. But we're very careful. No litter. No shit.'

We all smile at his joke. We are walkers – on his side by default. The Man is always in a smart car, with a beautiful wife and a beautiful house . . .

Today, the World Heritage Site is cautiously open to revellers who are more interested in druids than drugs; there are plenty of other festivals for that. But when I visited at the age of twenty in 1984, Stonehenge was truly Stonedhenge. The main dirt strip through the festival was lined with grimy tents flogging every kind of high; blackboards scrawled with chalk explained gear and prices.

I went with three other pals from Oxford. I was the nominated driver, but it wasn't my car; it belonged to a supremely generous Old Etonian called Sebastian who didn't even ask if I had insurance or not. I had only passed my test a few months earlier and it showed. At the turn-off from the A34, I put the car into a series of terrifying wobbles that made the tyres buck and squeal, but luckily we didn't roll. We stopped (as students do after every new experience) for a steadying cigarette, then it was back in the old motor, a Citroën estate, for the festival.

It must have been around midnight when we arrived. Within a short time, I felt I had been dropped into some kind of hellish post-apocalyptic world. Lost souls were everywhere, wraith-like. Girls wrapped in old duvets stood by the Portaloos, offering sex for drugs or money. A dozen or so Hells Angels roared up the central strip and then roared back again, checking us all out. Cars that had been parked there for days, it seemed, were up to their axles in dust that once had been mud.

In the tents along the strip, fires and lamps flickered. Owing to budgetary concerns we opted for super cheap 'hot knives' to set us up. This involved crouching in front of the fire while the demonically grinning knife man heated the blackened blade of a chunky kitchen knife until it was red hot. Then a small piece of hashish was dumped on the blade and squashed with another equally hot knife. The cleverness of the knife man involved angling the gap between the knives so that the sudden burst of harsh smoke went right down your lungs. Getting high was an unsubtle combination of oxygen starvation and hash smoke; you stumbled as you left the tent and hoped that was the effect of the dope but it was probably from crouching down and being half asphyxiated. You'd probably get just as high sticking your head in a bonfire of wet leaves and pretending it's Ventolin.

My pals wanted the full trip, so we congregated at the counter of a burger van that within its darkened serving slot sold all kinds of drugs, fast-food style. They chose the cheapest tab of acid available – a black cat, which looked like a tiny scrap of paper with a little cat printed on it.

If I had been offered said drug I would probably have succumbed, but I was thankful that miserly considerations carried the day. Unlike the £1 hot knives, these tabs were a fiver each and no one was springing for anyone else. Plus, with the self-concern that characterises successful drug users, they wanted their drive home assured and not terminated in acid-enhanced visions of flying. My reticence, apart from the usual fears of a bad trip, was driven from an early and influential reading of the Russian mystic Gurdjieff. Gurdjieff claimed that hallucinogens – and here I imagine he meant mushrooms of some kind – damaged your ability to pick up higher knowledge if taken without skilled instruction. And a bearded bloke in a bandanna, pushing three tabs in his nail-chewed paw, didn't count as skilled.

Higher knowledge . . . my pals wouldn't have scoffed (the scoffers had been ditched in that cull of premature friends that takes place in the second term) but they might have been bemused. It was something I thought about but never spoke of. What did higher knowledge even mean to me? I suppose foresight and better judgement. I lacked both and very much wanted to arrive at the place of all mystics – the place where you trust your intuition. And acid increasingly looked like a wrong turn.

But I wasn't getting off lightly. We spent the night in the car. I don't think we even made it to the stones. Well, two lads did, but they got freaked out halfway there and came back to the safety, or madness, of the car. The idea of a 'contact high' was prevalent. Was I getting one? It certainly felt like it. The unsystematic derangement of all the senses.

I was glad when dawn came. We heard a rumour that the police were arresting people as they left. Quite why, we never thought to ask. Pushing the car out of the soft ground, we made it back on to the road with the boys squawking and caterwauling around me. I felt like I was driving a car full of fruit bats. I was.

And back to Oxford. Parking outside Sebastian's residence in Walton Street, I left the car half blocking the street. I was strung out, I had lost my ability to park, had no willpower for driving left.

Yep. Stonehenge. It was strange because once again I felt like I was breaking in. A sign on the gate to the track that ran along the causeway said that access was denied as the path was too slippery. To hell with such nimbyism! We had been through far worse mud than this mere splatter of dirt. But as an elderly grey moustached official came striding with purpose towards us, long buried anxieties about being caught trespassing red-handed surfaced. I could tell Nigel was bracing himself too. But nothing. The man smiled benignly.

'Good morning!' he said cheerily.

We were a fenced-off field away from the stones but on their side of the road. Not wishing to pay to get closer and assuming we were way too early anyway (it wasn't yet 7 a.m.), it was with some interest and puzzlement that we could see the stones were already occupied. And there was drumming!

The people mooching around the monument were all Gore-Tex-clad normals; there were even some tiny kids in puffy all-weather gear designed for rolling in puddles. A family of incognito druids?

More likely foreign visitors willing to pay the hefty extra for an early morning private view.

The drummer was different. Dressed like an extra from *Braveheart*, he trod a slow and dignified route back and forth in front of the stones, the side away from the road. His drum was one of those large tambourine type ones you belabour with a double-headed drumstick. The sound was now faint, now clear in the early morning breeze, drum rolls building up to something.

The Druidical religion was brought to ancient Britain by the Celts. Stonehenge predates their arrival. To them, it might already have been an interesting ruin. Indeed, authors such as Graham Robb show that the Romans and Celts are perhaps better considered from the point of view of their similarities rather than differences; certainly both groups differ greatly from the Neolithic early inhabitants of Salisbury Plain.

Yet Druidism is what has captured the imagination. Just a few miles from Stonehenge (and only a mile from Sting's Lake House) we find Druid's Head farm, Druid's Head wood and Druid's Lodge on the map. When were they so named?

Drummer man wears a rough kind of headband, a woollen kilt (but as the proud wearer of the rain-kilt, I can't cavil) and one of those woollen waistcoats you find in the Himalayas. Yes, you can tell I am trying to take the piss – but I actually like the eerie sound of the drums at dawn. I'd rather there were sixty unearthly drummers drumming than six tourists roaming . . . But now there's shouting from behind us: thundering up the field comes a squad of about fifty soldiers; it's the army, out for a morning run in formation.

There was a marked path of pounded grass the other side of the fence from our track. These soldiers were youngsters and though hardly identifiable, the front three were all young women. All of them were youthful: eighteen or nineteen perhaps. One of the women had her face crunched into a mass of pain, but was keeping pace; the rest were mainly blank or red-faced. At the rear, two taller and heavier lads were lolloping with jarring strides that shook the mass of kit on their backs.

I wanted to shout encouragement but was a bit shy. A slightly older man running at the front in sweatshirt rather than uniform greeted us with friendly 'good morning' and Nigel and I rushed to 'good morning' him back. Then the army thundered on, off up a nearby hill. Imagine running past Stonehenge and a few random druids every day. I suppose you get used to it.

6

PLAIN TALK

I t is time to expatiate about poles. These poles were not just for walking, they were an essential part of the tent. One of the reasons my tent was so light was because it didn't need special poles; it simply used one of my walking poles fully extended as a central maypole-type support. It divided the space nicely: one side for sleeping, the other for kit.

The Pacerpoles made walking easier. You could push off them. This took some of the pressure off the feet. They were sturdy, if a tad heavy. I liked them and was careful to keep an eye on them.

But suddenly they were not there!

AAAAAGGHH!

We had walked round the army field, gone past Stonehenge and were making our way to Durrington Walls (just north of Woodhenge). We were at Ringbarrow Ridge – more barrows in a barrow-laden land. We then went on. And that is when I found I was poleless.

I knew immediately I had left the poles stuck in the ground by the information point at Ringbarrow Ridge. I had stopped to take a picture of an artist's impression of Stone Age folk. In the impression – in fact, in all the artists' impressions of the past I had seen so far on the walk – a strong wind was blowing their oatmeal coloured garments about. No bright colours. No green even. Surely those ancient Brits would have been more nattily dressed, like Ötzi the Iceman? Probably in bark and adorned with brightly coloured feathers. The artists were following that age-old convention of trying to make the past look more believable by making it more boring than it probably was. For all we know, they could have been inked like MS-13 gangsters; Ötzi had sixty-one tattoos . . .

Such thoughts lasted only a millisecond for now I had to head

back. Another group of soldiers went by and I thought that someone by now would surely have nicked my poles. An unreasoning fear
gripped me and, ditching my pack with Nigel, I started to run. Yes,
knackered and footsore though I was, I began running. More soldiers
ran in the opposite direction. A great glut of them, all chunky and
fit. I streamed through them, sweating and stumbling. There was a
sort of stunned silence as I made my way against the tide, swimming
upstream along the busy track to where I dearly hoped my poles
stood upright and waiting for me. The soldiers took in the fact of my
running and then, as I exited the peloton so to speak, expelled from
the colonic bulge of the group, a cheer went up – a celebration with,
I admit, a few ironic tones, but mainly not. I felt quite welcomed by
it all.

Past a courting couple in matching red Osprey rucksacks and no,
not my poles, they had Leki folding ones. I said all out of breath: 'Have
you seen my pole . . . zer?' They said no and I hurried on, upping my
stride. In the distance lay trees and the outdoor information point
with its dumb drawing. And—

Noooo! No poles!

But still I ran on and on. The poles had gone . . . no, they hadn't!
Some kind soul had unplugged them from the ground and laid
them against a silvery felled and sawed log. Great God above! I felt
blessed.

I ran back for a hundred yards or so. Fuck it. Nigel could wait,
find some daft mushrooms or scry the firmament for rare birds. He
was good like that, the kind of bloke you could keep waiting and it
wouldn't matter even if he took the piss for it; it wouldn't matter.

Yes, so, Woodhenge. Really it should be called Concretehenge because all the wooden postholes have been filled in with concrete nub-
ends, so the whole place is like a parkour training area in which, if
you were a mighty jumper, your feet need never touch the ground,
leaping from nub-end to nub-end to the pathetic small flint-studded
burial spot in the middle where they found a child's skeleton, probably laid to rest long after Woodhenge was at its height. Now its

height was only a couple of feet and I felt cheated. The place was an archaeologist's con trick.

It was first noticed from above by Squadron Leader Gilbert Insall in 1926 (an incredible war hero who was awarded the Victoria Cross for a daring combination of shooting up a German plane, then crash-landing and then repairing his own plane before flying home . . . and then in another escapade getting captured and finally escaping on the third attempt). He also found by aerial scanning one of the rare East Anglian ancient sites at Arminghall. Though Woodhenge had been half identified in the nineteenth century as a disc barrow, it was his glimpsing it as a fairy ring from the cockpit that confirmed it was a huge henge instead. It was the sort of a circle that you can see in all kinds of fields if, in dry weather, you take a lowish flight in a prop plane over Blighty.

Excavation was disappointing; the marks seen were empty pit holes where the wood had rotted away. Also found were two chalk axes that could have cut nothing and must have been ceremonial. The nearby Cuckoo Stone, a nondescript giant badger-turd of a rock in a nearby field, was more impressive. Wood just doesn't really cut it.

We had now 'done' two major sites on the Great North Line. It was time for a hearty breakfast in a coach inn we had spied. Yes, coach and not coaching: this inn was waiting for the lunchtime hordes who descend each day on the henges. We were early and ordered the usual rash plateful of fried muck running with yoke, baked bean juice and toms as red and skinless as a movie burns victim. The black pudding came in a single huge slice, big as a pineapple wheel, with hard white eyes of fat – rather good in fact.

Three 'executives' of the pub chain that owned the coach inn were crammed round a brown, circular, shiny-topped table, their laptops vying with the dribbly red and yellow condiment containers. It felt like a microcosm of modern Britain. A nerdy but chunky young man who 'knew about computers' berated in a confident yet toothless way the two resigned older folk – man and woman, tired, lined, hanging on to their jobs and maybe even shagging each other in desperate solace as matey boy, boss boy bossed them about with PowerPoint and spreadsheets. Silently they took it, as silently they must draw their salary and thank God they are not downsized into something small and useless; a Nectar point away from oblivion.

Nige gave me the rolling eyeball. He'd done his time in corporate land and his last job (before divorce blew up the company he shared with his wife) was doing that most thankless of tasks: corporate training. He and I both. The money was good but you always earned it. It was sow's ear needlework at its most refined.

And so we trudged on.

My boots were beginning to hurt again as we entered the silent army town, Larkhill – appropriate as on leaving, we'd hear the larks. But Larkhill today is a name associated with bullying and the suicides of young soldiers. There was no one about as we walked between the rows of neat houses – the married quarters and all the married soldiers away – cutting through the estate of grey boxes and communal play areas. In the middle of one such grassy expanse was a discarded red plastic car with a yellow roof, the kind tots sit in and paddle along with their feet. My son had one when he was small. Then that acute feeling of nostalgia that you counter with false bravado, a cease and desist order to the emotions while you remain face pressed against the wire, worried about their first day at school, how they still can't tie their laces . . . so I took a photo of it.

Through the army suburb we emerged on the southern edge of the Plain. This was quite an exciting moment for me. Salisbury Plain, like the Pennine Way, had always loomed large in my childhood imagination as a place of adventure. It is the biggest open space in southern England, and much of it forbidden to walkers – what secrets it must hide . . .

But from here, sun shining, the Plain looks like a bland spread of low rolling hills. The thing of note, though, is the smartly packaged woods and copses. All of them precisely defined, as if they have been cultivated solely to appear on a military map. There is no ambiguity to their shapes, all straight sided and yet unfenced as the tanks have to be able to crash in through the side. That strikes you too:

the general openness – kind of like the rolling prairies of the old West . . .

We start our long hike north, which hugs the eastern perimeter of the Plain. The track is for vehicles but we see none for hours. Alone and empty. One brief period of distant gunfire – booming not crackling, must be some sort of artillery – then silence, and larks. Nigel is happy.

Larks are becoming an almost constant companion.

They twitter and trill high above, almost out of sight, circling higher; wind brings the sound in ebb and flow; larks rise to the edge of the upper atmosphere one feels, beyond human endurance, higher than mountains, sparklingly out of sight. Hard to imagine hunting larks, and eating them for breakfast, which people used to do. Shows how many there must have been. Women falconers, and young knaves, out at dawn with their kestrels, would take them down, ten in one outing, easy prey.

We had seen a few kestrels already, the wind-hover bird, hanging in the air before dropping step-fashion to survey closer the ground. The kestrel's hover seems to hoodwink the messiness of nature, not going with the flow, the wind, the waves, but making a solitary stand of perfect dignity, unruffled, slightly ruffled, eye sharp, pin sharp, frictionless vibrato of wings, feathered dominance of exact space. The wind-hovering kestrel is bigger than that other lark killer, the merlin, who flies in darting gestures often close to the contour, seeking cover from sharp-eyed birds above.

'Larks,' says Nige.

'Yep.'

'Love larks.'

'Yep . . . You know people used to eat them. A delicacy in the middle ages. Their tongues.'

Nige paused and squinted skyward. 'All that singing. Must build up your tongue muscles.'

The track, made from crushed chalk and blindingly white in the morning sun, led us to the next ancient site, Casterley Camp. Of Iron

Age origin, it's not much to look at but covers a large area, over sixty acres. And it provides an important clue: the ditches and ramparts have a symbolic as well as functional role. Think land art, Robert Smithson's *Spiral Jetty* and Flevoland – we like these things aesthetically, symbolically and, hey, they also work as walls and fences too. But Casterley as a defensive structure is laughable; on one side there is a twenty-foot drop from the top of the rampart to the bottom of the ditch, while on the other side a strange curved slope juts out, as if the fort's enclosure is giving birth.

In the centre, there's a pit which contained a post a metre in diameter, suggesting a huge tree trunk – possibly a sky pole of some kind, which later becomes the maypole of Merrie England (sky poles are found everywhere from North America to Nagaland). Dispersed around the post hole were fourteen red deer antlers and four human burials. It is, of course, a place of religious significance. 'Ritual function' as the archaeologists like to say, putting it on the same level as a regular bowel movement . . .

Casterley is Celtic, extending into Roman times, though it is thought the place was one of significance before it became a hillfort. The ditches were built long after Stonehenge, but the place may have been revered much earlier. After all, it is on the Line.

A tricked-out Land Rover surprised us and we had to move fast, be-rucksacked and inelegant, for the verge. But then it anchored up in the middle of the track and for a moment I was trepidatious, that old English walker's fear of trespassing never far away – maybe it is in our DNA from feudal times. Spray painted with mud, the Landy had an external roll cage and tyres as bloated as something nourished on whey powder and steroids. I braced myself for some sort of confrontation. But the youngish guy in his twenties with his smiling girlfriend and a bounding dog had stopped simply to ask for directions. He was friendly but clueless and treated Nigel's map as something arcane and fragile: his GPS had gone down and he'd been driving in circles all around the Plain.

Decently out of earshot, we slagged him off. 'Hard to get lost when on one side it's all "no entry, danger of death" signs and the other side it's a main road.'

'GPS victim.'

'Can't beat a proper map. He could hardly read it!'

'Exactly. But did you clock his bird?'

'No wonder he was distracted.'

'Probably looking for England's only layby under regular artillery bombardment.'

We continued in this laddish vein for a while, enacting the ritual revenge of the walker against those travelling in faster and more comfortable ways.

Then more signs. The signs the army erected had their own flavour, for example:

'Danger! Impact area. Keep out!'

'Danger! Unexploded Military Debris!'

Or the more arcane: 'VP 13 Casterley GR113537'.

This was actually quite useful; having a grid reference painted on the side of a hut in two foot letters made it very easy to find where we were.

Along the road from this unexplained locked hut was a row of giant shells painted white. Empty of detonator and charge, they stood penguin-like at the roadside, some a little wonky with rust dribbles around the nose. Signs of neglect; like the tattered red flag, tight and flapping on its high pole, its edge looking like it had been chewed by a giant hound. Surely the army, despite all the cuts, most know that such signs signal defeat, withdrawal in some sense? They'll be handing Salisbury Plain back next. Good.

I changed to my trainers as we left the Plain. Salisbury Plain takes a day's hike to cross through big, empty, open country on a single, endless track. But though it was marked as a track, and was gravelled, it was just as hard on the feet as a road. And now some mysterious and unwelcome pain had started in my Achilles tendons. Ah! The sheer relief of trainers. Why wear anything else unless it's seriously boggy and wet? I began to get the gnawing sense of impending failure you always get on a walk, often repeatedly. 'Is this it?' you ask yourself. 'The moment I give up?' That's why rest days are essential, one in every seven. Schedule them in as Amundsen did. And Scott didn't.

We, or rather I, limped down off the Plain. Nigel was striding pretty well. But he was still depressed and to my surprise I was beginning to catch it myself again. Gone was the buoyant banter of earlier. Common subjects had dried up. I could feel the sense of slippage that precedes depression; the inner hollowness, almost an ache, the creeping sense of pointlessness. The one sure sign is that you can't 'snap out of it', which is what all those who have not experienced depression expect you to do. The growing fear that you may never 'snap out of it'. That it's a permanent slide down.

The answer of course lies in halting, even briefly, the inward look. You need to look outwards. Stop assuming your ego is the 'real you'. Depression, like shyness, seemed to me then an ego problem: your self-image has taken a blow. You aren't quite the person you thought you were. You are somehow less, but in a crumpled, unformed and vulnerable way.

Ego blows are sustainable when you have good mental hygiene, when your life is ordered; but I had been living a disordered life for a while now and a certain small number of setbacks had slowed me down. What would have been, in the past, trivial, became a series of ego blows, seemingly endless: sponsorship declined, book plans refused, payment deferred. But I can see, even now, that this rather detached tone doesn't really suit any discussion of depression. Its major characteristic is how the onset of depression magnifies the personal, makes the subjective almost everything, blots out the entire world . . .

And it is terribly serious. You're down. You're slipping. And the only way out, is out. Looking outwards. And for me that came from reading a single story, in a book I had packed solely because it a) was very slim and b) had been sent to me free. But this is how life saves us . . . It was a story from Rumi's *The Hundred Tales of Wisdom*.[5]

In it, the Caliph Usman complains that his wealth keeps increasing despite him giving it away to charitable causes. He is used to wealth and finds it no novelty, in fact a burden because of the cares it brings, and he desires the freedom of poverty. Rumi explains that all he has to do is become ungrateful for good fortune. Oddly enough, good fortune does not succeed gratitude; it precedes it.

If someone had told me, 'Just be grateful for what you have', I'd have ignored them. I mean, what's in it for me? But the additional hook for the ego – gratitude will result in riches – found a chink in my self-centred carapace. So I started to list all the things I had to be grateful for.

And quite quickly I started to emerge from the dark, self-referential bubble of proto-depression. Gratitude opens you up; you face out-wards, you lighten up, the world is good again. Make a list of five things you are grateful for . . .

Off the Plain, down steep, deep paths cut by centuries of use and dangling with clematis we hurried, just in time to see Marden Henge before nightfall. Right on the Line and the largest henge monument in Britain (in fact, there is another henge less than a mile south of Marden that is thought to be part of the same huge complex, bigger than Stonehenge or Avebury), Marden Henge encircles Hatfield Farm and is bordered on the south by the nascent River Avon, wandering east before it strikes south towards Durrington Walls. The Avon had been the key linking every monument so far.

A Neolithic sweat lodge had been unearthed at Marden, consid-ered one of the most complete Neolithic buildings south of Orkney. Graves and grave goods had been found, including a jadeite axe head from the Aegean, amber from the Baltic and a dagger made from walrus ivory probably from Norway or Russia. One woman was buried with a gold-wrapped disc of bone, thought to be her own trepanation memento . . .

As a henge, with its ditch inside rather than outside the external bank of earth, we can exclude a defensive purpose. These huge earth rings symbolised the progress made to self-realisation in the sha-manic journey. Just as the mysterious – and almost endless – cup and ring marks found engraved on northern outcrops do. The labyrinth is another version. It is the metaphor of the journey through man's successive layers, crudely carved, but understood by all as a symbol of the path.

At Marden, a fifty foot high artificial hill, perhaps something like Silbury Hill near Avebury, was extensively mined and burrowed into in the late eighteenth and early nineteenth century. It collapsed in 1807, weakened by existing and recently dug shafts honeycombing the structure. With an admirable lack of concern, the hill was ploughed under and nothing really remains of it today apart from the odd suggestive rise in a network of fields, best viewed from a drone or other aerial vantage point. From this we can conclude that what is left of Britain's ancient monuments is what survived because it was on poor land. There must have been a great number of earth structures on good agricultural land that long ago were rifled and levelled by ploughing. The dearth of monuments in the fertile lands of eastern England may be because of this.

Material gifts from faraway suggest other gifts might also have travelled: ideas, potent shamanic ideas about orientation, the Pole Star, trances induced by heat, drumming or ingesting fly agaric fungi. That the henges were gathering places we know from the large quantities of bones left after feasting. A dozen pig skeletons have been found in one place at Marden – a big feast indeed. Why did they gather? To make more real the notions of alignment and inner journeying, the key elements of the shamanic path. If certain suggestive images are burnt into your consciousness you will make connections that otherwise you might miss. Humans think in analogies, largely, so having your brain first stocked with the right analogies is important.

We know now that paying attention to one thing rather than another, over time, increases neural connectivity in that area of the brain. And if you engage more of the senses and bodily movement when studying this thing, be it guitar playing or shamanistic beliefs, you'll physically change your brain. Do you believe before you have proof, as they tend to in the mysterious East? Or do you demand proof before you believe, as we like to do in the West? Well, the believing might be a necessary precursor to the neural build necessary to observe the proof when it appears. But *belief* may be the wrong word here – maybe we just need to know enough of the right kind of stories . . .

Ah, but death was still on the horizon. Our low mood (gratitude training takes a few days to kick in) was made worse by not finding a good camping spot. In the end, Nigel favoured a triangle of wood that was run through with quad bike tracks and pheasant cages, blue pellet containers and feed troughs. Would the owner return and find our lowly dwellings? Fuck 'im, was our official statement, though I was still at this stage surprisingly nervous.

These nerves were not helped when, after pitching, we took a stroll to the end of the wood only fifty yards from Nigel's tent and found the whiff of something very off. Three dead foxes, two with their tails cut off, were laid out in long grass, legs sticking front and back as if they had died jumping. Victims of quadbike-pheasant-man (I already pictured him as a fat sod, sweatily setting out his cages), but why keep the rotting bodies? To scare off other foxes? As some kind of totem?

Gamekeepers used to nail grey squirrels to trees as a warning, and I've heard it works, though admittedly that was from a gamekeeper. Both totem and revenge, the king's head on a pole at the city gates. My grandfather had a farm producing hen's eggs and had suffered enough from foxes to be no friend of theirs. I had inherited something of this aversion, yet who could not be sad at seeing a wild creature like that killed and discarded in this way?

Then we heard the sound of a quad bike coming. I looked at Nigel, who looked at me, making his jokey 'ominous' face. What should we do? It was nearly dusk, but you'd see our tents if you came down the main path.

The revving growl of a quadbike going up and down slopes hung in the night air for ages. And in the hours of twilight on a still night sound really does travel further. Exhausted and dispirited, we agreed on no fire and slunk off to our respective tents.

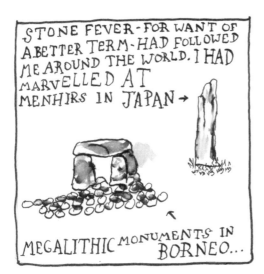

STONE FEVER - FOR WANT OF A BETTER TERM - HAD FOLLOWED ME AROUND THE WORLD. I HAD MARVELLED AT MENHIRS IN JAPAN →

MEGALITHIC MONUMENTS IN BORNEO...

...AND STONE CIRCLES IN THE EGYPTIAN SAHARA

ALL ALONG, THE REAL MYSTERY WAS BACK IN ENGLAND...

AND IT HAD TO DO WITH A LINE OF LONGITUDE:

1° 50' WEST

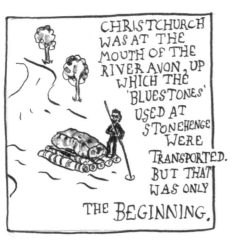

CHRISTCHURCH WAS AT THE MOUTH OF THE RIVER AVON, UP WHICH THE 'BLUESTONES' USED AT STONEHENGE WERE TRANSPORTED. BUT THAT WAS ONLY THE BEGINNING.

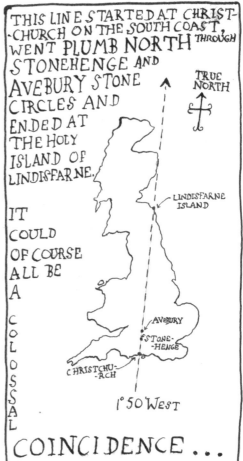

THIS LINE STARTED AT CHRIST-CHURCH ON THE SOUTH COAST, WENT PLUMB NORTH THROUGH STONEHENGE AND AVEBURY STONE CIRCLES AND ENDED AT THE HOLY ISLAND OF LINDISFARNE.

IT COULD OF COURSE ALL BE A COLOSSAL

TRUE NORTH

LINDISFARNE ISLAND

AVEBURY
STONE-HENGE

CHRISTCHU-RCH

1° 50' WEST

COINCIDENCE...

7

A POETICAL DUCK AND WITCHES

Avoiding the indecisive fox killer (he had taken two brushes, I found one discarded a few feet away; he'd cut it off, then changed his mind), we were alert even at this dark and damp early hour to the intrusive sound of another quad bike near by – the sound of the modern shepherd and country dweller. The rangy, rake-thin, striding countryman of yore had evolved into today's beefy, blowhard John Bull on his Kingquad 500. Such thoughts on farm labour were on my mind as we walked at dawn through the village of Charlton, where the annual Duck Feast is held in honour of the farm labourer poet Stephen Duck (*c.*1705–1756).

You can't help liking Stephen Duck – if only for the fact, that, already owning a name to relish – he married a woman called Sarah Big who then changed her name to the double-barrelled Sarah Big Duck. As a clever lad Stephen was encouraged by the local squire, schoolmaster and rector into reading Milton, Dryden and the Bible, and was soon writing poetry himself. Though a pious man who later wrote religious poetry, he was thankfully encouraged then to write about his everyday life. And at the age of twenty-five, he wrote 'The Thresher's Labour', a rather good poem about the fairly awful working life of an agricultural worker in the post-medieval but pre-mechanical age, where 25 per cent of a labourer's time was spent threshing in dark, stuffy, sweaty barns, the rural equivalent of the dark satanic mills.

The need for grain from increasing urbanisation, the enclosure of common land and commodification of grain production, the gradual stripping away of 'Holy Days' and other medieval festivals all meant farm workers were worked to the bone:

The Sweat, the Dust, and suffocating Smoak
Make us so much like Ethiopians *look,*
[. . .]
Week after week, we this dull Task pursue
Unless when winn'wing Days produce a New:
A new, indeed, but frequently a Worse!

But the young Duck was soon to leave the threshing nightmare behind. Taken up by Swift and Pope, 'The Thresher's Labour' was read at court to Queen Caroline in 1830. Duck became a famous man overnight and received an annuity and a small house to live in at Kew (which is where he married Caroline's housekeeper, Sarah Big). In 1735, in a move that may have rankled, he was made keeper of Merlin's Cave in Richmond – a thatched folly complete with waxworks.

He was later ordained and, after stints as a chaplain, finally became a popular parish priest in Byfleet. But at the age of fifty-one, he committed suicide by drowning himself in the river at Reading. Some claimed the social divide he had traversed had finally caught up with him; that he felt out of his depth in the company he kept. But is this credible? Duck had been a professional poet (and hermit) longer than he had been a thresher. As with all suicides, one suspects something more complex. Queen Caroline, his main sponsor had died; Pope and Swift were also dead. He had swapped poetry for the more socially acceptable role of vicar. Betrayal of the Muse? Something to muse on, as Nigel and I sipped our morning milk – bought in a glass bottle from a milk float that hovered out of the morning mist with a Tardis-like groan at 6 a.m.

No more threshers in the immaculate village of Charlton, and even the milk float, still in old-style livery, smacked of some kind of retro-simulation, but such serendipitous encounters involving food or drink are much valued by the walker. We set off across wet fields of thyme and mint owned by Vitacress (pulling up a few strands for addition to the supper pot), and though the path was ploughed over and boot claggy, we were in much better spirits than before.

Stephen Duck, a fellow poet and descendant of threshers, as I was; I could sympathise with every step of his journey away from working-class tedium. My sister, along with an uncle, was obsessive about family history. My shallow interest in genealogy had been in any famous or royal or 'big' characters I could colourfully yarn about. But apart from a mayor of Lichfield, our forebears were modest folk, mostly agricultural workers. No wonder everyone in my family likes gardening so much.

Casting myself back to when I was in my twenties, doing manual work, writing poetry and generally skiving – i.e. a young man interested in verse and the life of the mind – I could sympathise with Stephen Duck's horror at dull physical labour. He even contrasts it with the shepherd's life, which allows for contemplation and wonderful views. Yet I had discovered, after the age of twenty-five, that you can get into dull repetitive work – and even get a kind of high from it. The kind of high that drives people to Stakhanovite excesses. But Duck left that life before he'd discovered this. It's something Neal Cassady of the Beat Poets learnt later in life, swinging a hammer and working on the railways. Despite his humble origins, Duck was a true intellectual: he'd forgotten he had a body. Mind you, like Cassady he knew there was another reason why the workers did not revolt. In 'A Description of a Journey to Marlborough, Bath, Portsmouth, &c.', he describes the scene after the harvest is in:

> No Cares, no Toils, no troubles now appear,
> For Troubles, Toils and Cares are drown'd in beer.

The sun was up now. Our spirits were raised even higher by legging it over the main train line, the straight double rails, splinters of steel shining to the horizon; you wait and check nervously then saunter across, thinking all the time, 'What happens if I trip?' No larking about here, as if we ever would – Nigel and I were sensible schoolboys, not the kind to play chicken on the railway track. And once across, almost instantly, the *vroom* and painful shriek of a high-speed train ... It made us laugh with nervousness, as if we had escaped something unpleasant by our wit and skill.

We were now entering places I knew a little. 'There's a pub in Honeystreet,' I told Nigel. 'We can get some lunch there, perhaps.' But the pub, which had been the local for crop circle enthusiasts from the late Nineties until recently, had just shut. Canal boats lined the banks near by, no longer able to suckle from the mothership.

One man, full of himself, as some are when they confront walkers listlessly lying by a shut pub and brewing up on a tiny stove, regaled us with the fantastic success of his life post-miserable divorce and losing his small house in Cheam. He had cashed in his half of the settlement to buy a canal boat, which had been too big to get under many of the bridges he subsequently encountered. But having sawn off the top of the front cabin (which was still fairly commanding – we were given a tour), he'd discovered that if he filled his water tanks he was able to scrape under any bridge he was likely to encounter. He was a good-hearted man, a rugby enthusiast, a big man alone on an over-buoyant boat. He planned next to take it to France, 'and who knows where after that!' But as he was more or less completely uninterested in our own adventure, we wrote him off as a pillock.

The Kennet and Avon Canal, which we'd just crossed, lies at the foot of the downs, the downs that would lead us to Avebury. The village of Alton Priors (last stop before the downs, you can't help feeling) is a place of huge and ancient significance. Maybe something of this, twisted and distorted by our upside down culture, drove the rather desperate crop circle fad that flourished here twenty years ago, and perhaps led to the creation of the small roadside museum and photo gallery we passed. Inside, it was hung with small witch puppets, half-humorous, borderline creepy. Yes, we were entering witch territory, if indeed we had ever left it.

Wicca is a subset of paganism, which is claimed to be the fastest growing religion in the UK after Islam, and is spoken of by its adherents 'as a true British religion', the only one not imported. I've met a few pagans, and apart from a penchant for calling themselves after trees ('Ash, meet Oak, or is it Thorn?') they speak a lot of sense about the need to reconnect in some way with the everyday mysteries of nature, and of becoming wild again – as in, natural wild rather than out-of-control wild.

Some claim Wicca is the remnant of a native shamanism that flourished before the arrival of the Celts and their European druidism. Others with a wider perspective consider shamanism too to be an import, ultimately from Central Asia, some time after an Ice Age had receded. Certainly elements of Turanic shamanism have been reintroduced into Wicca, rather like the reconstruction of ancient dinosaurs from trapped blood in amber and frog DNA in *Jurassic Park*.

The interests and preoccupations of shamanic religion are apparent in everything that Stone Age (i.e. Palaeo- and Neolithic) man has left behind. This is the theory advanced by Mircea Eliade, rebuffed, and then massively shored up more recently, as I have mentioned, by David Lewis-Williams and Jean Clottes in their work on ancient cave dwellers.[6]

It was my growing belief that it was impossible *not* to interpret the distant past in this way. Having travelled with remote peoples living in a pre-modern way in Africa and many parts of Asia, I can safely say that their main preoccupation and references are dimensions other than the everyday. And though these people may be crushed in the face of diggers and chainsaws, they are very successful at the mundane things they do on their own terms, such as hunting and forest gardening. In fact, a multi-dimensional perspective helps these activities: as anthropologist Dr Jeremy Narby has shown,[7] many traditional people of the Amazon successfully enter altered states in order to better hunt or use natural resources. They literally dream their way to success. And the language of these shamanic dreamers is never direct and prosaic, it twists and turns and relies on puns and metaphors to bypass the rational mind that constantly throws up objections.

Interestingly, when Narby persuaded some Western botanists and scientists to take a jungle hallucinogen, to see if it helped their creativity, they reported that it did, but not significantly more than their own habits of daydreaming and contemplation. In other words, they already had their own way of getting into the altered state needed for some kinds of creativity.

It is beyond the scope of this book (oh how I love typing that phrase!) to try to persuade you that we should all become fur-clad shamans stalking the woods and streams of Albion. Nevertheless, if we want to understand the true unearthly–earthly mysteries of England, her ancient stones and our roots in Stone Age man, we must embrace a non-utilitarian, multi-dimensional view of man that ultimately conflicts with the modern academic position.

You see traces of this position in the almost troubled observations at the end of Jean Clottes' *What Is Paleolithic Art?*, when he travels with shamans in Siberia and concludes that there is a meaning of a deeper kind in the revelations of shamanic religion; that, unlike the arguments of the staunchly prosaic Lewis-Williams, the shamanic experience isn't just some sort of weird acid trip, all in the head, but actually connects to something bigger, more significant, more connected. In other words, it aligns.

The modern academic posture has to be (when it dares to venture into areas of religion) atheistic. Of course, many academics aren't atheists, but they either have to hide this, or refuse to research areas involving belief. Suggesting that a moral posture, a spiritual idea, an earthwork and the life of a people are really connected would earn you a round of laughter at a university conference, rather than a round of applause.

In the end, like Jean Clottes, like Jeremy Narby, you have to cross over to the other side. You have to get just a little bit weird.

Why? Because otherwise you may go mad. The madness of the past – the mass delusions – are different to our current desperate, non-social forms of despair. Melancholia existed of course, but was far less widespread than today; I suspect most madness in the past wasn't about lack of meaning in life; it was about being caught up in some form of hysteria. Now I see the roots of madness in everyone's attempts at sidestepping the big question: how do you live in a world that is – on the surface that it presents, the official version that it thrusts in your face – meaningless? For most of human history, mankind has interacted with, communed with, and got better and worse at understanding the ineffable and wordless zone of mystery that surrounds our very existence. And found meaning in it. But to find that meaning today you have to let go of the official version, drop Dawkins and look elsewhere.

It is to this mystery that Wicca – with its silly witches and burning men and circles and sacred spots – attempts to give significance. You see, the common argument about proof is misdirected. Religious activity is just as much about practice as belief. Practice without initial belief can lead to the flickering of belief. Belief can lead to more practice, and further practice can increase the importance one ascribes to those beliefs (and by belief I do not mean obsession, I mean something more dynamic and encouraging of openness to all kinds of experience). It is about giving ideas their due importance, rather than arguing, as a philosopher might, about the logical grounds for believing X rather than Y. In martial arts, a teacher will tell you that stance is the most important thing, but as a beginner you may take years to realise the significance of this statement.

This walk was my way, I was beginning to see, of shoving certain beliefs into the foreground, or walking the talk, so to speak, so that I could talk the walk better. I believed there was something odd and mysterious about this Line up England. Now I had to reveal it.

But witches and all that craziness? Well, we'd be getting into that all too soon . . .

If I had to nominate an unlikely charity to support, it would be the quiet and modest Churches Conservation Trust, who look after hundreds of disused churches in England. A place like this church in Alton Priors would, without that fine charity, have been sold off and converted into a split-level residence, the cool high-tech floor suspended dead centre of the nave windows; a couple of squat black cars reminiscent of jelly moulds in the drive, probably with humorously linked personalised number plates . . .

Instead we have a cool, damp church with an ancient yew tree in the graveyard. A church is a place that is always open; even the locked ones (which are few and far between, I would discover) have generous porches in which you can dry off and brew up tea on the gas stove. You can make a brew in any church porch as long as it isn't during a service; and for most churches in the wilds that is 99 per cent of the time, with vicars straddling about four churches at a time and doing one service a month in each.

Those churches that are open allow a glimpse into the stilled and slowed air of a reverent past. Deluded or not means naught alongside the carved wood finials shiny through use over hundreds of years, the dusty font, the light battling past stained-glass windows and leaded diamonds to break into the cool gloom.

Alton Priors: the name had a ring to it. I had heard it before, long ago, in a sunny schoolroom while studying the English poet and essayist Edward Thomas, whose poetry I had never wholeheartedly liked. I went back to his poem 'Lob' to find the reference to Alton Priors. It is where Thomas is sure he met an aged wise man who re-membered the opening of the barrows in his youth, and it speaks of a forlorn search for some ineffable form of English magic that Thomas masterfully evokes in the poem as a potent brew of folk tales, wise saws, slang, old words and ancient rhymes, the unchanging land-scape, the ancient burials.

(One piece of ancient lore, mundane perhaps but interesting, he reveals is the origin of the word 'skinflint'. Flint and steel were used to start a fire or light a pipe; when the flint was worn down with repeated use the miserly would 'skin it' with a knife to get a bit more use from it.)

The poem takes flight and the remembered old sage becomes Tall Tom, Herne the Hunter, old Lob, Young Jack the namer of things; it is he who knows why there is a Totteridge, a Totterdown and a Juggler's Lane. (And anyone who walks up England will spend some time trying to work out how places got their stupendously odd names.)

'Lob' is a *cri de coeur* for the same strangeness I was looking for: the pre-Christian, shamanic strangeness of old England that is there still at every turn if you half-shut your eyes and listen for the hum of insects, the sound of the cuckoo, the fast tumbling of a cold brook, the smell of wild thyme.

It was serendipity that brought us to this church (always more highly valued by the serendipped than those breathlessly told about it, but still); we had originally followed signs to a Saxon church in Alton Barnes, assuming that would be the interesting one to see. But by getting slightly lost and finding ourselves at the later Norman church here, we discovered one of the marvels of the Line: a church resting on sarsen stones.

All Saints' Church is built on raised ground, which is very often a sign that this was an even earlier special site. The circular walls of the graveyard, perhaps with incorporated sarsen stones, was another clue. As we walked round the church, it was clear one of the buttresses was supported with a sarsen stone. Just as the ancient Egyptians 'seeded' later temples with stones from earlier ones, not disguised, but celebrated, so, too, the sarsen stones here were clearly revered rather than seen as symbols of a disgraceful 'heathen' religion. Evidence that sarsen stones were not seen, even in Norman times, as simply 'stones' is, in the case of Alton Priors, to be found very excitingly by opening a trapdoor. Actually two: one on the right as you enter the church and another near the altar.

Nigel spotted the trapdoors. The first revealed a large, uneven stone with a hole drilled in it. Some have speculated that this might have been an oath stone, perhaps one used for 'handfasting' – a word of Norse and Germanic origin, meaning to make a commitment by shaking hands (and presumably inserting them into the hole for extra significance). Handfasting can also mean a commitment to marriage, which is something the Wiccans have latched on to, and 'handfasting' has, since the Sixties, become a form of pagan marriage. (Jim Morrison of the Doors was 'handfasted' to Patricia Kennealy in a pagan ceremony in 1970.)

The second stone, nearer the altar, is longer and more obviously resembles a standing stone. Several interesting questions must be asked. Why keep these stones? Why not use them in the construction of the building if the stones are simply structural objects? And, if this is a former holy spot, why wasn't the Saxon church built here first?

The answers must be those already speculated upon: that the stones were 'seeds' from an ancient site. And the site remained significant even after the conversion to Christianity. The presence of a yew, already five hundred years old when the church was built, suggests the ancient site had remained, with the stones, a place of significance despite the arrival of Christianity in Saxon times.

I had an inkling now why churches are special and should be preserved simply as sacred spots – because that is exactly what they are. People more attuned to the mysteries of the Earth than we are today chose this place – not for economic, agricultural or theoretical reasons; these were the power spots of old and by retaining them we protect something of value. Approach a village at dawn and the place may seem shut and irrelevant, but the church remains in its old spot, a portal to other dimensions.

Near most special stones you find water. And this was some water: none other than the sacred rising of the River Avon in a spring near the church. The name Avon comes from the ancient British word for river: *afon*. That's why there are five Avons in England. One can imagine a Roman invader enquiring of a surly Brit the name of the river they are standing by and getting a one-word riposte . . .

But this Avon is special: it's the only river to run a significant length of the Line, connecting the ancient sites from here all the way to the sea, and, almost certainly, the method for transporting the Welsh bluestones to Stonehenge.

The Avon has several sources, but none as magical as this, known as Broadwell or the Laughing Well. And it really is laughing. A beautiful circular pool in a dip with an upbubbling source in its centre. It reminded me of natural gas bubbling up through river water, but this is not gas; it is water bubbling up from the ground. A true sacred spring mentioned as early as the ninth century in the Saxon chronicles as *aweltun* – literally, a farmstead with a well – which has become Alton.

Naturally we had to have a brew by the spring and drink directly of its waters. The Line, as I have mentioned, very closely follows the watershed line up England – the line dividing rivers that flow either east or west. And the watershed line is always near the spring line; was it then the line of springs – of sacred water – that determined the ancient significance of the line?

Wood, stone and water: all three seemed always to be present at these ancient places. I thought I understood wood and water; stone I was learning about as I walked. But seeing this spring, I began to see water differently. Its deep significance. I imagined these sodden pastures as the remnants of the glaciers of the last Ice Age, which finally retreated only a hundred or so miles to the north. The place must have been running with water. Sarsen stones were often ripped from old riverbeds, worn flat on one side by flood waters; after the Ice Age, these early rivers must have been ferocious. Then, as England was repopulated and settlements grew rapidly, the water dwindled to this line of sacred springs, always there, always reliable.

But the economic argument is never sufficient, however superficially compelling. Whatever it takes to make a special spot, whatever humdrum components are needed, the specialness is not just for the sake of feeling good. It is a very definite and precise arena for creating an experience. The experience of greater and greater connection to all things on this planet ... and beyond. It was truly a place of alignment.

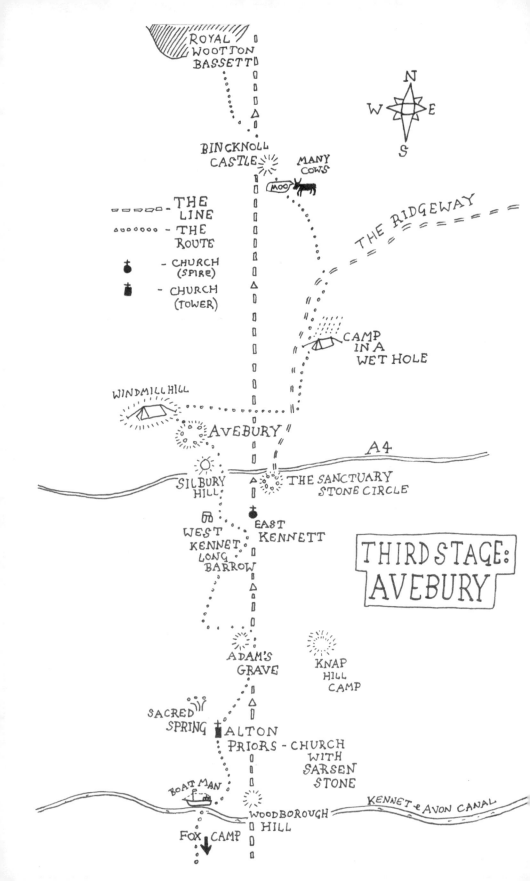

ROYAL
WOOTTON
BASSETT

N
W E
S

BINCKNOLL
CASTLE

MANY
COWS

MOO

THE RIDGEWAY

⊟⊟⊟⊟ - THE
LINE
∆∆∆∆ - THE
ROUTE
♠ - CHURCH
(SPIRE)
♣ - CHURCH
(TOWER)

CAMP
IN A
WET HOLE

WINDMILL HILL

AVEBURY

A4

SILBURY
HILL

THE SANCTUARY
STONE CIRCLE

WEST
KENNETT
LONG
BARROW

EAST
KENNETT

THIRD STAGE:
AVEBURY

ADAM'S
GRAVE

KNAP
HILL
CAMP

SACRED
SPRING

ALTON
PRIORS - CHURCH
WITH
SARSEN
STONE

BOAT MAN

KENNET & AVON CANAL

FOX CAMP

WOODBOROUGH
HILL

8

ON FROM ADAM'S GRAVE AND AVEBURY

The sacred entrance if you like, the enchanted gateway to the downs and to the new lands dominated by Avebury and West Kennet and beyond, lies between Knap Hill and the summit known as Adam's Grave. At this portal lies the significant crossroads (always a place of significance to the shaman, and subconsciously referenced in a macabre form by the ancient gibbet sited at a crossroads) of the Tan Hill Way and the continuation of the ancient route of the Ridgeway.

I grew up in the Vale of White Horse, the Uffington Horse, which lies on the Ridgeway. The landscape here holds some significant but homely milestones:

1. First visit to Wayland's Smithy long barrow and the White Horse, aged ten. Reverently draw maps of both places in a special note-book with a penguin on the cover which I still have.
2. Walk with two boys – Motty and David Plaine – twelve miles of the Ridgeway for a scout badge, aged thirteen. Years later David Plaine is shockingly beaten up on a scout camp by a group that included Motty because he had 'gone gay and put a safety pin through his ear' (it was the beginning of punk, a movement my conservative scout troop did not approve of).
3. Wearing a borrowed climbing helmet, ride the Ridgeway on a borrowed motorbike, aged twenty. Feel like Hunter S. Thompson until I get stuck in a deep rut and have to be hauled out by two proper off-roaders.
4. Very late at night, visit the tomb of Wayland's Smithy with poet Steve Micalef and wait for the sunrise, aged twenty-two. On the way back, we cycle past the village policeman in Uffington, out in

his front garden to exercise his falcon, the hooded bird sitting on his outstretched gauntlet-clad hand.

5. Fail to walk the Ridgeway owing to blisters and rain, aged thirty-two. Rescued at a chip shop by long-suffering parents.

6. Hold a launch event for a book about the search for a lost oasis in the Sahara at Wayland's Smithy, aged forty-three. This wacky (though for me rather significant) gathering was attended by a descendant of the explorer Mungo Park, who arrived in bare feet after navigating the Thames in a coracle made of horse hide . . .

The Ridgeway is surprisingly remote considering it snakes through the highly populated M4/M40 corridor, with reintroduced red kites circling over the motorway commuter traffic. It is, of course, a watershed route of its own: to get water you have to descend one side or the other, or make do with a dew pond settled in the fold of a hill. It was never a route linking places of population. In fact, the evidence suggests the most ancient routes that did that are probably buried under existing A- or B-roads – the rule being to build on the path that came before you. An animal path around an obstacle or across pastureland becomes the human track that becomes the winding road we have today.

So where does that leave the Ridgeway, which interestingly doesn't even go through sacred Avebury, but trails off a mile or so to the east . . .? A drovers' road – certainly. Before that, in times of unimaginably greater numbers of wildlife, enormous herds of deer and elk may have used it as a route from pasture to pasture, with wooded lands far below. In the wet times after the Ice Age, the hill that Nigel and I were puffing our way up would have been running with water; boggy marsh would have been the normal lowland state and the relatively dry Ridgeway would have been both a route for herds of ungulates and for the humans hunting them.

Relatively quickly humans spread out over England, producing a network of tracks and paths between homesteads and hamlets that would be recognisable today. But these were now submerged beneath tarmac and only paths through areas less frequented retained their ancient integrity.

We walked up to the hill. Nigel, who had been feeling worse than usual, stood for a long while in an *Angel of the North* posture on the top of Adam's Grave and somewhat revived himself. The 'grave' is technically a long barrow – and it is long, over sixty metres, though it seems, from its hilltop position with its side ditches, like a sort of micro henge; far too small to be for any defensive purpose and therefore symbolic and funerary in usage. There are traces of a sarsen stone burial chamber and in 1860 the remains of three skeletons and a beautiful leaf-shaped arrowhead were unearthed.

The view was tremendous, the wind ripping at our clothes and giving us earache as we walked over the neighbouring (or neighboring) white horse – a recent one carved in 1812 and therefore somehow, with our heads full of ancient lore and ancient sites, uninspiring.

There were walkers now along the ridge we followed, which would take us across the mysterious Wansdyke earthworks and up to West Kennet Long Barrow. The sun and the wind were cancelling each other out, leaving a cold brightness to the day. Thistles grew at the path edge; too early for orchids but I looked anyway. Flint shards spilt from scrapes of grey topsoil and chalk below.

It was hot walking and we wanted to cut through directly to West Kennet, but there were keep out signs everywhere. Men in a group of hangar-like buildings watched us careful as we discussed simply using a track that went past their homestead of dilapidated vehicles and piles of algae-covered tyres. Too many walkers, too many stone-lovers had obviously pissed them off. I wondered if this redneck hold-out had any interest in the ancient landscape. Probably just seen as a hippy thing. So we went the long way round to West Kennet.

I was glad of having to make this approach, up through a field of knobbly denuded cabbage stalks, where a wide track had formed from the foot traffic to the ancient grave. The gentle curve of the hill leant real grandeur to the approach; there is something royal about the West Kennet Long Barrow.

The deep dark chamber appealed to my love of caves and bunkers.

There weren't a huge number of caves where I grew up in Warwick-shire and I have always highly valued them, I am not sure why. On examination, it was easy to see that some of the stones that made up the barrow were sculpted by moving water – not merely rain, but a river in spate. These stones had been hauled from a river bed some-where, though others would have come from the scattered piles on the downland further north.

We wanted to be in Avebury before nightfall and now we were hurrying. We gave a cursory look at the sacred spring on the town's side of the downs. Then it was down to the pub in Avebury, a place of utilitarian functionality, less a gastro pub and more of a Bisto pub, the kind of place where you are best off choosing fish and chips, and not the expensive steak option as I did.

Dark and half-full of food and beer, we made our way with head torches up Windmill Hill, the ancient causewayed enclosure that overlooks Avebury less than a mile to the northwest. To sleep in an ancient site is not condoned or even allowed by the owners of such places. Nigel, then, was not too keen on camping on this revered and ancient monument. I pointed to the nosey sheep pushing closer as we messed with tent poles and sleeping gear.

'They're sleeping up here and they're animals,' I reasoned. 'And judging by their claggy arses, a lot less clean than us.'

But that old middle-class fear of being humiliated by an irate farmer only grows as you get older. Two fifty-year-old men acting like scared schoolboys. It was a barrier I was keen to break through. This land was our land . . . our ancient inheritance. Even though Nigel was stark naked from the waist down at one point as he changed into his long johns, we did not provoke interest, camping in the hidden bowl of the enclosure, which was invisible from below.

The air was chilly as the stars came out and we hunkered down in our separate tents. I wrestled once more with the too-small sleeping bag and vowed to get myself an even downier down bag, an extrava-gance I had denied myself for years . . .

Nigel would be parting ways with me here in the morning, leav-ing on a bus to Swindon,[8] and I could already hear him snoring. I unzipped the tent door to see the stars. Looking into a black infinity with the faintest reassurance of little lights, I could make out not a single recognisable constellation. There was something satisfying in not being bothered by this and I fell asleep.

All alone at last.

It's different when you're on your own but not in an obvious way. First you have more control over your time. If you want to mess about drying the tent or fiddle with your camera settings or read a bit from the *Penguin Guide to Prehistoric England and Wales*, you can. You don't have to be as careful about where you piss and shit. If you want to run, you can. If you have to keep stopping to adjust the lacing of your boots, you can. It's safer, in a way, because you go at your own pace instead of rushing to keep up or dawdling and getting bored.

Reinhold Messner, the first man to climb all the 8000-metre peaks without oxygen, prefers to go alone, and when he can't he goes at his own pace. Even if it means, as was the case when he went to the South Pole, leaving his companion so far behind, that said companion (Arved Fuchs) ends up hating you and vowing never to go on an expedition with you ever again . . . Such is the brutality needed to be a top explorer, who goes at his own pace.

When you walk alone, you scare away less wildlife because you're not talking. And you can make more mistakes and get lost without feeling such a fool. On the other hand, if you travel with someone who is observant like Nigel, you get the benefit of their eyes. Another time when you regret being alone is when you find a pub after doing more than your usual miles and that celebratory drink just isn't the same, really.

The tour buses had already started pouring people into Avebury. A pretty village ringed with standing stones was just too good a sight to miss – like a smaller Stonehenge but with a teashop and pub on hand. I had a strong urge to ignore again the usual siren call of the pub, but I succumbed for a 'final meal' – fish and chips, unlike the chewy old steak I had last time. 'Final meals' are a big part of a walk like mine; indeed, you can end up having them almost every day. You feel you have to make the most of what's on offer before you return to a diet of tinned mackerel and Pot Noodles. All the same, I told myself I was eager to leave after eating; even the prospect of a pub with an 86-foot well dating from 1600 in the bar palls after a while (though it does have ferns growing in it that you can see through the glass lid).

In the pub, the 'well table' was taken, but I had a good view of it. When the people who had been sitting there finished and left, a couple of women came in. They inspected the table as if they were about to buy it – with the well thrown in too, but only if they bargained cannily enough. Gravely, they asked the school-age server if the table was reserved. Discovering it wasn't, they pondered some more and made the weighty decision to take it.

I envied their involvement in their own lives. Like many people who can't take much of modern life seriously, I don't usually give a toss where I sit. I'm too busy rushing through my existence, tearing off chicken legs of experience and spitting the bones out without chewing properly . . . However, this lofty and dissociated feeling was not helped by the smell of my wet socks draped discreetly on my rucksack in an attempt to speed their drying. An Indian family came in for a meal and my barefoot appearance with stewing socks caused the pater familias to look at me with a sort of pitying recognition, before he ushered his people to a table at the other end of the restaurant.

I thought I probably 'ought to' make some kind of pilgrim-like walk around the stones, but somehow I couldn't find the inspiration. It seemed enough to walk across the rain-sodden grass to get a better look at one stone and check whether it had river erosion marks on it (it had). This was my big theory, then: that ancient stones came from rivers for a reason, a linking of earth and water. They would also have been easier to break off when water ran over them like a lip and created an overhang. But like all theories, it was just conjecture. In the end, only the stones remain, enigmatic and not a little mocking.

I was just not that interested in getting . . . what? All vibed up on the place? I was more excited about getting back to the Ridgeway, which for the next section of the walk followed the Great North Line.

*

I have alluded already to my attempt to walk the Ridgeway in 1996, which ended in a raging blisters and a chip shop debacle. I had started twice: once at its end at the market town of Tring, and once at its beginning at Avebury. I walked a bit from both ends but failed to join them up.

I was at the time living in London in a housing association flat under the assumed name of Hazel (the three of us who lived there had to pretend to be the middle-aged Jamaican woman called Hazel whose flat it was but who had fled back to Jamaica). Sometimes we would – well, Hazel would – be summoned to appear at the housing association but we would always make excuses. When it got desperate, our downstairs neighbour, who was coincidentally also called Hazel, went in and explained that the other Hazel was away and somehow that was just enough to hold them off.

The flat was grimy and had a huge bloodstain on the landing floor. I found a defunct air pistol, a tatty rucksack and a commando dagger in the loft. Even after we laid down some new carpet and lino, the place remained extremely downbeat. But it was exceptionally cheap. The kitchen table was a board resting on two paraffin heaters that provided the only heating in the place – but it was enough. All cooking was done on a two-ring electric cooker, until one of the rings broke which meant all our cooking was done on a single ring, which was slightly inconvenient but perfectly possible.

I was teaching English in a sporadic way and trying to get my first book published. I dreamt of escaping the city but was too lazy to do much about it. But the rucksack gave me an idea: walk the Ridgeway!

It was summer so I decided to do it lightweight style. I had no tent or waterproofs at that time (for a period in my twenties and early thirties I turned my back on my earlier interest in the outdoors). I had a pair of boots I'd bought at a thrift store in San Francisco. They were chunky and a little tight. They'll stretch with all the walking, I told myself. I didn't even have a sleeping bag.

I saw a rather small cycling poncho for sale in a discount bin at Halfords. It cost £3.50. This became both my waterproof coat and tent. I had a thick jumper for warmth and a large metal mug that I planned to use for cooking on fires. Not that I had ever done much cooking on fires, but I'd always liked lighting them. I took several books including a guide to the Ridgeway I had borrowed from a friend who had never walked it either. No map but the guide had narrow versions printed on every other page.

As the earlier list showed, the Ridgeway had assumed a sort of mythical status for me because it was the nearest long-distance path to where I lived. Long distance walking had been of intense interest to me and several of my friends when we were growing up; we regarded people who had 'done' the Pennine Way with considerable awe. I think we saw it as a rite of passage, something difficult and adventurous. My only attempt – walking the Cleveland Way when I was fourteen – ended in failure when I left the flysheet behind and my pal and I were soaked for forty-eight hours both inside and outside our tent. Oh yes, I was already used to failing on long distance walks.

The Ridgeway was near, my 'home' turf. Must be fairly easy. Anyway, I set off to Tring with high hopes and a couple of tins of sardines.

Of course it rained steadily as I tried to transform my electric blue cycling cape into some kind of shelter. When I stood up, it barely reached my waist, was more of a ruff than a cape, a fashion accessory designed for the shortened profile of a seated cyclist. I fondly imagined, after watching a few episodes of Ray Mears' TV series *Tracks* and having built a few dens in my youth, that I could create a hybrid leaf and cycling cape shelter.

I was in a wood near Chartwell. It was a wood full of foxes and owls and badgers and pheasants who made a great racket all night. I was awake all night so I was able to notice how different barks and squawks and squeals happened at different times, as if each wild creature had its own time slot. The cape sort of kept my head dry; the rest of me was soaked. As was the wood, so it was no fire and cold sardines and no pasta for me. My wet boots were already giving me blisters. They were made of a kind of leather that doesn't stretch when wet but actually shrinks quite considerably. In a few miles, I was daintily limping along a C-road in the Chilterns, acquainting myself with the exquisite agony of raging blisters and tight, unforgiving boots. The sun came out so the tarmac heated up, making it even worse.

My parents rescued me at a chip shop in Watlington, a town where a few episodes of *Midsomer Murders* have been filmed. After a day of rest, my good dad dropped me at Avebury. I was wearing the same boots. I still believed it was my 'soft feet' rather than the stupid foot-wear that was the problem. Fancifully I thought a day's walking would have 'hardened them up'. I managed a day before giving up again.

I'd set off from Avebury up the same track I was now walking. It was quiet, getting towards dusk (I'd mucked about getting supplies during the day, been rained on, been to the pub, etc.). Quite suddenly, a woman bore down on me on a mountain bike at high speed, as I was checking my map with my glasses hooked up (making me short sighted but good for checking maps). In a moment of impaired vision, I froze in the deep rut in which I was standing. Hurtling towards me in the same rut, she shouted very brusquely and loudly, 'Get out of the way!' And then as she passed, she rang her bell.

This was the clincher. This is what drove me to sheer unmitigated rage. I think she was trying to 'thank me' after the manner of cars which flash both indicators when you let them in ahead of you. But the bell could have been used earlier. Why shout – and had she no brakes? I had moved out of sheer, automatic fear of the authority in her voice. This too I naturally resented. No one likes to discover they're house trained. A better rider, I fumed, could have wheelied out of the rut. I could have; I was great at wheelies. Once. A long time ago.

Slowly sanity returned, as it tends to in the damp dusk, the crepuscular hour. But despite this being *l'heure du crépuscule*, it was still damp and a few spots of rain started to soak into my Buffalo top (which can manage half an inch of rain an hour but no more, according to the company website). I was on top of the landscape. Fields with rough piles of sarsen stones were on either side of the wide Ridgeway track. I started looking for shelter.

Farmers have long noticed that large stones have a propensity to rise up through their fields, as if coming up from the underworld. This is made even more apparent in post-Ice Age conditions where the land is thawing, and then subject to longer periods of frost than today. Since rock conducts heat better than earth, a large stone channels cold further into the earth and actually stands upon a frozen core. This can suck in more moisture from the surrounding earth as it freezes. Since ice is peculiar and occupies more volume than the equivalent water, the freezing of the sub-rock serves to shove the rock upwards. Known as 'frost heaving', its effects are exacerbated by wind erosion of the soil and tillage. Could ancient man have seen these boulders rising up from the earth and thought them special? It certainly would have added to their attraction.

I could camp on the track but it was windy and exposed. Climbing over a fence, I found a hollow some way down the hill. There were a few interested sheep but they kept their distance. But now I couldn't pretend I wasn't on private property. Livestock means a red-faced farmer lurking with a shotgun somewhere. I was wild camping *alone* for the first time on this trip – and this was how I was thinking.

Wild camping, stealth camping . . . I prefer the greater honesty of the term 'stealth camping'. For me, camping means being in a tent anywhere. The expression 'wild camping' seems like a way to jazz up the ordinariness of . . . camping. It's sort of borrowing some of the feral prestige of bears and wolves, except there aren't any in England where it's even pretty hard to get away from something as tame as road noise, at least in the South. It can't be that wild if you can hear a DAF truck grinding through its twenty gears on the opposite hill.

But stealth camping is different. It's hiding, being a bit canny, a bit criminal; a trespasser except, of course, no one knows you've been there – and you leave before dawn. Stealth camping is suited to the edgelands,[9] those places that are neither town nor country, not really rural but not urban, which is much of England now; in which villages are actually suburbs and farms a sort of local colour, their real value being the rising price of the land they occupy.

Stealth camping in the rain. Always stealthier, as quite wisely fewer folk are about looking for stealth campers to out; at the same time, you care less about being found, less about camping and more about the fact that you are being pissed on. I got the still-damp tent up (no opportunity to dry it during the day) in a patch of nettles in a dip that threatened to fill with water if the rain persisted. Fuck it.

Dawn rain. Misty drizzle. It had rained all night but my hole was simply spongey and not a small lake. Drops of water, seemingly enlarged, defying surface tension, huge in fact, were on every blade of grass. Stretching away down to the fields of wet sarsen stones, for I see I have camped on the edge of a valley of stones. Grey wethers they call them, and they do look a bit like sheep lying down in the rain. You can see why Avebury was a good site, so near to so much stone.

After a quick cup of coffee, I was on the move through the droplet-laden grass, trousers soaked immediately, too lazy to put on gaiters. Two rabbits lolloped off though the damp greenery, which was unusual as rabbits, like humans, hate the wet. Then I saw another and came up with no good reason why they were there, but was cheered by the early morning anomaly.

I was back on the track now, brolly up and enjoying the ring of drips that didn't affect me. A disturbance in the sky, two helicopters flying to Wootton Bassett; like dragonflies a-roar, they passed too low and too quickly overhead. Very soon, though, I was back in the little world I was walking through. I studied the ground, the healthy wide verges: meadow saxifrage, lady's bedstraw, clustered bellflower. And from out and under the brolly's edge again: lapwings, a single tree sparrow and always skylarks following my path; larks singing despite the drizzling rain.

A church is quadruple, quintuple as welcome in the rain. Some have a porch over the entrance to the graveyard, good enough for a quick break and brew. In others, you can sometimes shelter in the entrance, the narthex, which is traditionally, but not always, on the building's west side. It is therefore opposite the altar, which should face east; an intriguing 43 per cent of churches are supposedly built to face the sun rise on the day of the saint for whom the church is named. Many doors are on the south side, so you turn right for the altar and left for the bells and font. The wood, stone and water of ancient sites become transformed but serve similar purpose with graveyard yews, church and font.

Churches haven't always been oriented thus. Early ones were supposedly freer to face whatever way they wanted. But over time the old ways asserted themselves; the old worship of the sun and life in a new guise, a new dispensation. Since the purpose of religion is to provide a framework so that the participant may find God in or behind or involved in everything, it is not surprising the sun features a lot.

The rain showed little sign of letting up so I waited awhile in the church porch in Winterbourne Bassett. A sarsen stone incorporated into the north porch added to the welcome. I dropped a pound in the wall-mounted collection box, and there was the dull sound of the coin falling onto a mound of cash; it obviously hadn't been emptied a while. The slot was all nibble edged, the result of various prying attempts to get at the money. I thought of Genet, before he became a writer, who used a licked postage stamp glued to the bottom of a pencil to lift up coins from such boxes.

On the edge of the village were two barrows and the remains of a stone circle said to be sixty-five metres in diameter. Some of the stones were missing or broken; perhaps they ended up in the church. Bang on the Line.

The path now went vaguely north along the escarpment, a wet and slippery trail that veered in and out of the micro-valleys that punctured the scarp. I got lost at one point and had to backtrack to find Bincknoll Castle, an ancient hillfort that occupies a triangular spit jutting out from the scarp, with great views looking north to the next valley system and the next subtle change in the landscape. You look for differences and see them. It is quite different to traversing a huge continent where it may take two hundred or five hundred miles for anything to significantly change.

Bincknoll, or Binoll as it is locally known, is probably of Iron Age origin and was continually improved owing to its strategic location. Roman pottery has been found at the site and in Norman times it was enlarged into a motte-and-bailey castle, long since ruined. I climbed up and faced a herd of bored, timid-nosey bullocks who insisted on following me through the deep, schlocky, hoof-pocked mud. I got out onto the furthest most part of the spit that looked north and descended a slippery single-track path, far too steep for cattle, I thought. Two held back and looked on, heads branching out skyward above me, snorting in the misty rain, but a fearless one pushed through and followed, skidding down the steep path. Then another and another and soon I was chased down and off Bincknoll like a Pied Piper of bored bovines.

After legging it indecently fast over a gate, I turned and swore at the dumb beasts, while taking close-up pics of their snorting pink-blubber nose holes. Knowing I was all alone, I took uninhibited pleasure in insulting them with the most horrible names. For quite a long time. Then I turned to see a girl of about twelve on a pony had silently approached. She didn't smile but instead regarded me sternly from under her riding hat as you might a fallen tree or a bad case of littering.

Hurry on down.

9

A ROYAL WELCOME

Instead of crossing the main railway line harping out of Swindon, I followed it and the canal due west a few miles to gain entrance to Royal Wootton Bassett, my first town, albeit a very small one, since Salisbury.

So many warrior tombs lie on the Line, it seemed wholly appropriate that a spontaneous reverence for fallen soldiers should have arisen in the early years of the twenty-first century at a town right on the same meridian. This 'people's memorialising' was the reason the town was granted royal patronage by the Queen. The two others to be honoured in this way by monarchs was for the benefit they provided as spas: Tunbridge Wells in 1909 and Leamington Spa in 1838. But dig a little deeper and Wootton Bassett is a sort of spa town too – albeit spouting mud, not mineral water.

Just past the canal were rare mud springs that bubbled up from over a hundred metres down. Several cubic metres of mud a day are forced to the surface. Danger lurks and signs abound which read: 'Warning. Mud Springs. Danger of Entrapment.' In the past, attempts were made to fill in the mud springs, but they just keep bubbling up. The site has now been preserved as one of special scientific interest. And of course it is. But I can't help feeling that we revered pristine water in the past and now we revere . . . mud. Such revelations come fairly naturally when you are liberally daubed with the stuff – as I was, after my encounters with cattle at Bincknoll.

More grot to traverse as I entered the edge of town where the dustbin lorries were parked. I resisted writing 'garbage truck' here, but that would have conjured up the loitering ripe and rotten smell better. Nothing dusty about it. It was a Sunday and not much was going on as I passed the shut tyre-replacement shops and empty-looking pubs.

In the wide high street under the ancient raised town hall, I ate a pasty from the Co-op and drank a takeaway coffee. Here I broke out my old-style phone and called up David, a good friend who owned a farm a few miles away.

It seemed essential to stay with anyone I knew who lived near the Line. David and his wife, Sonali, were two of my oldest and most loyal friends; she had championed my writing long before I was published, had faith in me when others didn't (another of her discoveries was Will Fiennes of *The Snow Geese* fame). But Sonali was looking after their daughter in London, which was fine as it would give David and me time to talk on our own.

David spent some of his time in London, where he ran a successful company, and the rest on his farm, which had been run by his father before him. That sounds neutral and a bit ordinary, which David wasn't. The main thing being, to my rather petty mind, that David was descended from landowners and royalty whereas I was descended from navvies and farmworkers who would probably in the past have toiled long and hard for David's forebears. And willingly so, because David, like many members of the gentry in my humble working-class hero experience, has a well-developed sense of *noblesse oblige*. Oh, you wouldn't find me cavilling at his refined accent and extolling my class origins, oh no, because I am an ardent forelock tugger when it comes to posh people with *noblesse oblige* stamped into their DNA. And good old David was such a chap, with generous donations of time and money (far more than I ever had of either) to help folk far less well off than he.

The way David and I bridged the gap in our lifestyles and modes of earning a living was through a mutual interest in adventurous travel. David had been on expeditions to Spitsbergen and other wild locations, and while he was at Oxford he had been one of the earliest members of the Dangerous Sports Club. There is an amazing levelling effect when you genuinely share an interest with someone. It's one reason why the way you often meet people in England is by joining a club devoted to your special hobby or interest – be it pigeon fancying, alpine gardening, martial arts or topiary. Safe in your clubhouse, you can talk the same lingo without ever having to broach the terrifying subject of class differences. But here I was, about to enter the most sacred domain of an Englishman's life: his castle.

Years earlier, I'd been working as a van courier and I'd dropped by a friend's flat in London with another van courier, a Yorkshireman called Tim. When I suggested we both go in to meet my pal, he said, 'Oh, I don't like meeting people for the first time in their houses.' A few years out of that great leveller university, I thought this odd and a little paranoid. But now I knew different.

Still, I was vouchsafed by my nomadic garb and my nomad's purpose. And there is no madness like nomadness . . . I could play gypsy to David's settler.

As we drove to the farmhouse in the Audi estate (preferred drive of the discreet rural wealthy), I said, 'So what are you exactly, a gentleman farmer?' David laughed. But when we arrived I saw that the farmhouse was actually a mini stately home complete with ha-ha and indoor pool and sauna and other stuff that farms of the humbler kind usually do without.

David had cooked a proper meal for me, with roast meat and vegetables, and he served a fine wine, more than enough, but I was getting sleepy by 9.30 p.m, having risen at dawn in the drizzle. Our chat was good and wide ranging but I sensed it was not going to go on into the small hours. Which was fine: David was an action man, not a bon viveur. I forgot the essential difference in our states – beggar and baron – and enjoyed the luxury for what it was. I took a bath in the huge tub. I didn't go swimming in the piping hot, steamy chlorinated pool, but I could have. I slept well, if disbelievingly, on the super comfortable bed. I read some poetry too.

Next morning there was a strange moment as David gamely helped me to pack up the muddy litter that constituted my gear. He picked up the light blue foam mat I was using to sleep on (perfectly functional and comfortable beneath a Therm-a-Rest mat, but David did not know this). The thing was, the mat on its own – thin, torn, holed in places, duct taped in others, daubed with days of mud – looked like something a homeless person would reject as being beneath them (or not, in fact). David waved it in the direction of the large, functional bin in the drying room, the kind of wave where assent is assumed. I had to lunge to save my super-useful bit of rubbish. In that moment I felt a smidgen of the shame that the newly homeless must feel when their few possessions are looked on with derision, or, perhaps worse, pity.

David drove me in his Audi to my drop-off in Wootton Bassett central. He gave me a half a cooked chicken and would have pressed more goodies upon me but I refused, fearing the added weight more than their corrupting influence.

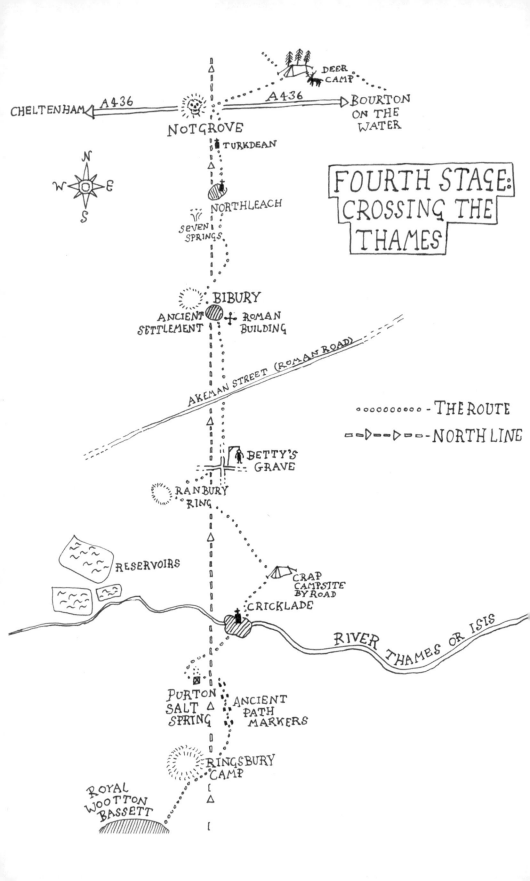

FOURTH STAGE: CROSSING THE THAMES

CHELTENHAM ◁ A436 — NOTGROVE — A436 ▷ BOURTON ON THE WATER

DEER CAMP

TURKDEAN

NORTHLEACH

SEVEN SPRINGS

BIBURY
ANCIENT SETTLEMENT ROMAN BUILDING

AKEMAN STREET (ROMAN ROAD)

∘∘∘∘∘∘∘∘∘ - THE ROUTE
▭⊳▬⊳▬⊳▭ - NORTH LINE

BETTY'S GRAVE

RANBURY RING

RESERVOIRS

CRAP CAMPSITE BY ROAD

CRICKLADE

RIVER THAMES OR ISIS

PURTON SALT SPRING

ANCIENT PATH MARKERS

RINGSBURY CAMP

ROYAL WOOTTON BASSETT

N W E S

10

TAKING THE WATERS

There had been a loose arrangement for more friends to drive from Bath and meet me in Purton. A certain excitement gripped me, though it had only been a day since I'd left the grand luxury of David's house, I was very quickly back to my rainy and lonesome self. I imagined the warm pub we would meet at and all the news they would bring. It only takes about a day away from everyday life to start entertaining the fantasy that you're the lone survivor of some terrible apocalypse, an old school explorer or a Romani traveller of the byways and highways.

But first, Ringsbury Camp. Two circular ditches; the middle had been ploughed flat. Before I reached it, I saw the first bluebells of the trip behind a barbed wire fence, blue-violet streams through woodland only recently come into leaf. The camp, a bit further on, had a path between the two ditches, rather like Castle Ditches further south. This was not so large. At this point I was beginning to think that camps, henges and forts all look more similar than different: ditches and banks, some inside and outside, some doubled or even trebled, but the palate was limited. It was like sandcastle building with kids – the same shapes predominate. Not that I was falling into that familiar and terrible trap of thinking I was somehow smarter than my ancestors – no siree! – but it did set me to pondering if it wasn't just the materials that had limited the construction techniques of the past. There was an urge to do things as they had been done before, to preserve a continuity. In storytelling terms, it was like retelling the same myths and stories in a subtle new way, rather than inventing whole new stories each time.

In contrast, in our modern culture, things are judged creatively on the large differences, not the small ones. The larger the difference you can get away with, the better. We have lost all regard for a formal sense of continuity being anything other than 'nice', or 'comforting' for old people. And what this has done is force endless hurdles, endless transitions into our lives. Everyone has to invent a life for themselves from scratch – and that's very stressful.

Transitions; some people are better at them than others. Of my two children, one was much better at simple transitions such as school to home, playing to eating, than the other, who needed warning and coaxing. In the end, we found a ritual of some sort, however small, worked to bridge the transition. Warnings at five minutes and two minutes. A special chair for meals. And inadvertently we'd stumbled on the real reason for ritual. It's not because ancient or traditional people are kind of stupid and childish and like celebrating all the time; it's because they have a sophisticated grasp of the limitations of being human.

Life is a balance between obsession and change, between attachment to things, places and people, and detachment from things, places and people. You need to focus, become attached to get something done. But then you need to be able to detach to move on, do something else. All religions work on both principles. Some focus more on attachment, cultivating obsessive behaviour in some cases. Others encourage detachment to such a degree that the believer can no longer function except as a beggar. Religions that lose their way over-emphasise one or the other. True freedom is to be able to switch regularly and often between the two. Ideally it is how we should live – and ritual is the pain-free and easy way to aid that transition.

It works on every level. The big transitions in life, from childhood to adulthood, say; and the small ones, such as going from awake to bed through the steps of book, drink, pyjamas, sleep.

But what happens when we get transition overload coupled with the death of ritual as a feature in our lives? The result seems to be a widespread increase in anxiety, especially among those in transition phases, such as the young and the middle-aged. Some people are creative enough to cope. My good friend Rich Lisney celebrated his fiftieth birthday for fifty days. He said he got a bit tired of it by the end, which is how a ritual should feel. (The Japanese are brilliant at rituals, especially in martial arts, and by the end you're always a bit bored, a bit restless – in other words, keen to move on to the next phase.) But not everyone is creative in this way, or wants to be. So they live life with anxiety and change rather than calmness and ritual.

In my book *Being a Man in the Lousy Modern World*, I looked at the need for a difficult and potentially dangerous rite of passage for young men. I suggested a long distance walk in the wilderness might serve that function to some degree. It's not just that you get time to mull things over; what you really get is a series of ritual acts: getting up, doing your miles, making your food, camping each night.

On a month-long desert walk, I was accompanied by a doctor who was thinking about whether he should get divorced or not. He'd come on the walk to help him decide. On the last day, in a coffee shop in Siwa Oasis, I asked him if he'd made up his mind. 'No,' he said, 'but it just doesn't seem as important as before.'

Ritual shifts importance – and shifting the pressing nature, the obsessive neurone-hogging nature of something, is the real battle. Solving the problem is always secondary, easily done when you have the right perspective.

Ringsbury, a ring, circles within circles, a continuity and not a pointless departure. Ringsbury is, like many old forts, known as a 'Roman camp', but it predates the Romans. Ploughing and agricultural use of the central eight acres mean very few artefacts have been found. But its outer shape reminds us of the core design: circles within circles that can be breached at certain special points. An esoteric, shamanic representation of life. We live circular lives, we repeat patterns – and once we recognise a pattern we can break out of it, into a higher level of personal and therefore (given the all-connected world view of the mystic) universal being.

High thoughts for a damp day. Walking in the rain, looking for a pub in which to meet my particular and rather picky group of friends, I found that none in Purton appealed. Instead, I found a farm shop that sold coffee and homemade cake.

Inside, there was a comfy-looking seating area with an old cloth-covered sofa, a movable gas heater and a low table with magazines. A sign said this was a private area for staff only, but it looked so inviting. The woman running the place was Swedish, from Gothenburg, and much more reasonable than the average Brit under such circumstances: 'Yes, you can sit there. No one is in today so it doesn't matter.' When I ritually whinged about the damp, she said, 'But this is the best weather for walking – you don't sweat!' And I had to agree. What brought her to Purton? 'Well, first I came to Swindon' (why Swindon of all places? It was never really disclosed) 'but my boyfriend lives here, so I came here and here I am!'

Ah, total relief, warm drying comfort from the gas fire, cosy soft sofa, the feeling of damp leaving layers of clothing, the warm fug of it. Just being shut out for a few hours made this an acute pleasure. Another flat white, please; another slice of apple cake with clotted cream, please.

Just as I was tucking in I got a new message. The friends were not only coming, they had arrived; well, one had: my great pal, the highly acclaimed writer Tahir Shah. I sent directions, eager as always for new company.

Writers meet a lot of other writers, or they can if they want to. It's one of the perks. Literary festivals, launches, the odd party (rarer these days, what with tightening budgets and ever expanding conglomerates). Some writers are nice, some have huge egos, well hidden or not. Ego size does not seem to affect how timid most writers are, but they usually manage to be a bit wacky, a bit creative. From time to time, though, you come across an author who's not only original, but who goes against the grain in every imaginable way.

Tahir has managed that, though I had no hint of what he was to become when he turned up to live on my floor in Tokyo in the early Nineties. I was holed up in what was, even by Japanese standards, a remarkably small flat. The only way to reach it was to walk through a graveyard. Without much floor space to go around, my writer guest took to sleeping under the dining table. He was completely broke – largely because he refused to teach English like the rest of us. For food he would pinch ceremonial cabbages from Ueno Park, lugging them back through the cemetery to the flat, where he would brew them into thin soup, flavoured with powdered MSG. As a treat he'd heat up *gyoza* on an upturned iron.

Tahir was descended from a noble Afghan family, though he had been born and brought up in England, before embarking on a bizarre and even magical life – dedicated mainly to originality, with lots of hardship thrown in for good measure.

Tahir had already written one book by the time he was twenty-four, his age when he ended up in Japan. Being the son of the Afghan writer and thinker Idries Shah (whose work I admire immensely), he'd grown up in a family where writing was simply what one did: his grandfather, Sirdar Ikbal Ali Shah, had been a prolific writer too. Tahir was raised in the most unconventional ways. While other kids were out on their skateboards, Tahir was being steeped in *The Thousand and One Nights*, instructed in the kind of life lessons that matter, and taught to seek out what was really going on.

I hadn't seen him in several years. Whenever I messaged him, he would reply from some distant land (by the age of twenty-four, he had already travelled through almost all of Africa and South America, and the pace has never ceased). Usually, he was on the trail of an extraordinary quest. Like the British travel writer Bruce Chatwin, he was 'always arriving, or about to leave'. Like Chatwin, Tahir is never still for a moment; he constantly spouts ideas, random details, incredible stories. He's that very rare thing: an original thinker; even when the idea is wrapped up in the familiar, the core will be different. And usually very helpful. He gave me the idea of micromastery, which became the centre of a book I wrote later about polymathy. Oddly enough, unlike most people educated in the UK, he has, I think, a fear of silence. Maybe it's his greatest fear.

Another text came. Of course he was in the graveyard. On a bench. Was it near? It was. He really liked graveyards; once we had gone on a mission together, instigated by him, to see the renovated tomb of the explorer Richard Francis Burton, laid to rest in Mortlake cemetery.

Tahir was sitting on the bench when I found him, his eyes wide, as though he'd just swallowed too much coffee or been zapped by a Taser. Now in his early fifties, he was wearing a third-hand British Army waterproof poncho, and a pair of American Altama jungle boots. As soon as he saw me, he leapt up, hugged me hard and started on an idea he had conjured probably two minutes before.

The idea involved treating common phobias with fairy tales. For several hours we walked and talked, knocking the idea back and forth. As we neared a clearing of tall beech trees, Tahir suddenly exclaimed that he had been blessed in a rare and fabulous way – a way that allowed him to perceive the world around him differently.

'Through stories?' I prompted.

'Yes, yes, but not only that, there's something else.'

'What?'

'Everything I see, hear, smell, touch, or taste is distorted as it reaches me.'

'Distorted how?'

Tahir hesitated, scratching a hand over his closely cropped hair. 'It's as though the information is being bounced from one beacon to another, and another, in a wild rumpus of relay.' (Rumpus is a favourite word of his.)

'What effect does it have?'

Again, Tahir reflected before answering. 'It means that my senses are actually kaleidoscopic.'

'Is that a good thing?' I asked.

'Oh yes!' he beamed. 'It's better than good.'

'Why?'

'Because it means I achieve a full spectrum of Zigzag Think!'

What did he mean? I've always set great store by the indirect effect his ideas have on me, so I didn't ask. In our walking, we hadn't gone far – zigzagging, even – and he now had to leave me to get back to Purton where he'd parked his car. I thought about zigzagging a lot after that, because it conflicted with what I was trying to do: go in a dead straight line.

*

I was at last getting my eye in with regard to which footpaths were likely to be fruitful and which weren't. Straighter paths were usually older, especially if they ran parallel to a road between two villages. If the road subsumed the original track then no such alternative path would exist; you'd just have the usual pattern of dog-leg footpaths round fields beloved of village dog walkers. But if the original track was somehow unsuitable for wheeled traffic, too steep or too wet, then the oldest track would be still there.

This is what I found, and an additional sign of antiquity, at every field entrance was some kind of stonework. Sometimes laid flat, sometimes double stones parked close together – the rudimentary stile, too wide for a sheep but narrow enough for a human to squeeze through. Sometimes just a marker sarsen stone. This continued for several miles and was so predictable it was not mere accident. Again I realised why so many religious monuments mimic gates – from the Japanese *torii* to Stonehenge's trilithons – because these are transition points. And crossing from field to field is a transition: the stone acknowledges this, a symbolic reminder of what we need in life.

But where was this ancient and preserved path leading? To water, of course, to one of the few rural mineral wells in England. The 'salt spring' at Purton (some way from Purton village but within the parish) has been used since ancient times for curing all kinds of infirmities. A creative etymology for 'wellness' might include visiting a well . . .

'Well' documented for healing since 1700 (and no doubt in use before then), the Salt's Hole at Purton was enclosed in a summerhouse-type structure. The small octagonal building with leaded windows stands locked behind a weed-tangled, rusty, white gate with the letters 'SPA' worked into the metal. Inside, a piece of round wood, about the size of a manhole cover, occludes the ten-foot mineral well beneath. Adjoining the well building are two thoughtful loos; this small establishment is all there is of the Purton Spa.

In 1881, it was reported that one long-lived local, an Isaac Beasley, 'when in the 94th year of his age, and being still in possession of extraordinary powers of memory and great physical strength for his years, avowed that all his life he had been in the habit, when out of health, of drinking this water, and it was certain to put him right. He remembered his father took this water as a physic, and that large numbers of folks in his youthful days took the water from Salt's Hole for all manner of diseases, and it mostly cured them.'[10]

It is reported, though, that at this time, the gentry and the local doctor were sceptical about the healing properties of the well. So much so that a new landowner tried to drain it . . .

> At Purton . . . is a field which time out of mind has been called Salt's Hole . . . some years back it became the property of the present owner, S. C. Sadler Esq., JP etc. for Wilts, who at that time caused it to be drained, in doing which a well of water from which the field took its name, was filled in and destroyed. This circumstance, it appears, at the time gave rise to much murmuring and dissatisfaction on the part of many of the poor people in the parish, who stated that when they were ill they could always be cured by drinking the water; and one old man in particular . . . had given such fabulous accounts of the diseases cured in olden time by the water from Salt's Hole, that the owner was induced to search for the locale of the well, which was, after some trouble, found indicated by a slight sinking of the earth, the surface of which had a white efflorescent appearance. A small excavation being made, the water quickly came bubbling up . . .'[11]

The well water was tested by a Dr Voelker of Cirencester Agricultural College. A small stone plaque at the well records the 'saline water' to be 'sulphated and iodated'. The canny Mr Sadler started selling the stuff and an advertisement of the time assures readers that the water cures 'Numberless cases of skin diseases, scrofula, consumption, enlarged glands, ulcerated legs, stomach and liver affections [sic], piles, gout, rheumatism, female irregularities, dropsies and all urinary diseases.' In 1900, the price was the same as beer: 2d a pint.

On and off the water was sold locally until 1952 but somehow Purton never became a second Harrogate or Ilkley, fashionable spa towns in the nineteenth and early twentieth centuries. Oddly enough (or maybe not, given the proximity of the Line to England's watershed), I would eventually be passing through both those old Yorkshire spa towns. If I made it that far.

If only the Salt's Hole well had been unlocked, I could have revived myself with a glug of Purton's finest. But I wasn't unduly worried. Think of it as a zig. Or a zag.

11

THE PRICE OF PROPERTY

I'm sitting alert in a wood as dusk falls. The trees are sparse, as if they've had a hard time growing. Moss on the floor. Dead branches for a fire, but a fire would be seen. I'm as far as I can get from the road, about twenty metres away. Behind me a single, sagging strand of barbed wire and then a vast acreage of cabbage field, no hedges for miles and no buildings – but I can hear barking. Dogs bark at sunset just like in 101 *Dalmatians* and the peculiar combination of air temperature and stillness at dusk means the bark travels for miles, much further than during the day. It feels as if I am in the farmyard I can't yet see, but I check the map and I'm half a mile away.

Decisions. Should I pitch my bright green tent now or after dark? Still not sure if it is luminous or not. Surely I can check? No, it can't be, but a niggling doubt remains, the kind you only have when you are totally alone.

Walking through the posh village to get here, I saw a man watering plants; he didn't look my way. A couple, elderly, gamely getting out of a Morgan Plus 8, low to the ground so a bit of a struggle. As a twelve-year-old, I dreamt of getting a car like that. Despite their bourgeois country cottage, thatched with all the trimmings, I think warmly of them for having this car.

Bourgeois? You mean just like me. That couple could be my mum and dad. But everything changes when you're homeless. All the time I am furtively awaiting a call, 'Oi! Where are you sleeping tonight?' Of course it never comes. But I wait for it. As Orwell exquisitely points out in *Down and Out in Paris and London*, middle-class inhibition and shame are stubborn. They stay with you long after they serve any useful purpose . . .

When I came up with the idea to 'walk the stones', I blithely told people I'd be camping along the way. I thought it would be a laugh, but so far it's proving to be the opposite. A rather unpleasant event at the end of each day. Anxiety when you want relaxation. I can cook my meal, that's always welcome. And I can do that with the tent still down. So I can look like I am moving on. All this subterfuge. The alibis I have ready.

And yet this is part of it. This walk is about England, and England is a place where property has replaced gold as the safe store of value. It has replaced industry as the way to make money. We are returning to a new kind of feudalism where having land is the gateway to having everything else. The funny old days when landed gentry had to give away their land to the National Trust to look after are long gone. Any landowner who survived the tax regimes and the downturns of the late twentieth century is laughing now. Set up for life.

It would be easy to be bitter, but a part of me revels in this new challenge of living without a roof over my head. It highlights the pointlessness of homeownership as the supreme goal in life. It makes any choice, like mine, to become homeless for a while all the more stark; vagabonding, a modern nomad among the grasping and fearful settlers who are afraid of having their land invaded or taken away.

The number of 'keep out', 'private', 'neighbourhood watch', 'farm-watch' and 'no trespassing' signs is extraordinary. Signage keeps pace with property prices. Burglary rates are down, we are told, but people remain paranoid. I am too when I am back home. Watching out for strangers mooching round my neighbourhood. The man next door had two statues stolen from his garden. Can't be too careful.

I wonder if it is going to be like this every night, for the whole trip. I have 350 miles or more to go. If I'm like this now, what'll I be like by the end?

The anxiety had started at about 4 p.m. You can't stop at this point in the day, but you're getting a better idea of where you'll most likely end up. This is when I'd checked the map for likely spots ahead and calculated my walking speed.

Then something subtly changed when I saw a deer halt on the track in front of me. That magical moment of connection with a wild beast that is bigger than it ought to be; I mean England is all parcelled up, controlled, penned in, surely rabbits are about the maximum that should be 'allowed'? Even a hare, standing tall with its tufted ears and thumping great legs, is a bit cheeky, a bit on the large size. But deer break the rules; they can be big, big as a trespasser, an interloper, a fence jumper and crop spoiler – someone like me.

You often see more wildlife in the edgelands than in the endless patchwork of fields that is most of rurality. As I walked up Blind Lane to Cricklade, the roe deer took two steps in front of me and looked back with quick assurance, then ran fast away.

My mood altered; wild animals somehow mean that freedom is still possible (should you be a bit down and doubting such a thing). The extreme importance in maintaining our population of visible wild creatures is all about maintaining a reverence for freedom. A few minutes later this path, littered with dumped corrugated tin and the parts of washing machine, fully in keeping with nearing the urban, was now overhung by more strangeness: what looked like a roosting fruit bat. Or a double black bag of God knows what. Getting closer, I saw it was actually a large black bra hanging from a branch. It was such an odd sight, why so large? Why black? Why here?

Cricklade. Humour was here in the cock-and-balls underpass graffiti titled 'your mum jumps on my dick' to the 'His and Hairs' barbers. There was a smell of Sunday roasts filling the alleys as I walked to the town centre; then, as I left, the smell of dope on the high street. I bought a pasty from the Co-op and ate it on a bench. I didn't feel I'd earned a late pub lunch myself, so it was time to get moving again along the nascent Thames path, the path actually a series of long puddles I splashed through in boots I now knew to be holed rather than merely leaky. I saw a woman in pink leggings and lime-green top yomping along in front of me, her walking poles and feet making little white splashes, as if she was walking on water.

Bricks overgrown with weeds, a neat stack of four plastic chairs on a piece of plywood sitting incongruously next to a holed and rusty-springed trampoline, on which someone had balanced a great number of empty beer cans like a found-art installation alongside the trackway from the river to the Basin, a restored section of the Thames and Severn Canal. Built in 1789 and finally abandoned in 1941, the canal fulfilled a long-held dream to link west and east from Bristol to London. It struggled on but always suffered from a lack of water, or the inability to keep the water in the canal, and was never as successful as the Kennet and Avon Canal, which I'd crossed earlier. The trouble was the canal passed through the spring-rich country of the Avon and Thames watershed (both rivers rising within three miles of each other), and the springs continually broke through the canal's bottom, leading to massive leakage. At the highest point of the canal, a million gallons a day were lost into the porous limestone beneath.

Dusk was coming and I walked on fast, enjoying the evening as I strolled through Down Ampney, birthplace of Ralph Vaughan Williams. He was born in the vicarage, a substantial but modest building in comparison to Down Ampney house, a rather nice fifteenth- and sixteenth-century building (internet estimate of value: £4.6 million). I noted with envious scorn yet another prissy 'Private' sign on the house's front gate and the paranoid keypad for getting in . . .

A man, walking the dog just before night fall, smiled in a friendly way as he passed in his country gent's gear of Barbour and wellies. These days he could be anyone, from the land manager to the owner to a bloke in the pub . . .

Thoughts of fine houses and the fine prices they command gave way at last to the old nagging worry: the search for a berth, a bolt hole, preferably far from prying eyes. A wood would be good.

First, look at the map and identify woodland far from any housing – always hard in the South. Near to a road seems less like trespassing than it does in some remote corner of a farm. In my law-fearing mind, I started my usual extemporising of ludicrous excuses (sometimes even aloud if I was quite alone, testing them out). Excuses such as 'I was hitchhiking and had to just bed down near the road', 'I'm only resting, I'll move on soon', to the outright ridiculous 'I'm part of an academic project studying patterns of homelessness'.

I saw on the map an interesting crossroads named 'Betty's Grave', but it was too dark to walk much further. A sliver of wood a few miles north of Down Ampney would have to do. I could still see headlights through the sparse birch and alder tree cover, and I imagined as always my tent glowing luminous green in the full beam glare. Fuck it.

12

BETTY'S GRAVE

Betty's Grave. Just a crossroads, but crossroads can be special. I didn't like the fact that the sign affixed to the road sign, saying Betty's Grave, was obviously handmade. I could tell locals were proud of the name while the local authorities were less sure. But it seemed to me an obviously important crossroads, a carrefour.

The carrefour, and I use the term advisedly as it was once a common word in English for a crossroads, comes from the French and Latin, and means a fork with four prongs – though it is often transcribed as four forks, which would make eight roads, which is not a crossroads. The name of the Carfax junction in Oxford similarly comes from the Middle English word carfourkes.

In voodoo, derived from West African magical practices, the carrefour is a vitally important place. It is a node point of energy. When I spent time in Port-au-Prince searching for bona fide zombies (they exist but that's another story), the then president Jean-Bertrand Aristide was under grave suspicion of being a *houngan*, a witch doctor. I was once told that Aristide had changed all the traffic directions in the capital. Considering Haiti's many woes, this seemed a rather petty complaint. But the people were vastly angry. (And think of how angry we get when the traffic direction is changed in our own towns.) In the case of Port-au-Prince, this meant that the directional energy of carrefours had been changed, in the way they either contributed energy or depleted it from the city. (I also heard that if you lifted Aristide's French-tailored jacket, the silk lining was pattered with a *veve*, a voodoo diagram used to summon dark forces.)

Human energy exists on parallel levels. At the most mundane, the crossroads is the best place for business. My very good friend Frank Nasre, one of Australia's leading Iranian rug dealers, said that his grandfather had only one bit of advice for starting a shop: make sure it is at the crossroads, because that is where the foot traffic is . . . It's no accident one of the world's largest hypermarket chains is called Carrefour.

Moreover, all that human energy buzzing around creates its own zone of significance. The main symbolism of the crossroads is that it marks the place where you must seek directions. Unlike the fork, in which both prongs might conceivably go in similar directions, the carrefour sends you in diametrically opposed directions. You must either *know* your way here or you must ask. Ask who? Either a wise man or woman, or that inner quiet place inside us all where we connect with the wisdom we all carry around with us. The crossroads is traditionally a place of contemplation. Hence the common image of the dervish wrapped in his cloak, deep in contemplation at the crossroads. In North Africa, a crossroads may have a Sufi shrine, a place where a local wise man was buried that has since become a place of pilgrimage.

Churches, as we've seen, are often sited on ancient mounds or at crossroads. Sometimes the two coincide. Over the centuries, the confusion between wisdom and witchcraft grew to fever pitch, especially in places where a predominantly oral culture became overtaken by a written one and the old stories were discarded as childish relics. Printing encouraged a textual appreciation of religion, a left-brain shift away from the holistic mind needed to appreciate the shamanic reality. It lead to the Reformation and revolution in England, with the world soon to follow. A world turned upside down – with the wise woman or man now thought a witch, something evil. The carrefour became a site for the excommunicated, the expelled, the gibbet cage swinging with a rotting murderer's body inside, the site of the suicide's grave – all things designed to kill the influence of witchcraft and kill the reverence for the carrefour.

Still it goes on. Betty's Grave has many stories attached: in one, Betty is a suicide from around 1780 (most of the stories involve a date around this time). In another, a poor woman who could not speak was taken for a witch and killed at the crossroads.

So Betty (who is also a bastard child in other stories) had her grave at the crossroads. But what makes me believe she was a witch was that bunches of flowers would be left either at the slight mound that might mark the grave (or a mark stone) or at the foot of the sign post itself. This stopped for a while in the 1970s until Betty was reported to be haunting people as far away as Fairford. Mysteriously the flowers reappeared; Betty had been appeased and the haunting ceased.

This was a day of carrefours. The next, after a delightful road plod, was where I crossed Akeman Street, a Roman road. The tiny hamlet at the crossroads was called Ready Token, either a corruption of an ancient name or a reference to the old pub that used to stand there. It might mean the pub was ready to accept (as some were) any token, such as defaced or odd currency. My first thought, though, was that this was the kind of place where a tax or toll might have been charged, so you better get your token ready.

Further up was the crossing of the old Salt Way and the Roman Fosse Way. The salt ways were some of the older trading tracks, reflected in names like Sale, Salterton, Salway Ash, Salcot and Salt-ley, Salford and Saltash, not to mention ruins named Salt Barn and Saltway Farm. Though it seems now that a salary wasn't all salt; nor did the Romans build these tracks – salt was needed long before 55 BC. The salt ways are straight too, evidence perhaps that the Romans built on existing routes, which is what Graham Robb suggests very compellingly when he shows the extent of Celtic straight track build-ing in pre-Roman Europe.

The C-roads (yellow on the map) were at last quiet enough to walk on for miles. It was a huge difference to further south, which in many places seems like one huge suburb, with regular fast traffic on even the smallest roads. I was returned to my childhood, walking the back roads of Warwickshire to the pub at Whatcote and back at night without seeing a single car between Fulready and Pillerton Priors.

Barrows at crossroads, ancient sites, and a straight road connect-ing all, bang on the Line. I felt I was in a place which had retained much of its ancient connection to the past.

I headed down into Bibury – jam-packed full of Japanese; we can thank Emperor Hirohito for that, as he visited the place on a world tour, perhaps because William Morris called it the 'most beautiful village in England'. Bibury is at the special crossroads of the old Salt Way and the River Coln. Not surprisingly, the Romans liked the place: there are the remains of a villa here. It is a place of water meadows, fine Cotswold architecture and . . . tour buses. Youngish Japanese sat staring at their paperback-sized smartphones, a row of them on the wall by the river, all bent over with curved spines, entranced by the virtual world.

Beyond Bibury I saw a hare. I'd seen a few big rabbits bolt off earlier that day and been second-guessing: are those really hares? But when you see a hare you know instantly. There is no doubt.

I was going from a patch of sunlight to a gateway overhung by trees, shady and cool. I didn't see the hare sitting there, and I think my poles confused it, made it think I was some kind of strange ungulate. The hare is rightly a shamanic beast, and a creature to be enjoyed as true royalty of the wilderness. His old bulgy eye and knobbly head turned, twitched, and then he was off, huge back legs pumping hard.

I planned to camp at Notgrove, a significant long barrow at the side of the A436, which leads to Cheltenham. I thought it would be a memorable place to stay even if it was near the road. To get there, I managed to get into a huge walled field of turnips, with double barbed wire strands above the walling. This is a particularly tricky one to master with a pack on. You need to be careful of knocking stones off the wall at the same time as not getting hooked up on the wire. Poles should be thrown over first, as long as you are confident in following them. I spent a long while looking for gates or even holes in the wall, but there were none and I got majorly snagged up both times, but at least I didn't have to walk along the road.

But when I arrived at Notgrove I felt for the first time a bad vibe (no better word appropriate) from an ancient site. I checked my gazetteer and it confirmed this had been a burial site for at least six adults, three children and a newborn baby. But surely all ancient sites have somebody buried in or near them? The stone chambers branching off a 12-metre long passageway are oriented north–south, while the passage is on an east–west axis. Alignment is never far away. At the west end is a possible older mound, or round barrow, with a standing stone at one corner. But now the stonework is covered in earth and grass, and has been since 1976.

So it actually looks like an old grassed-over quarry or demolished house. It had been excavated twice – i.e. grave-robbed – in 1881 and in 1934, but there was evidence it had been interfered with non-professionally, so to speak, since Roman times, rather like the sites in Egypt. Nevertheless, for 2000 years several skeletons, a leaf arrowhead, some jet beads and a quantity of flints had remained. No longer, though. Of course it is all probably safer in Cheltenham Museum, but you can't help feeling a little sad that these places were safe for hundreds of years until the nineteenth century, when scientific digging took over . . .

A well desecrated grave, then. Was that the reason for the odd feeling I had? Or was I simply tired and irritated from yomping through two turnip fields? Whatever the reason, this was the one and only time I felt almost a repugnance at an ancient site.

And so the search was on. Where to kip in the manicured lands of the Cotswolds? I headed along a disused railway track that was being used for clay pigeon shooting and pheasant rearing – the telltale cobalt-blue plastic food dispensers visible through the light but thorny and nettly woodland. I had to cut under the railway through a nasty, brick-loose culvert, dark and dripping. I was fearful of a brick dropping on my head, but all I felt were cold drops of water. Out the other side, I was in a mysterious, beautiful valley heading past the lost medieval village of Aylworth into the valley of the River Windrush – surely one of the best names for a river (though I also like the neighbouring Evenlode too).

I passed a big house and two women in fawn jodhpurs on horseback. One had a skittery horse and irritably said, 'Are you coming through, then?' Bloody horse riders, always think they own the place. I scuttled by, but soon recovered with thoughts of sneaking onto a nearby golf course and kipping in a bunker. I'd done it before in France, along with dossing down once in the grounds of a crematorium . . .

But I saw a better place: a wood, or rather a plantation of pines, up the hill ahead of me, with the bubbling river down below. I climbed up along a wide ridge and cut through the dark, musty, spindle-twigged trees. Commercial firs but not too closely packed.

It was in fact a magical grove. But dark inside. My tinted glasses took a while to recover from the evening direct-in-my-eyes sunset but as they did, I suspected something was inside the grove, looking at me. First a shamanic hare, now a deer edging towards me; no white markings I could see, so not a fallow, but a bit big for a roe, a red deer maybe. We watched each other for a while before it reversed awkwardly while watching me then turned and clattered away.

Grave and grove. Grave, meaning serious, comes from the Latin; grave, as in hole for the buried, from the Germanic. Grove from the old English for a thicket or copse. Groove, from the old Dutch for a channel, maybe a lengthy grave. The trees on many barrows – often Scots pines, our only native pine – form a grove on a grave.

There was no flat ground in this grove. A few deer coughs and barks in the night. Cold for hours. And in the morning, a frost in the field below. Sun reflecting a dazzling silver. All this beauty – and yet from nowhere it seemed came doubt, I could hardly see the point of what I was doing. I backtracked through the events of the previous day and got nowhere. A growing feeling of malaise, pointlessness; I decided to pack it in and walk to the nearest town.

13

OLD BOOTS AND MODERN SHAMANS

Bourton-on-the-Water: nice water, shame about the tour buses and the milling crowds. Not even a decent bacon butty shop that wasn't full up. Too fragile to wait even a minute, I spotted a real bus leaving for Cheltenham; I ran and jumped on board, feeling spontaneous.

I went back up the road past Notgrove. I was thinking about boots, sleeping bags and the writer Geoff Dyer. My own boots had split and were wet and cold from the glorious walk to Bourton that morning. I needed new ones; I could get them in Cheltenham – birthplace of Geoff. And I could get a sleeping bag that actually fitted. I could also buy Sealskinz socks – cunning wool/Gore-Tex wetsuit sock combinations. Hardcore hikers wear them inside trainers to combat getting drenched when walking through wet fields.

Because this is the heart of the boot problem. Or maybe the left ventricle. Trainers are great for most walking until you are faced with a field of dew-drenched grass. Your feet are dripping in seconds. Your socks, soaked. And your pasty, patty-like footsies and tootsies are soon pink and creased like a baby too long in the bath.

When I'd walked that riverside path, so beautiful in the silvery frosty morning, so damp and chilly were my feet from dew that I was plodding along cursing. If I hadn't been taking photographs every few seconds like some mad street photographer I'd have been thoroughly depressed.

But now that would change in Geoff-town. Geoff deserves all the attention he gets. For years, he was known only to the cognoscenti, but after the publication of his travel book *Yoga for People Who Can't Be Bothered to Do It*, Geoff went viral. Geoff was once a famous doper and acid taker, and this has always made his intellectual status a bit more hip and groovy. He knows the precise value of drugs to change a writing perspective, and as a seemingly daring counterweight to travelling. *One acid trip in Cheltenham = a trip to India*; it's a lot cheaper too.

Geoff's novel *Paris Trance* has a great chapter near the end in which the characters are walking through the sunny French countryside while off their heads and tripping. It's nature writing but not like any you've read before. For a start, Geoff doesn't know any plant or tree names and has the courage to come clean about that. It doesn't stop him looking, being deeply observant. But no names, no fact drill. Ignorance as bliss. Geoff's most radical, and I think, most important gift as an intellectual in the twenty-first century is his embrace of ignorance.

In *Yoga*, Geoff becomes obsessed with visiting Leptis Magna in Libya. Yet, at the same time, he can't be arsed to read the guidebook or indeed learn anything about the place. It's genius, not just because it validates our own contradictory feelings about such tourism, but because, I think, for the first time in the Western Intellectual Tradition (WIT) *yet-more-information* is put in its place. (The bus is now rumbling past the outskirts, the Cheltenham racetrack.) He's echoing something expressed by Eastern philosophers and sages: that the amount of information and theory we have about a thing must not be allowed to outpace our experience of that thing. And following the information explosion of the twentieth century, we simply have too much information about most things.

I know. This sounds like a slacker's get-out-of-jail-free card. It sounds like an excuse to not do your homework. And who doesn't like a juicy Wikipedia titbit from time to time? In fact, if anything, we've become *more* addicted to factoids rather than less. I suppose what I'm edging towards is Geoff's refusal to 'package' his writing with information, names, details, data. He's going it alone. He's taking the backpacker ethic into ordinary life. (And I have to say, when I did the same thing by taking up gardening but refusing to read a single book on the subject, the results were very pleasing and more successful than many of my book-led ventures.)

Embrace ignorance. Refuse to amend and check and insert the names of every creature you see. I had been struggling with the weight of my bird guide – time to ditch it. I had been assiduously conning my *Penguin Guide to Prehistoric England and Wales* – bin it (apart from the map references to find the sites).

Now the bus was passing the area where the Cheltenham Literature Festival is held, a place where I had once appeared. I tried to feel nostalgically happy. As festivals go it was OK, though they put me next to Wilbur Smith in the signing tent, who'd just come out of retirement for 'one last book'. His queue stretched twice round the entire marquee, blocking the entrance. Thus stopping my own loyal fans from getting to me . . . at least that's what I told myself.

Embrace ignorance. Be as fearless as Geoff; be like the raft guide I once met on the Zambezi, who called a fish eagle a chicken; be like the boy in Oxford who I saw point to a swan and call it 'a great big white duck'. It's a hard path to travel. Information is nice and cosy, and when you're a writer it's easy to pad your work out with lots of it . . .

I am in town now and have seen the outdoors shops and avoided them. Instead I am watching buskers in the sun and drinking a flat white at Waterstones, looking down from their terrace onto the pedestrianised street below. The spirit of Geoff is indeed influential. A young writer told me that reading *Yoga* destroyed his writing ability for six months. Even the esteemed MP Rory Stewart has evinced an admiration for Geoff. Enough of this. I would take the single lesson: we are drowning in data. We don't even take it all in, we're too busy skimming and skipping; we're driving too fast. Don't be Robert Macfarlane, be Robert Macnearlane or even Robert Machardshoulder

Another flat white. Another almond croissant with a light dusting of icing sugar. Time to consider Geoff as shaman. I don't mean in any literal sense, but in his embrace of backpacker culture (drugs, Burning Man, the author Hakim Bey) he was tracing the outline of a path, and that path was shamanic.

The drugs/travel equation is the age-old terrain of the shaman. In a sense, the backpacker is mimicking the path of a seeker. I could never understand the insatiable desire to visit Hindu temples that backpackers show in India, but that's all part of the deal. The drugs, too, even though they're for fun really, rather than enlightenment; it's all part of the same act.

Walking the Line, an attempt to investigate alignment, was a new take on the old concerns of the shaman. Could there ever be a modern shaman in the developed West? I sometimes thought novelists were like shamans; hence society's high regard for writers and the almost universal desire of people to pen a novel at some stage in their lives. Novelists slip into other worlds and bring back news. We expect also some measure of direction; they should tell us how to live better. But they don't do that very well, or they do it very obliquely, through accurate observation of inner states.

I didn't think Geoff would want to be thought anything more than a writer. For him, I suspected, most subjects were just grist to his writing mill. But I was less sure. I believed that walking up England might be a sort of magic in its own right. But now it was time to visit the gear shop.

I drank a final flat white, which, along with the kerosene fridge and the dual flush toilet, is a truly great Australian invention. Time to visit the boot shop. The shop assistant, a too-thin, pencil-moustached man about forty, told me he had taken this job out of desperation. Admittedly he had the good sense to tell me this after I had hesitated for about an hour over a new sleeping bag (which I tried while fully clothed on the floor of the shop – it was huge) and new boots, which were also huge, and waterproof socks, which I looked forward to using greatly. As he rang through my hefty bill, the shop man told me he had applied for over two hundred jobs in telecoms – he'd ten years' experience in his chosen field – but not got a single interview. He'd been using the internet to find jobs and it hadn't worked. Then he'd walked into this shop and asked about a job and got one.

'It's a start,' he said wearily.

'Much easier to get a job when you already have one,' I chirruped.

'Yes, they do say that.' Then he'd told me he'd had health issues, which was why he'd quit his old telecoms job. Normally I would have been nosey and asked more, but his hurt was too apparent, too recent. Brightening, he said he'd use his staff discount to buy a tent and go backpacking. He'd never been camping before, even though he was selling all the gear.

'Doing day hikes mainly,' he said a little defensively.

I told him he'd made my day what with the Sealskinz socks and the new boots. He looked a tad happier as I exited the shop for my bus back to the actual nightmare of backpacking.

Nightmare? I needed to be a little more grateful, a little less self-centred . . . I needed to worry a little less. And I'd start by being a bit more ignorant, a bit less well-informed, a bit more shamanic, a bit more backpacker, a bit more go with the flow, a bit more Geoff.

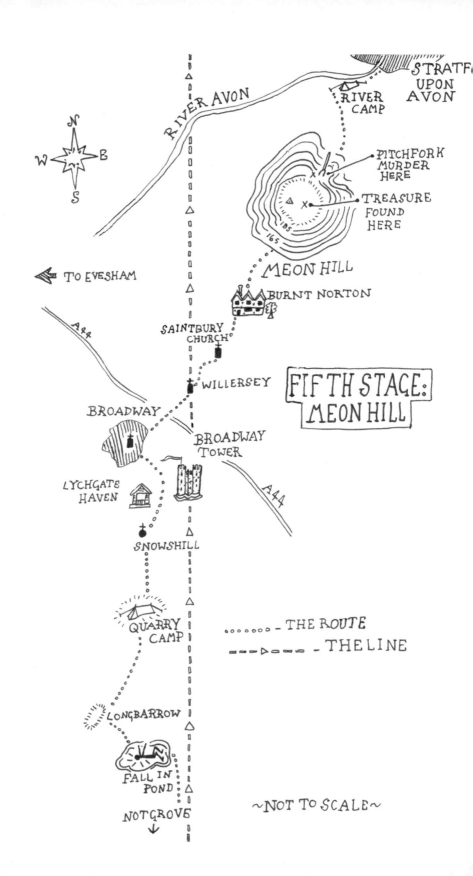

FIFTH STAGE:
MEON HILL

RIVER AVON

STRATF
UPON
AVON

RIVER
CAMP

PITCHFORK
MURDER
HERE

TREASURE
FOUND
HERE

N
W E
S

TO EVESHAM

MEON HILL

165 185

A44

BURNT NORTON

SAINTBURY
CHURCH

WILLERSEY

BROADWAY

BROADWAY
TOWER

A44

LYCHGATE
HAVEN

SNOWSHILL

•••••••• – THE ROUTE
– ▷ – – – THE LINE

QUARRY
CAMP

LONGBARROW

FALL IN
POND

NOTGROVE
↓

~NOT TO SCALE~

14

DRINKING TO THE ANCESTORS

Happy in my new boots (old ones, dumped, old sleeping bag posted home), I got off the bus from Cheltenham opposite the bad-vibe barrow of Notgrove. I then headed north past what looked like another ancient site near Cloud Hill. In among the trees and bright green grass hummocks, there appeared to be a ditch and rampart, though there was something wrong about them. Too lumpy. I checked the map; sure enough, the site was marked as an old quarry. To obtain the smoothness of a real barrow or henge takes longer than a few centuries, it seems. I was pleased, though, that I was getting a feel for what was genuine and what wasn't. Intensive immersion is the only way I seem to be able to learn – and this was an intensive course in ancient places.

It was getting late as I passed what looked like a keeper's cottage and entered the wood at Winchcombe, back on the Line again. I've had a few run-ins with gamekeepers in the past and I was anxious to avoid contact. Maybe it's in the blood as one of my illustrious ancestors, a poacher called Robert Twigger of Warwick was tried, along with three others, for the murder of a gamekeeper in 1819. He was condemned to death but then the keeper made a miraculous recovery. Robert's sentence was commuted at Warwick assizes to transportation for life to Van Diemen's Land. He was nineteen. After behaving himself in Tasmania for seven years and then Australia for five years, he was eventually given his freedom and allowed to settle down and get married.

The path up to the wood was called the Warden's Way and led past a barrow deep in the trees. It would have been a fine place to camp but I had no water. Far off, I heard the double report of a shotgunner out for an evening's sport, the sound clearly carrying, as it always does in the evening, although I couldn't tell where from. Poachers rely on the fact that it's very hard to tell the exact direction of where a sound comes from at twilight, owing to atmospheric differences at that time of day. I moved on past the dark woodlands with their gnarled deciduous trees, hoping for at least a small stream. Nothing. Then I was suddenly out on a tarmac road again, albeit one running alongside water.

It was a dammed river that formed a series of small lakes. One had a rotting swimming platform and a half-sunk boat tied up. I used my trusty Sawyer filter bag to suck up two litres of lake water. First I had to get clear of the shallows, and saw I could hang out over the water by holding on to a tree branch . . .

First bottle done. Another car went by, slowing down to scope me out as I hung out, one-handed over the water. It was apparently satisfied and accelerated away just as the bark began to feel loose – and the branch gave way with a crack. With the doomed heaviness that only a surprise fall can bring, I hit the water side on, grateful as I went in that I didn't have my rucksack on.

KerSPLASH!

I reared up like a water monster to be left standing knee-deep in wet boots. Not as sopping as I'd have thought, but still immensely wet down one side, and feeling foolish yet deeply grateful at the same time that no car-load of nosey locals had witnessed my shallow dive into the swamp. Notebook OK but wallet soaked. I emptied out all the cards and the tiny amount of cash onto my blue quick-dry towel. I changed my top half and socks but left on the wet trousers to dry as I walked. I even felt a growing cheerfulness, as if the silly shame of vagabondage had been lifted. It hadn't been bad at all really. Twenty minutes later, I found the quarry just off a gloomy uphill track. It was about thirty feet deep with a grassy bottom no more than a hundred feet across. Thin hazels sprouted from cracks in the limestone, and earth-covered piles of old stone made ramps at various places on each side.

It's not so very surprising, I suppose, that most quarries also double as shooting ranges. I tried to find a place away from the smashed glass, punctured rusty tins and shards of clay pigeon. There was a corner that backed uphill a bit which was relatively clear. The good thing about quarries is that they feel quite a bit less like trespassing. It was as if you could say, if challenged: 'You may own the quarry, but actually you only own the right to quarry, not the quarry itself, which is, in fact, under Saxon law, a free campsite.' Which was nice to say to oneself inside a tent thrumming with rain, a drum tattoo of knitting needles on the flysheet easing one into untroubled sleep.

I woke to more rain, my Buffalo top and trousers almost dry from hanging up in the damp tent all night. Dry enough to wear, at least.

All this day I would be walking through the Cotswolds, coming down deep lanes, ancient tracks from the high pastures, now tarmacked over. Lanes that worked well as running streams. As well as calling home I was thinking about calling my uncle, who lived right on the Line in a village north of Broadway, only a few miles away. The coincidence of that (and the coincidence of my grandfather having had a farm on the Line about twenty miles further on) was too much to miss. I would have to drop by.

Raining. The umbrella was punctured but still working, a few drips a minute, nothing to worry about. The pac-a-bac was working admirably to keep the drips off. The rain kilt was in place and so were the gaiters. I looked like one of those shelters the homeless build from scraps of tarpaulin and polythene sheet. But rain has this advantage: no one else is out in it, certainly not the mockers. I could keep going for ever in this weather, in this gear.

So it rained without stopping and under my brolly I was still thinking about calling my uncle. It was a little tricky. I had offered to help his wife with a writing project and I had not really done what I'd said I'd do. I'd been a bit tardy. Plenty of excuses, of course, but the reality was: a let-down. In the end, I came to the conclusion that I'd call from a B&B in Broadway, a village bang on the Line with its ancient beacon hill, one of the highest in the Cotswolds. That way they'd be under no pressure to put me up or even feed me . . .

Ah, better, now a decision had been made. But I was in need of a brew. The village of Snowshill offered nothing but the usual expensive village houses and parked cars slicked with rain. I tried the phone box – some still worked in out of the way places – but this one was for 999 calls only. Inside the relatively clean box, it still had a hint of the old odour: damp directories, cigarette ash, a scent of long-evaporated urine . . . and it was just too cramped a place for a decent brew. Still raining all through Snowshill and out, until I saw a church. Doors locked at this time of day, it had an elaborate lychgate – a covered gateway in the hedge surrounding the graveyard.

This lychgate was yet another magical portal on my journey. From an inscription I saw it was dedicated to the American painter Francis David Millet, a friend of Mark Twain and William Morris, Rossetti and the other Pre-Raphaelites. Millet had lived and worked in Broadway in the late nineteenth century, spending time at Broadway Tower, among other places, the folly that William Morris had restored and lived in that decorated Beacon Hill. And another nugget I'd store away: Broadway Tower had originally been built at the suggestion of Capability Brown, the prolific eighteenth-century garden designer.

Millet had become a painter later in life, a life cut short when he had the immense ill fortune to drown with the *Titanic*. (I felt sad reading this, an emotion reinforced by watching the running water pouring off the porch roof.) He was last seen helping women and children into lifeboats.

When I stumped into Broadway village itself, the sun finally came out. Too inert to look for a B&B, I booked into a pub for a night, true luxury, especially when I was shown where the sachets of tea and coffee and treble packs of shortbread were kept. Stocking up with tubules of instant coffee and sugar and salt and pepper shows the true pathos of the vagabond's revenge on the settler. William Morris would have understood my childhood disbelief when I discovered (age ten or so) that people actually paid money simply to live somewhere. Instinctively I was against rent and landlordism. It still doesn't make any sense . . .

*

Uncle Pat was home and of course invited me to stay the next night. The book thing was all in the past. Two nights indoors also meant my kit would dry. What's more, I could catch up on some family history. Uncle Pat, along with my sister, is the family historian. A lifelong rugby player who worked his way up from labourer to managing director of a big building company, Uncle Pat is not someone you'd want to mess with, even though he's nearly eighty.

He and his second wife, Cath, entertained me most royally and we sat up late into the night discussing the intrigues and intricacies of Twigger history. It was yet another aspect of alignment. Do you reject the general gist of your family past or do you cleave to it? Unless you reinvent yourself, it is best not to turn your back; that seemed evident. But Twiggers were an odd lot. My great-grandfather, Harry, to whom I felt particularly close in terms of what he attempted, was an early photographer and poet, but useless with money; he largely survived on 'remittance' from his businessman father, the one-time mayor of Lichfield. In fact, Harry was to spend time in the debtors' gaol in Birmingham. His postcards of Warwickshire churches are sought after by collectors to this day; I bought on eBay a pamphlet of his poems and photographs of Guy's Cliffe House, an ancient fortified manor house that obsessed me as a child (though Harry had been long dead when I was born). While Harry had been despised by his son, my grandfather, who became a professional soldier (whereas Harry was a pacifist), it was heartening that his creative work was still out there, his name was still known.

Despite financial failure, Harry had seen that his own destiny, his own path, lay in creating something new. His son found his path in becoming an army engineer, whose most memorable work was in building army camps and hospitals. His sons in turn were both involved in building and construction, and then my own path of writing books sort of returns us back to Harry. The cycles of the past generations are but a harmonic of the cycles in our own lives ... Alignment is about harnessing those cycles, so that forward motion and satisfactory progress are made. Progress in the widest sense of the word.

Uncle Pat and I drank late into the night, three whiskies each on top of the wine. He told me stories about my strange old grandfather, how he preferred outdoors or a bunkhouse to normal life in a house. How he made 16mm films of the Naga headhunters on the Burmese–Indian border. How he ran a Cotswold honey business and drove everyone mad who lived with him. Then Pat fixed me with a stare: 'What you going to do when you can't walk?'

15

MEON HILL AND BURNT NORTON

Damn headache from drinking. Said nothing to Uncle Pat, of course, when leaving, but now, huffing up a hill, I can feel it. Alcohol sucks the oxygen out of your blood. Hence snoring when inebriated. Hence out of breath now. Mist rising off hills, everything coming into the brightness of green. Coming up Saintbury Hill, you can see earthworks beneath the fields, like buried giants. (Are long barrows the origin of giant myths?) The church is up there all alone because something ancient was here first. And the name saint-plus-bury – a cross, a fort, a mound, a square-spired church. Everything about the Line is here.

Except I'm lost. And being lost with a hangover is especially crap; crapulous in a cap. In a fit of 'efficiency' I had posted home the previous map and only retained a hand-drawn sketch to get me on to the next sheet. Of course the sketch map was crap and now I don't know where I am. Words of my uncle come back to me clearly: 'Oh, I always like to know where I am.' This after my breezy boast that I am happy not knowing my exact position, implying I can live with ambiguity.

I can't. It's bloody annoying, especially as I can't take footpaths as I don't know where they will take me. I resort to walking on roads and using the compass, which I now find has a bubble in it. This makes the needle wobble, another annoyance for the liverish lost lover of the Line.

An age of head-down walking; I must be back on the map but where am I? Headache. No fucking clue. Feet hot from plodding along tarmac. Finally a National Trust sign: Dover's Hill. I look at the map – how obvious – staring me in the face. But it's as if people can read my only-just-departed state of lostness. On Dover's Hill a

Cotswold ranger comes up and asks: 'Hello there! Are you looking for the Cotswold Way?'

'No.' But I must relent, he is too nice a man. 'Actually I'm walking due north to Lindisfarne.'

'You don't say! A pilgrimage?'

'Of sorts.'

He's a man of about sixty or so, overweight and unhealthy looking but full of information about the Cotswold Way. He says he finds someone lost every day he is out walking his allotted seven-mile stretch . . .

Then an American couple, who I know are American from fifty yards away as they smile and wave at me . . . is it me? I look behind in case they are signalling someone else. They're just happy to make contact with anyone.

'Wow! Walking to Lindisfarne – that's amazing. And wild camping too!' The husband is also over sixty and has the tired but well-kempt face of stress ameliorated by wealth: they let slip they live in Palo Alto.

She is younger, super vibrant and healthy. 'Yeah, we're just heading for our B&B – we love them!'

'And how do you like the Cotswolds?' I ask, angling for flattery. And because they are nice to talk to.

'Great, just great! But you know, just between the two of us, I preferred the Peddars Way . . .'

'The Peddars Way?'

'In Norrfoke, we walked it last year. Stunning.'

Leaving them behind I stride on, glad to be back on the map and knowing exactly where I am. This is important, as finding Burnt Norton next would be impossible by dead reckoning.

To see a place you've read and thought about for years is deeply satisfying. Oddly, just seeing that the sign or place name exists in the real world is almost enough.

Burnt Norton, after which T. S. Eliot named one of the *Four Quartets*, is a seventeenth-century, grey-stone manor house, beautiful as almost all surviving houses of that time are. It has a wing as a writer's centre but I was too early for any writers to be about. You can still wander parts of the formal garden, though. The 'drained pool' of the poem, which I imagined as a reader to be a cracked, concrete swimming pool, is slope sided and long, rectangular, a little like an excavated mass grave. Eliot and Emily Hale, an early girlfriend, walked from Chipping Camden a few miles east and then around these gardens, of what was then a deserted old house. He wrote 1131 letters to her – only released in January 2020. . . . At one point they almost married. And she seems to have been a muse for most of his life.

Burnt Norton is all about time: in fact, it puts forward the shamanic idea of time's reality being an eternal present, of which past, present and future are but human constructs, ways of making sense of something too overwhelming – too real. Stillness, the still point at the centre of a feeling of timelessness, is one intimation of the reality of the eternal present. All the paradoxes of an eternal present – that nothing could be other than it is – provide material for the poem; it is essentially an Eastern religious idea and it is there to support Eliot's religious mysticism, a quality which also lies at the heart of the shaman's path. And it is true to what I contend is evident all along the Line: that a shamanic style of religion inspired the landscape of ancient Britain, and is still there to this day.

Alignment is about finding your place in the landscape, your 'spot', as shamanic author Carlos Castaneda would have it. Ley lines are sometimes seen as 'power' lines connecting up such spots. What I am suggesting is that the metaphorical power of a Line up England may receive some assistance from geomagnetic or geoelectrical forces we may yet discover. But even if the Line is just a metaphor, it is still tremendously useful.

The ancients knew the power of symbols: the circle within two or three rings, cup and ring engravings, henges and camps all signify the movement towards greater enlightenment. The spiral, so common in shamanic art, is another variant. Gates or entrances through the banks of a henge are symbolic entry points to higher levels of consciousness; a greater appreciation of unity, connectedness, a place where time stands still.

Even in the hands of Eliot, unable to convince a religious doubter like George Orwell, you may think this kind of talk oversteps some kind of acceptable boundary of belief. But these words connect to real experience. Their problem is they are merely words – worn out and overused. For those who have experienced a greater sense of unity – either through contemplation and feeling a sense of awe, through art or looking at the stars, or perhaps by chugging down a bowl of magic mushrooms – it is above all else an experience that counts even if the words lag far behind. Yet symbols keep you looking, hopeful and aware. The Line is there to be walked.

I plodded on, walking a small stretch of the Cotswold Way until I wasn't. As I approached Mickleton, a roadside diner with the sign 'Decades Café' drew me in with its own timeless bacon-sizzling charm. The friendly place was crowded with women and pushchairs, and the Formica-topped (plus all sauces) simplicity of the interior was enlivened by Seventies posters. An old MUFC line-up, *Starsky & Hutch*, Noddy Holder in a soft top hat with Slade, Niki Lauda and James Hunt, Borg and McEnroe in their goofy headbands. The pictures encouraged reminiscence. A fat lady next to me told her pal, 'In the past, I used to be able to arabesque . . .' Imagining her on tiptoes *avec hauteur* was . . . tricky.

Ian, the middle-aged man who made me a tasty bacon sandwich, told me about his hobbies. Bird watching, mainly, was his thing. He'd seen a barn owl out at Long Marston. 'But any bird will do,' he added, squirting cleaner and polishing the serving top. On the radio, as if in tribute, Slade played, followed by Ultravox's 'Vienna'. The windows steamed up and I rubbed a patch to look out.

But as I walked back into fields, the mood changed. In a long grassy field, a headless lamb lay bloody. And then another lamb about thirty yards further on. These were small lambs, maybe only a week old or less. But why the missing heads? It was macabre, and not out of keeping with the place where I found them – close to Meon Hill.

It is a very striking, large hill, looking almost manmade, so regular is its sawn-off cone shape, flat on top. The ditches and ramparts of a

Neolithic structure are visible at the sides but the top has been levelled by constant ploughing.

I had come here as an eight-year-old boy, brought by my parents at my own suggestion. I loved ancient forts and ruins. But to my consternation there were others about. I had been scared off from reaching the top, where the fort's remains are, by local boys (one or two of whom came by bus to my school in Ettington, about ten miles away); like something out of a poem by Eliot, they giggled and made pheasant calls from behind bushes near the top. My parents had only laughed at this behaviour and found it to be quaintly rural.

Lower Quinton, which nestles on the northern side, was my destination as I started to climb Meon from the south. All the tracks are private and there are none that attack the hill from the north, my direction. But nothing was going to stop me this time round. Head still a little fragile despite the coffee and bacon sarnie, I powered on up the hill expecting to be warned off the land. I felt all eyes on me. Meon Hill has a reputation. Apparently Tolkien used it as the inspiration for Weathertop. Time to keep an eye open for hobbits. In *Lord of the Rings*, they come over the hill from the north.

In 1824, an Iron Age hoard of 394 currency bars were found just behind the ramparts of the camp that remains on one side of the hilltop. The bars were sword-shaped and made of iron. Other finds of sword-shaped or chisel-shaped bars have been found in rivers, including the Avon, where they are bundled together like offerings. The Arthurian romance of throwing a sword into a lake perhaps is the mythological version of the bundled sword-shaped currency bars laid in the river.

Iron is dangerous stuff, hot to handle in every sense. Even today, in parts of sub-Saharan Africa, the metal worker is held in doubtful esteem. Working metal is not only unpleasant work, it is morally suspect. In Istanbul, at the Byzantine church of Chora, iron nails are depicted as the work of the devil.

Iron is hard to make. It needs hundreds of pounds of charcoal to smelt one pound of pig iron. Iron had a value, yet it wasn't like gold.

No one was throwing gold into rivers. Iron has something dark about it. It can be used for killing or for making ploughshares. Anything this ambiguous must be appeased by the appropriate ceremony. In order to transfer the spirit of iron to the side of light, there needs to be a sacrifice from time to time.

In Warwickshire, 1945, there was the worst winter for decades. A man's body was found in a farmhouse on the slopes of Meon Hill, stabbed through the chest with a pitchfork, his throat cut with a hedge slasher. Iron can do work like that. The man, Charles Walton, was a local farmworker and when CID investigated, they began to suspect that the crime had a ritual element. A local farmer for whom Walton worked, Robert Potter, was the chief suspect, though no charges were ever brought. It remains the oldest unsolved murder on the books of Warwickshire police.

Potter, it was claimed, blamed Walton for the death by drowning of one of his heifers. Witches were traditionally blamed for the death of valuable beasts, and there had been poor harvests and other grievances that only a ritual killing would atone for. Fifteen years earlier, a woman, also said to be a witch, was murdered with a pitch fork in Chipping Campden, some ten miles away.

Walton's murder occurred on Valentine's Day, a fortnight after St Brigid's Day, also known as the ancient festival of Imbolc; halfway between the winter and spring solstice. Some ancient monuments are aligned with the sun's rise at this time, including the Mound of the Hostages on the Hill of Tara in Ireland.

Was it a sacrificial murder? We shall most likely never know. Even today, the people of Lower Quinton refuse to talk about the murder; when a publican tried to cash in with a witch motif at the local pub, he was told by the locals to take it all down.

Robert Fabian of the Yard, England's top detective at the time, wrote: 'I advise anybody who is tempted at any time to venture into Black Magic, witchcraft, Shamanism – call it what you will – to remember Charles Walton and to think of his death, which was clearly the ghastly climax of a pagan rite. There is no stronger argument for keeping as far away as possible from the villains with their swords, incense and mumbo-jumbo. It is prudence on which your future peace of mind and even your life could depend.'

At the top of Meon Hill, I had to toil through the damp ploughed field, mud glutinously sticking to the cleated soles on my boots, to the tiny concrete island supporting a trig point. Like the OS map, the trig point is an essential part of the English walking experience. Though England was more accurately mapped than any other country in the world (and remains so), trig points were laid out in the 1930s to help with an even more accurate mapping, and as a child I was brought up to relish finding one. As you get older, standing on them and being photographed in a howling gale is all part of a young walker's initiation into the arcane rituals of rambling. Most points are around four foot high, a micro obelisk made of concrete. When you find one on a high and hard to get to hill, you wonder just how far the trig-point makers must have carried the cement. The top has inlaid a triangular grooved shape with an inset ring in the middle to hold a bolted-down theodolite.

Trig points are good for a brew. The base makes a handy solid stand for the stove and the obelisk itself acts as a windbreak. I crouched below the trig point sipping coffee, sitting on the lip of its extending base.

Getting up and over to Lower Quinton was easier. I followed the diamond pattern of a mountain-bike tread down fields and along a muddy track, a private footpath but I didn't care. The village lay inert and dull before me, under low clouds. Boys were playing football on the green, descendants of those who'd refused to say a word to the police about the murder. Of course they ignored me as they swearily played on, attacking with gusto a single goalmouth.

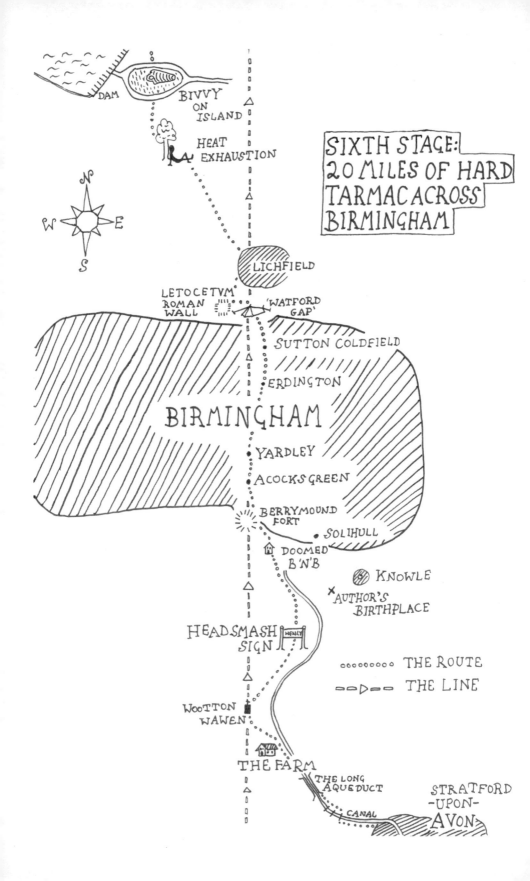

16

HEAD SMASHED IN TOWN

Nearing Stratford along a long straight track, the path of the old railway, I could at last see the river. A new Avon, joined a couple of miles hence by a new Stour. (The Dorset Stour joins the other Avon exactly 100 miles to the south in Christchurch.) There are six Stours and four Avons in England (with two more Avons in Scotland and an Afan in Wales). We've seen that 'Avon' means river, but what does Stour mean? A tributary of the Elbe is the Stoer, while two tributaries of the Po are named Stura; is Stour, like Avon, an invader's mistake? No one is sure. Though there is a link to the Celtic word *sturr*, meaning strong, most Stours are not very big rivers. But nor are they easily fordable. Perhaps a legionnaire asked its name and learnt that he couldn't cross because it was too *sturr*.

Another coincidence, Stours and Avons joining; I would have liked to camp at the confluence for its added shamanic benefits but give up all too easily as it's getting dark and I'm wading through tall grass, trying to find somewhere not too damp, nor too close to the backwash from the periodic party boats from Stratford that blast past, all lights and sudden bursts of crashing, jangly music.

Found the spot now and the tent goes up fast. (Getting better at this.) Yes, it feels good to be camping by a river. I should do more of this. In an extension of the idea of freedom of access between high and low water on any UK beach, the margin of any river (say the nearest ten feet) seems less owned than the rest of the field it happens to be in. Camping by a river, like camping by the side of a national trail like the Pennine Way, seems more of a right than an act of trespass.

A good night then, and everything saturated with dew the next morning. When I peer out of the tent door there is mist in mysterious layers, like loft insulation rolled out over the fields; I watch as the sun breaks the horizon to become a precise red dot in the haze. It is then I hear the far-off stentorian gasp of a hot air balloon roaring its way to fulfilment. The morning is dead still and above the haze is icy cold clearness; what will be a blue sky, perfect for ballooning. Rolling up the drenched tent, cramming it into a Co-op 10p bag (so much more waterproof than a natty silnylon stuff sack), I then down the last of the coffee. Now excavate with fingers the coffee grounds from the WindBurner pot and flick them onto the riverbank. Quite a mess considering. I pack and walk towards the roaring.

It's a Virgin-sponsored balloon, in fact there are several; some kind of event in the fields by the side of Stratford. Another is being filled up like a dopey Humpty Dumpty. There is a studious stupidity about it, all that waiting and wobbling in slow response to the on–off of the rasping burners. In the lifting basket, all sorts of people wait with satisfied, expectant looks.

Virgin is everywhere; Branson is always busy. I suppose everyone has some sort of attitude towards Richard Branson; in the 1980s, I used to do publicity for Virgin Books and delivered packages to Branson's houseboat in Maida Vale. My then boss, who knew him, said Branson always finished dinner in forty-five minutes; no leisurely small talk at all. I cross an ancient iron viaduct and then surface in the residential end of Stratford. I need to cross the town to exit north along the Stratford-upon-Avon Canal. It's Saturday, still very early – not even 7 a.m. – but I know the market will be opening in the centre; we used to go often when I was younger.

The streets are empty, but then two men in their thirties or forties, dressed in dull, grubby-looking clothing that looks hastily thrown on, too many buttons open, catch my eye on the other side of the road.

One says, in an accent I can't place, 'Any shops open now?' I am about to launch into helpful mode but something hostile is coming off both of them. I say nothing and he insists: 'Any shops selling beer round here?'

'No idea,' I say breezily, but this guy is not the kind to be fobbed off. In harder tones, he says, 'You got any beer on you? Anything to drink?' which I know is a prelude to asking me to pay for booze, and if I say I don't drink, he'll have an excuse to act insulted.

'Sorry, mate, bit early for me. I think there's a Tesco over that way; the service station will probably be open.'

Grumpily they wander off and I realise they probably had me pegged as a fellow hobo. Pretty much the only hassle I've had in English towns has been the morning after, around this time when you think everyone will be either bright and cheery or deep asleep. You tend to forget about the all-nighters returning home still thirsty.

The market people are setting up. Scaffold poles, polyester tarps with faded pink stripes held by giant clips like those used to jump start a car. Clothes, tools and nails in black buckets labelled with starburst Day-Glo price tags, a discount fishing tackle stall. No sign of my favourite stall of the past: SONA Surplus, where aged eight, I bought my commando cap comforter and navy-issue clasp knife. No army surplus stall at all in fact.

The stall people banter among themselves. They haven't officially opened so people talk around me, over my head. In fact, no one pays me a blind bit of notice. I get a typically terrible cappuccino (instant, of course) but an excellent bacon roll from a van.

I say to the bacon man, who has tinted glasses, 'Looks like a good day.'

'Hot one, yeah.' He flips my bacon from the square, oil-smoking plate into pre-warmed bun halves. 'But cloudy is better for us.'

'Saturday must always be fairly good.'

'Actually Monday is often our best day.'

Towns draw you in. Even a day on the trail, well, maybe two days, and a town seems welcome. Supermarkets chock-full of goodies. Cafés. But just as quickly they pall. Just as an introvert needs time to recharge away from others, and can't understand the extrovert's need for constant company, the walker, who can survive perfectly well in the wilderness (if needs be and given enough supplies), soon tires of the prosthetic nature of the town. Prosthetic? Sure, it seems to me sometimes that towns are best suited to people who are a bit ill, a bit low energy; everything is so easy in a town that if you are of a normal fitness level, it becomes about doing things as quickly and efficiently as possible. Oh, I know: what about the browsing, the bargain hunting? Well, again, if it's too easy, you start becoming 'efficient' at it, i.e. rushing. Obviously the best solution is an easy oscillation from town to country and back again; the kind of life lived by the Roman gentleman farmer, transhumance shepherd folk, or the oasis-hopping nomad. But we can't all live like that. Mostly we get stuck in towns all the time. Grrr.

On the way out, I look for the New Leaf Bookshop where my sisters and I queued for hours (it seemed) to get Richard Adams to sign our copies of *Watership Down*. It's now an outlet of The Works (I think); I don't really mind for some reason (usually I can manage at least five minutes of righteous anger at the thought of another independent going bust), maybe because Stratford for me is very much a place sealed in my past. The modern Stratford has little or no connection with that time. Anyway, I am soon heading out of town, along the sunny canal towpath that will bring me to my grandfather's old farm.

Unlike the Railway Children I've always preferred canals to railways. Uncle Pat has found that many of our ancestors were 'canal navigators'. In my ignorance, I thought that meant being a sort of inland river pilot. Er, no. A navvy actually.[12]

Canals played a more sinister part in our family history: my great-grandfather was murdered and thrown in one, in the far end of this one, on the other side of Birmingham. This is where I'm going next, following first the Stratford-upon-Avon Canal and then the Grand Union.

Murdered aged twenty-three; I used to look at his soft features and moustache in the large sepia photograph my grandmother had of him. He looked much older than his years, already married with two children. He worked as a plain clothes detective for the Transport Police, tasked with breaking up the Railway Gangs that operated at the turn of the century. He cannot have been working long when he was caught out, bludgeoned to death and thrown in the canal. When I was younger, I used to imagine the door of a moving train, a cattle truck of some kind, sliding open and him being thrown out into the canal running below. Splashing and drowning.

Today, of course, it's all lovely. Sun. Joggers. A couple of well-off, well-turned-out pensioners, the kind with Fitbits and iPhones, stop and question me on their way into Stratford to buy fine cheeses and the *FT Weekend*. I am more than happy to boast about my walk, and they are friendly enough and preferable to the next person, a bloke in his fifties in a tracksuit top. He does the usual, 'It's brilliant that, what you're doing,' and then spends ten minutes telling me about his green credentials and his daughter's walking holiday in Yosemite. Bait and switch!

The woman I like best is blonde, tubby and a bit distracted, who is waddling to Stratford to fill her pitcher, she tells me, showing me a white plastic jug with a screw top. 'Got to get my diet drink!' It seems she fills the pitcher at a health food shop. She asks for a donation to the charity (she's vague about which one) that she supports because she lost her partner this year. Then she swerves away, turns and asks, 'When you get to Solihull, what you going to do? If it doesn't sound nosey?'

'I'm going to sleep.'

Solihull is my next destination, but I don't add it's where I was born, according to my passport. In fact, I was born just outside Solihull, between Knowle and Dorridge, in a small village called Bentley Heath. Born on the Line ... well not quite, maybe five miles off it. This is a rather distinguished part of the world. Jasper Carrott is the most living famous resident of Knowle. And John Wyndham of *The Day of the Triffids* fame was born in Dorridge.

By now I'm at the aqueduct. This was somewhere I only heard about as a child. I was never allowed to cross it. Wootton Wawen aqueduct carries the canal skyward over roads for more than a hundred metres. It is supposedly one of the longest in England. The footpath is level with the riveted metal base, the trough of water that carries the boats, so you are at nose level to the water when walking. It's always surprising how narrow canals are. A longboat goes by loaded with partying twenty-year-olds; one, older at the tiller, all with beers at 9.30 a.m. It's weird being below their level; they look down on me, literally, but give friendly beer-charged greetings which I return in a generic way. I catch the eye of the tiller man and he gives me a 'these kids!' kind of look, which I know is meant to comfort me in case I'm one of those oldsters who hate people having fun . . .

From the aqueduct I can see the old farmhouse clearly. The whole place was sold and went out of our family for good in the 1970s. The owner doesn't farm any more, just rents the land out to other farmers. The bungalow that my grandparents built and retired in is surrounded by fir trees grown tall in the last forty years. Barns that I remember being full of egg-laying hens are still there. The long path over two cattle grids to the main road, walked everyday by Grandpa Tom, is much shorter than I remember . . . of course. Walking by the canal I think of Grandpa Tom, with his glass eye and missing ring finger (both lost in the First World War), finding a wallet on the tow path and another time a penknife. Even in his late eighties, he maintained a childlike interest in the world.

At a local farm-shop café I get breakfast. It's an upmarket place. A bald bloke with a body builder's physique and a beautiful girl (though with skew-whiff eyes) arrive freshly showered in a matt black Beamer. Both have tasteful tatts; they order brunch then sit in silence. Finally she says, 'But if we go to Solihull what is there to do except . . .' But she doesn't finish as their eggs Benedict have arrived and silence again rules.

I pass another body builder at work in his garden, a neat-freak in a Nike tick singlet, with a spick-and-span roadside split-level house, a jelly-mould Nissan in the drive – black, of course – and a churning leaf blower in his meaty paw. It's summer for Christ's sake! Leave those leaves alone!

St Peter's in Wootton Wawen is a Saxon church, the oldest in Warwickshire, and describes itself as a 'one stop encyclopaedia of English history'. There is a mysterious tump in the graveyard, almost certainly an ancient leftover; this is another church built on ground sacred to pre-Christians. I arrange like dirty washing (well, it is dirty washing) my tent, sleeping bag and damp socks on the alloy five-bar gate that opens next to the church entrance. A hot sun must not be ignored and the tent was dripping after its night next to the river.

But now I am all churched out for some reason. King Charles II, I note wearily, passed through here. The interior is large and fine, much improved on its Saxon origins. There is speculation that it was sacked by Vikings – impressive as Wootton Wawen is, it is about as far from the sea as you can get in Britain.

Back to the hot canal, and a certain dread is building: tomorrow the Line goes bang through Birmingham; just missing the Bull Ring. I once asked my grandmother if Birmingham was a nicer place before they built the Bull Ring shopping centre. 'Oh no,' she replied. 'Birmingham's always been ugly.'

Walking through deeply urban areas, maybe dodgy areas, I'm feeling a little vulnerable. A friend was recently mugged in Coventry alongside the canal; wearing a backpack and raingear, a walker is an easy mark … but not if he has a sharpened walking pole! At some point the titanium stud had dropped off one of my poles, leaving the bare aluminium to be worn into an interesting looking and sharp-edged stump. Wouldn't want that in my foot, or calf, or thigh. A swordstick of sorts; should be illegal, I don't doubt. Makes me feel both better but also uneasy at feeling uneasy.

And at about that moment, approaching to cross a busy A-road between wide grass verges, a delicate curve out of Henley-in-Arden, looking down, not paying much attention, I walked between the poles of a road sign and then BANG! KERUNCCHH! A very unpleasant sound to have coming from your head: the munching, soft-crunching sound of a hard-edged aluminium sign cutting through the scalp and hitting the skull. BANG! KERUNCCHH! I was suddenly flat on my back, my rucksack turtle-shelling, blood pouring down around my ears.

First thought: bugger, I'll have to get stitches, go to a hospital. Second thought: at least I didn't black out. Third thought: head wounds always bleed like crazy. Fourth thought: glad my glasses are still on (hanging by one ear). Find the first aid kit. Stop the bleeding.

Toilet roll wadded up into a thick pad; bleeds through immediately. Slap another one on, then another. Keep up the pressure. Cars drive by. Some slow, look, then speed up. Probably don't really know what I'm doing.

Resting on the grass, my rucksack like a sort of backrest, I look up at the brilliant blue sky. In the distance I see the brightly coloured hot air balloons, too far and too high to hear. Like fruit waiting to be picked from the heavens above . . .

And so I make it at long last, by 7 p.m., to the outskirts of Hockley Heath, near enough to Solihull. Fuck Knowle and Dorridge, I'm not about to deviate an inch to do some sentimental sightseeing: stick to the Line. I photograph the sign (at least I don't bang into this one) and then continue along the canal again, a nice straight path. My head aches but the bleeding has stopped. I've taped the toilet-roll dressing down with duct tape. The gash might have needed a stitch but if I'm careful it will be fine. There's a nasty lump, though, which I can gingerly feel through the matted hair.

When I pop up from the canal, the first thing I see is a shop selling McLaren cars. These Birmingham suburbs are now a wealthy place. Head aching, all done in, I look for a B&B and after some hard tarmac walking, find one. I ring the doorbell, covering my wounded poll and assorted dressings with my tatty baseball cap. The male voice that answers the intercom says they've recently closed but he's willing to do a single night without breakfast for the same price: £50. I don't argue. A man around my age opens the door.

Inside I try to start a conversation. 'So you're selling up then?'

Rather sharply, he replies, 'Yes, you want to buy?'

17

FOOTING IT THROUGH BRUM

There is always something a bit mean, a bit calculating, about B&Bs that aren't successful. Even if all the amenities are there – the tiny kettle shoved up against the tooth glass capped by a paper thing, the dark plastic/wood mini-tray never stuffed with enough tubules of Nescafé, teabags in paper envelopes, the two shortbreads that sometimes have to double for breakfast (in my case, given that brekkie was shamefully off the menu here), the two small white towels and the two big white towels – it is as if the minutely calculated, so-called generosity of the B&B is exposed in all its stupidity and rigidity. Success lies elsewhere, except the failed B&B owner devoutly believes, even now, that these 'extras' will somehow confer success.

I was on the ground floor in a room that felt like it should be a bedroom looking out from higher up. Not that I had any complaints. I washed all my gear. I dried all my gear. I made a fair amount of mess. I slept OK. For some reason I had no interest in the TV. I read instead. Maybe all this walking was undermining my dreadful addiction to crap television. We'd see.

The next day, eager to be off, I was outside, loaded up and Pacerpole pacing in my Hoka ultramarathon running shoes by 8 a.m. I didn't want to wear my new boots. I wanted to look 'street' or even 'homeless', rather than 'lost backpacker'. But I love walking with poles so much that I still walked with them here. Click click click.

The distance to the next bit of green, fields and trees and places where you could reasonably kip, was twenty-eight miles. That was a fair bit more than my sixteen to eighteen miles (or sometimes less) that I was plodding each day. And tarmac miles were killers in my experience.

If I had managed the supremely simple task of registering with Airbnb, I could have simply dialled up a potential billet halfway across town. But something had stopped me from doing that. I've found that there are some tasks, seemingly very simple, that completely stump me and then – with a half-click of the Rubik's cube, a tiny act of realignment – and I happily do something two or three times as onerous and time-consuming like using a film camera instead of a digital one or building a shed from scratch rather than from a kit. It's not about the money; when things are too mechanical I start to lose traction, impending meaninglessness is my enemy, not time or effort.

The map looked grim. Completely unfolded, it was two-thirds covered with the battleship grey that signifies heavy urbanisation threaded thinly with the red veins of roads, plus a few blue motorway arteries – total urban blot.

So you start walking, thankfully along a relatively quiet A-road. It's Sunday, everyone is in bed. When you cross up and over the M42, the sun is shining and there are still very few cars. Now it's just about keeping the pace up, not too many rests, taking the direct route north.

What do you think about when you're road walking through suburbs? Just typing the word 'suburb' is enough to cause a creative block. You think about those disturbingly and gratuitously too-wide roads that feed off roundabouts to out-of-town DIY stores and you wait for a decent gap in the traffic and finally, head down, you leg it. And hope some psycho or half-asleep driver doesn't hit you. You think about who's coming towards you on the pavement. You think about the shops being open or shut. You think about getting a haircut, given the many hairdressing shops you walk past, the name of my favourite being 'Ali's Barbers'.

There are very few ancient sites on this stretch. They were obliterated long ago. West Midlands has one entry to Wiltshire's sixty-eight sites in my guidebook. Berry Mound in Solihull is an oval fort 'much reduced in recent times'. It is a sign of how rural and non-urban

England really is that, Brum excepting, so much ancient stonework is still on show.

My opinion might change as I push up later through Huddersfield and Halifax, Bradford and Bingley (evidence that building societies really did build), but so far I've confirmed an insight that I gained when flying down Britain in a prop plane from Glasgow to Exeter. England is all green! A multicoloured palate of green maybe – slate, ash, stone, earth, lime, olive, emerald, pea, pear – but still overwhelmingly green. This is my growing hunch: England is as it has always been, in the main: a patchwork of fields linked by filament-thin roads and tracks and paths. Towns appear like foxing on an ancient page, not even noticeable unless you're looking for them. Townies think they're the biz, and by a headcount of course they are. But the land exerts complex forces upon us, upon our psyche – collective and individual. By hook or by crook that land, although owned each year by varying numbers of people (going back to 1066, when it all belonged to one man), has remained much the same, which is rather incredible given the pace of change in so many areas of human existence.

Where you live, who you live with and what you do most of the time are the three main factors that control, at a conservative estimate, at least 80 per cent of your life. To live in England, with English people, doing English things; well, don't be surprised if you start to become a bit ... anglicised. Everything that goes into a salt mine eventually becomes salt.

Such are the thoughts as you pass from the millionaire mansions in Solihull to the grittier reaches of the city where immigration is most apparent. A few years after I was born, my family moved to Leamington Spa. Until the age of six, I lived on a street with Poles, Pakistanis and West Indians. I loved it. In a couple of hours' time, I'd be passing through Stechford, birthplace of Enoch Powell, five miles east of Birmingham city centre. I once heard Powell described by a very bright MP (they do exist) as the 'most intelligent man' he had ever met, and went with high hopes in 1987 to hear Powell talk about his hero Nietzsche but the lecture was ... very dry. But first, on the outskirts of Hall Green, an Indian wedding at 9.30 in the morning, everyone spilling out cheerful in pinks and whites and greys from a community centre. It feels good to see a wedding, even though I don't particularly like attending them. I realise it's the most life I've seen so far today.

Then on to Stechford itself – over the railway line, a splay of tracks like stuck-together spaghetti being pulled apart. Few people pass me: old folk, poor folk. In some stretches, all are Indian or Pakistani. In others, a sudden knot of Poles. Then long (and they are long) stretches of largely silent middle-class homes with cars securely lodged in the drives.

By lunchtime, I'm at a shopping centre built on an old industrial expanse below road height. It has a good enough coffee shop with flat whites and almond croissants. I rest my road-bashed feet. I find I cling to my outdoorsness here; even indoors, I feel apart from all the tubby shoppers with their trolleys and ice creams; they live here, I'm just passing through – the best feeling. But I lose my way in the shopping centre and find myself aimlessly wandering past pound shops and appliance outlets. Everyone is buying things, I'm the odd one out.

Now on again, past Erdington where mad Uncle Harry lived: garage owner, inventor, imprisoned for a year in the Lubyanka in Moscow for fighting alongside the White Russians; never forgave Churchill for sending the Cossacks back to be killed by Stalin. Voted Labour in 1945 and Labour ever afterwards in a family of staunch Conservatives.

Past Sutton Coldfield and its rather pleasant town centre; everyone sitting al fresco, enjoying the sun, and a bookshop where I get more maps. And still I pound on. Still urban the setting, but now the houses are getting larger. A few people in their gardens, trimming hedges, watering. Well-off looking kids with earphones walk by, staring at their phones. Looking at your phone is so much the default setting that anyone not looking at their phone signals their difference immediately here. Anyone up to no good better hide it with a pretence of phone fixation.

*

Finally, I approach Watford Gap: it's a real place, marked on the OS map as a crossroads off the Lichfield Road, north of Sutton Cold-field. Research reveals Watford Gap is an old name, centuries old, a place where a toll was exacted from those going further north. The other Watford Gap (nowhere near Watford town, but named after the village of Watford in Northamptonshire) is where North and South collide. The way you speak becomes significantly more 'northern inflected' as you pass up through the gap (a valley between hills convenient for road and rail, hence the motorway services of the same name). Watford Gap was also where the Danes were pushed back and agreed to stay (loaded with their Danegeld, a tax that some would call the ancient equivalent of an EU payment). This other Watford Gap, on Watford Gap Road, remains mysterious, but it is bang on the Line . . .

My feet are really numb and stinging a bit now. My calves have the feeling that they have been shock loaded, over loaded, shortened by excessive pounding, dulled into dead but still complaining muscle. Watford Gap, the crossroads, really does mark the beginning of the countryside again. Fields all of a sudden. I am released from the torment of town walking. So glad to have done it, so glad it's over. I find a wood off the main road and sleep almost immediately.

18

SUPERHEATER

I woke in a tiny triangle of low trees, down a track past three white ponies and a warehouse surrounded by piles of earth spotted with lumps of stone, as if they were in the process of burying an entire stone cottage. The three white ponies became my instant friends. That may sound like desperation, the words of a man starved of conversation after walking through the second most populous city in Britain; nevertheless it is true. Horses are obviously better than cows at quick friendship. These ponies looked at me with an infinite longing for freedom in the dampness of the morning as I passed by. They seemed to remember me from the night before, when I had paid them little notice in the dusk, quickstepping as I was towards the woodland, hopeful of a billet. But now the ponies watched me, the man who was free on the other side of the wall topped with barbed wire, leaving their lives forever – and I loved them for it . . .

My first stop before breakfast was the Roman settlement of Letocetvm in the village of Wall, next to the A5 and the M6 toll. Neolithic flints have been found there; Wall has been lived in for thousands of years. But why is the place called Wall? There are certainly a lot of low walls left: all that remains of the Roman buildings. And the fort probably once had a substantial wall too. Apparently, its Roman name of Letocetvmis derived from a local one meaning 'grey wood'. So Wall must have come later. It's a good name, though. It must be nice to say you come from Wall. (Maybe if you live in a crap house in Wall, you can get away with saying you live in a hole in Wall . . .)

The church stood on a knoll above the village, which I suspected was an ancient site. The churchyard very conveniently had a tap for filling jam jars for flowers for the graves. I filled up my bottles greedily; I was going to need them today. Below the church, among the remains of the Roman mansion and baths, I brewed up a morning coffee. By now, it was about 8 a.m. No one about. Shamefully, I admit to discarding coffee grounds within that ancient and preserved enclave.

But then on the way out, after I had snuck another look into the church, a woman bustled up, all friendliness. She did not enquire what I was up to, nor did I offer an explanation, trusting to cheeriness and walking gear to dispel the suspicion that I was a tramp. Her expression, which bore a sort of monstrous smiling fixity, told me I was not entirely successful in dispelling these suspicions.

Lichfield: 'You'll want to go there,' advised Uncle Pat. I duly set off in search of my great-great-grandfather, a former trooper in the army who made good as a director of the Prudential Insurance Company, finally becoming Mayor of Lichfield. But what made his name was his successful suppression of the infamous 'baby farms' on Cannock Chase. When life insurance was first offered, clever yet unscrupulous folk realised they could insure a baby and then engineer its demise . . . thus collecting a fat wodge. This was 150 years ago, maybe less, and it sounds like something you'd read about in another part of the world. Mind you, there have been recent cases of slavery in Staffordshire, with people locked up and forced to work for no pay. Maybe this stuff is just cyclical.

The house where my great-great-grandfather ended his successful career was called Boston House. As a little lad, my grandfather (the nutty one who kept bees, not the farmer) had spent his Christmases there amidst servants singing carols and hams hanging from the ceiling and all sorts of Dickensian cheer . . . I discovered it was now the Rosemary Lodge Residential Care Home, a big red building with landscaped gardens and twenty-six small but well-equipped bedrooms on the Walsall Road; on its website, the wording: 'affectionately remembered by locals as Boston House'.

For a brief and not very pleasant moment, I imagined a trajectory that ended with residence in one of the twenty-six rooms in such a home. My grandfather actually spent his last four years in a place like this. Maybe if he'd lived a year or two longer he could have been situated here. How strange that would have been: ending his days as a paying guest in a room in a house that was once his family home.

There's only one pub open in the village. Today, I belatedly realise after seeing many shut shops, is bank holiday Monday. After I've waded through efficiently farmed, endless cornfields, it's lunchtime. There is a holiday atmosphere in the pub; at least I infer one after the large lady behind the bar tells me her husband is barbecuing burgers in the beer garden. She is the kind of slightly intimidating landlady who is simultaneously kind and considerate but also very good at banter. And I fear her husband will be a macho northerner (after a day in the official North, it really does feel 'northern' here in Staffordshire, though many would think of it as still being in the Midlands) and will find something to rib me about due to my admittedly odd appearance. My Buffalo top is now unzipped on both sides with the sleeves rolled up – and still I'm sweating; short of going about in an undervest, I have nothing cooler to wear.

Such ribbing is never as bad as the humiliation and social ostracism one imagines, yet the mere thought of it is sometimes enough for me to avoid pubs . . . except when I am dying of thirst, like now. Anyway, the man appears and I see immediately he is the silent type who lets his wife take centre stage. But he is no wimp; he simply nods at my order, so I am not sure whether it has sunk in that I am actually ordering rather than enquiring.

To hell with the macho need to buy pints of lager. I drink two pints of shandy and feel more hydrated. As I suspected, there is some confusion about my burger order. Lots of locals, friends of the landlady and her husband, are quipping back and forth in the small public bar while I sit at a dark table, sipping. Then the lady finally remembers my food and takes it upon herself to get it to me, dispatching her extremely polite and personable teenage son to do the job.

This son is evidence that the pub-owning couple have done a good job. Increasingly I am shocked at how polite boys are in places of work. Partly, it's the importation of the American 'sir' (unknown in my youth), but something else is at work. Politeness, sad to say, usually exists where people are fearful of the consequences, like the 'carry' bar I once went to in Arizona where everyone was exceedingly polite – no one wanted to get shot.

The landlady spots my not-yet-proffered water bottle as I approach the bar and says, 'You'll want water.' People are very happy to give me free refills of 'tap water' in any café or pub I frequent. They want to help me, as long as it doesn't cost anything . . . As I leave, she cautions, 'Take care, keep covered up – it's hot out there.' Her concern for me is very heartening. As well as feeling sweaty, I feel warm inside too. She's like my mum and I've only known her ninety minutes! And she's wise. It's 2 p.m., hottest part of the day.

Right next to the pub is the Trent and Mersey Canal. It runs right alongside an old mill building that is now being used for something else, so still working but a shadow of its former glory. I can't help thinking how wet it must have been in the past, with the canal right up against your wall. Unfortunately the tow path is not in the shade and only when I scuttle under bridges is there any relief from the heat. No one is about. All indoors if they have any sense. A great stultifying stillness lies over the land.

After a few miles of the canal I'm into empty fields, also without shade. And my pace is getting slower and slower. Then all of a sudden I realise I'm going to blow a gasket soon if I don't stop. I am melting in this heat. The only shade, though, comes from the pathetic shrub-like bushes that are all that is left of a ripped-out hedge in a mega-field of green wheat. About 400 yards ahead is a bigger tree, promising more shade. This last stretch, once I've decided to stop, is like a stroll past an open pizza oven going full blast . . .

The shade isn't complete darkness – it is the flickery, patchy shade you get through leaf cover – but it works. I lie back and fall deeply asleep.

Late in the afternoon and the walking now is through privileged land with well-maintained cottages, retirement homes maybe, farms with shooting grounds, picturesque fields. I'm still a bit disoriented and dry mouthed from my slumber. And low on water; I'll need to camp near a supply. Then I'm into a valley, one end barred by a dam, a big reservoir present but invisible on the other side of the ridge. It's like being in the rain shadow of it, with only a few dribbly streams allowed to seep out through the earthen dam wall, which could just be a ridge of low hill from where I am walking.

Low-lying land, boggy in many places, not a good place to camp. I am summoned by a glimpse of woodland, the only trees I can see for miles. It turns out to be on a piece of land that is effectively an island, cut off by a ditch that enters a river. Dumping my burdensome pack, and avoiding two honking geese, I have to hop over the ditch to get on to the island. Then over a tangle of barbed wire, which I manage easily without my pack on. There are nettles everywhere and in the distance a blue barrel signifying a pheasant rearing zone (used for feed). The only un-nettly place is under the sloping gravel base of a willow tree bordering the river. The spot is in the sight line of a farm about 400 metres away. I duck down until I am hobbit height, hiding behind the high stingers. Now I cannot be seen, the nettles are too high. It'll do.

Back to my pack lying at the confluence of ditch and river. This is cow country, and there is hoof-pocked mud to the water's edge. A fluff-hung barbed wire strand, slack between rotting posts, marks a vague boundary. And those geese again. Which I am prepared to drive away brutally with flailing walking sticks. Honking and wingtip splashing, they depart after only a few well-chosen but supremely harsh and guttural oaths. Cow water, but fast water, and fast water is good water; I step out on wobbly stones and a submerged log to fill my bottles and laboriously filter a couple of litres. Remembering my last splashy fall, I am super methodical, like someone remembering a pre-flight checklist: put bottle down. Screw on top. Put filter down, etc., etc.

Now I'm watered up, it is now a great test to get over the ditch and wire to the island with my pack. In the end I throw it up and over into nettles. But there is something a little worrying. This ducking down business. I can hide but my tent will be too high. It might be seen. I am camping in a pheasant patch within spitting distance of the enemy.

The sky is clear. It's been a hot day. I don't need my high tent. Time to sleep out under the stars. Now it actually becomes fun. In fact, keeping low has a fun all of its own. It reminds me of ducking down as a child to avoid being seen during hide and seek. It reminds me that hiding is almost as much a pleasure as seeking, maybe more so for some people. When you hide you're outwitting people, proving how clever you are. When you're seeking, it's less about a single genius idea and more about energy and methodical looking. The hider has to see possibilities, be creative and then all the work is done. Hiding presumably appeals to lazier folk . . .

So from being a bit shitty, this becomes a great campsite. It is lovely and cool too, near the fast-running river; just enough babble to be pleasant and not noisy. I keep my head torch angled down, and on 'red' some of the time. I cook my meal on the hissing blueness of the gas stove, extra blue in the encroaching darkness, and it still feels good to be keeping low. It is like being in the trenches: keep your head below the parapet and you'll be fine.

19

DOWN THE TUNNEL

Terence McKenna, following R. Gordon Wasson's seminal book *Soma: Divine Mushroom of Immortality*, has been highly influential in promoting the idea that shamanic intoxication and subsequent transfer to another dimension is the driver of human evolution. According to this theory, ancient man was like an Amazonian Indian or maybe a crouching Turanian on the steppes of Central Asia. It is a step forward from the earlier model of ancient man as uneducated fellow who used magic instead of science. It opens up the possibility of realities other than the mundane one on the TV news.

Our society, the one we inhabit now, does not formally acknowledge any other reality. As far as the State goes, this is it. You may have a shamanistic 'real' name but you certainly don't use it when you claim your tax back. (Or plead that your poetic self does not pay tax.) But imagine a society where multiple realities are accepted. Perhaps they are signified by circles within circles. Perhaps getting from one reality to another would require a little help, the kind of help you might need to climb a rampart or cross a ditch. You might make markings and engrave rocks with the same cup and ring symbology. You are sending your heirs a message they will understand long after the language you spoke has died.

Away early from my crouching lair, I trogged across mist-laden, deep-ploughed fields, curved slabs of dark clayey soil, like an endless line of scoops of chocolate ice cream. Not overly wet but clingy and sticky; what my grandfather would call six-horse land – the number of horses needed to plough it effectively. The soil clogged up my boots and I quickly grew a pair of mud wellingtons, each weighing kilograms. Poke off the mud with a stick and the stick got clogged too; it was like trying to be rid of a persistent bit of hard snot stuck to your hand.

The mist burnt off and I found myself walking through a boarding school before the start of lessons. The grounds were well mowed and beautifully kempt, no one about. I checked several times before launching across the cricket pitch as the footpath really did go that way. It's always a nice feeling to enjoy a sense of trespass without actually doing it. The school, as I rather meanly checked later on, had its fair share of alumni you've never heard of, but who were still celebrities of some kind, including Kelly England Prehn, international fashion model and now a famous fashion person at large. Her Wikipedia entry notes she is 'considered one of the most influential people in the fashion industry in China' and that she successfully won a pair of Jackie Collins earrings at a celebrity auction for charity in 2017. She has been described as 'the Pride of the Potteries' for her work championing Staffordshire pottery. I know. Mean.

In Uttoxeter there are none of the usual coffee chains that I could see, so I sidled into Ted's 'T' Rooms because I erroneously believed it would do a good bacon bap. But once I was inside, I realised my catastrophic error. Ted's was the epitome of net-curtain twitching good taste – doily central with real china cups with skinny handles. The servers and the woman (maybe Teddy the owner) standing at the till were cut from the same forbidding cloth: they minded their ps and qs when serving t.

I ordered coffee and was told, 'Our coffee, dear, is a full cafetière, only £1.70', and this filled me with nostalgic hope. I would get to experience the last place in England still serving coffee in a cafetière, all the rage in the 1980s. You always pray with a cafetière that it will be filled by a real coffee drinker but it never is. There is never enough coffee in it. The common experience in days gone by was for the humble serving person to have only known instant coffee, and thusly dole the merest teaspoon of the real stuff into the pot. But surely now it had all changed?

As it turned out, not really. But I didn't mind. The weak but over-caffeinated brew was like a taste of history. I was a time traveller, indeed in another dimension. Surfing the late 1980s when everything was still to come: downfall of communism, Bosnia, the internet, 9/11, Iraq, Brexit. Time to enter another crawl space; another coffee, please.

Nastily pumped on coffee, clumping past the 'Khanphone Warehouse' next door to the tearooms, I think I catch a glimpse of Khan, smiling. Good for him, keep the jokes coming. The way out of Uttoexeter follows a cycle path, where a guy in grey trackie pants is tootling on a joint. The powerful smell of it roils over the path ahead. I keep pace with him, I do not pass; I am looking for a culvert under the A-road.

I find it. Culverts are truly mysterious places. They are places to hide in, crouch down in (ah, yes, crouching again), yet also places that allow transit across a difficult barrier. Whether you share the culvert with a pitiful stream, or, as in this case, a real river like the Dove, the idea of being in a tunnel-constrained watercourse is somehow ... sublime. It is sewer-like and therefore perhaps reminiscent of the ultimate cloaca, the ultimate wastepipe. It has echoes of Arne Saknussemm's journey to the centre of the Earth in my favourite story by Jules Verne. It mimics a sacred spring, a cave from which water flows ...

It was a long walk under and the river looked deep and dark; you wouldn't want to fall in it here.

No stone circles for a while now. There was Castle Ring at Cannock but that was ten miles off the Line. Now there was a different kind of stonework: mills and pill boxes.

I went through the old Roman town of Rocester, which is less noted today for its ruins than for the more recent development in 1792 of a water-powered mill for making cotton. This was one of the inventor Richard Arkwright's last factories (he built many) and though it has been scrubbed up by JCB, who use it as their training centre, there is no reason to disagree with Blake about mills. For a start, they are usually found in damp river valleys with powerful streams, sublime places in the true meaning of sublime – teetering on the brink of being a bit creepy and unpleasant as well as awe inspiring etc. The nasty mill takes away the awe and just leaves the creepiness. The same with abandoned railway tunnels and old mines. But this was one of the first mills on the Line; there would be many more, as mills need the water found around watershed areas.

And after the heavy stone of the mill, there was the unforgiving stone and concrete of a pillbox on the River Dove. It's hard to believe they thought the Germans would get this far. If they did, surely it would all be over, bar the rounding up? Pillboxes were built without recourse to a central map; there wasn't one, in case it fell into enemy hands. There were agreed lines that needed to be defended; a very definite one emerges from Bristol to Reading under London to around Dungeness. Another chops off Devon and Cornwall from the rest of England. But pillboxes running down the centre of the country, even as a defence against glider troops, is a farfetched idea. Nevertheless, a keen Home Guard unit could have gained permission to build their own pillbox. Perhaps this was one, up on the bank with its dark door promising the usual pillbox fare of urine, old fertiliser bags, discarded bricks, maybe a turd or too. As a kid I loved the idea of them – it's just the reality that is so unappetising.

Past the pillbox I followed the River Dove, hoping to camp by it. That time was upon me again. Like something you put off all day, such as making dinner for an ungrateful family, it couldn't be either enjoyed or avoided. I needed to camp somewhere – and by golly I wanted to camp by the river.

I walked past some dreary woods but they were on a dramatic incline and camping on a slope is never much fun. And something drew me on; I knew not what except that I would soon be traipsing through the grounds of an ex-stately home. The kind that had once been owned by a member of the landed gentry but had now been divided into two or three for an exclusive lifestyle at a price. Nicely sculpted groups of conifers and wide pastures without ugly fencing told me I was now on the land of the stately home. I kept looking for trees or even bushes by the river but there were none. Basically there was a bloody great lawn that ran down to the river. Behind the row of enormous conifers, about 100 metres from the river, was the big house.

I scanned along the bank for shelter but there was none. And the river looked so nice. Then, all of a sudden, or so it seemed, I was at the end of the lawn and there was a large freshly ploughed field, just like the ones I'd toiled across that morning, all wet clay and furrows you stumble in. I could go on but what's the point?

And that's when some kind of rebellious peasant revolt instinct kicked in. Fuck it. I will not move on. I WILL impose myself on the scheme of things, or, in this case, the giant lawn of a stately home. Like those Lancashire weavers who smashed up looms, I had had enough. Of hiding. As if making some obscure point, I chose a corner which had longer grass and a few nettles and thistles, which I stomped down to lay out my groundsheet. I sat thusly for a long while, making a brew and generally consolidating my new position, my new bolshiness. Then it started to rain so I quickly put up the tent and crawled inside, thankful because people don't tend to look around at 6 p.m. for someone camping in the rain.

I was cooking up a tasty combination of mackerel in spicy tomato sauce, half a sachet of chili con carne powder and the guts of a Pot Noodle when it stopped raining. In fact, the setting sun came out. Which would have been nice under normal circumstances . . . And, yes, though I tried to pretend to myself I could hear voices carrying from far away, I knew full well these were kid's voices tittering and mucking about near by. Then that silence and a greater intensity of chatter – they'd clocked me for sure. Then they were gone. Oh well, wait for it . . .

Sure enough, the sound of a vehicle coming and an old Land Rover Freelander drove into view. An oldish bloke got, fleece waistcoat speckled with wood shavings. The gamekeeper or estate manager. Coming my way.

I stuck my head out of the tent door and said, 'Hi there.'

'Hello . . . you've got quite the spot there.'

'It's not bad.'

'Made yourself at home, eh?'

'Hope so.'

'You staying a while?'

'Nope, I'm off at the crack of dawn. Just here for now. Then I'm off. I'm hiking to . . .'

A sudden thought assailed him. 'What you doing for food?'

'I've got food with me. Cooking it on this stove. Look.'

'Not fishing then?'

'No. Not at all.'

'Ah, well, should be all right. They don't like just anyone fishing here.'

'Fair enough. The famous River Dove.'

'Should be all right,' he said, and went on his way. He was a cautious, friendly bloke, but he was a bit unsure about me, I could tell.

Half an hour later, I heard a dog bark and then: 'Roxy, come here, good girl, come here . . .'

A collie bounded over to my tent door. I patted the dog, expecting the owner to show himself. His voice was not landowner posh. It was executive neutral and belonged to a bloke of about forty-five or so, I guessed. Roxy pretty much ignored him.

Rule One: Men who cannot control their dogs do not need to be obeyed . . .

'Leave that alone, Roxy, come here . . .' He still hadn't introduced himself or even knocked on my tent door, so to speak.

Rule Two: Let them do the heavy lifting.

He went away.

Around 9 p.m., the clanking sound of the Land Rover towing a trailer. It was the gamekeeper again.

'Oh, hello,' I said.

'You still here, then?'

'Yep. Be gone by 6 a.m.'

He looked around at the skyline, the trees. 'You had a good meal, I take it?'

'Oh yes, always aim to eat well.'

Then with sudden vehemence: 'There's no shops near by. No supermarket near here.'

'Nope.'

'Well, good night.'

'Good night.'

What was that 'no shops near' outburst about? Was it a reference to the proximity of the fish-loaded river and all its temptations? I had little time to ponder it before I heard, again, 'Roxy, good girl. No, don't go over there, don't go . . .'

Bloody hell, the gutless owner was back again. It was not yet dark, but getting there. No one walks the dog twice in the same place on the same evening. He was out checking up on me. Yet too scared to engage in conversation. What did he think would happen?

I had started this walk thinking it would be about the stones I'd see, but it was turning out slightly differently. People used to use the expression 'he's bought his stones', meaning to buy a house (rather than purchasing some gonads, which is another possible reading). Yet England today was in a period when owning your stones was getting harder and harder, where living rough was becoming more common. Being a tramp, an honest vagabond, a traveller, a gypsy even, was not about a lifestyle choice; it had become a kind of victim's mantle. Anyone not living in a Barratt home was a loser maybe, but a victim for sure. That left people like this landowner stumped. He felt a bit guilty; after all, I was doing no harm. But he didn't want to get too close. Victims aren't nice. They aren't who you really want to know.

Of course I could have held out my olive branch to him. Offered him a cup of tea. But I didn't.

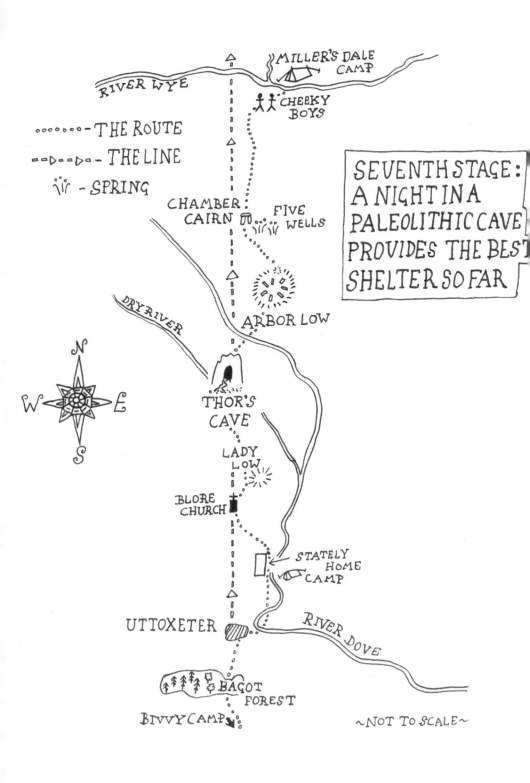

RIVER WYE

MILLER'S DALE CAMP

CHEEKY BOYS

········· - THE ROUTE
■■▷■▷▷ - THE LINE
ιⱳ - SPRING

CHAMBER CAIRN

FIVE WELLS

SEVENTH STAGE: A NIGHT IN A PALEOLITHIC CAVE PROVIDES THE BEST SHELTER SO FAR

DRY RIVER

ARBOR LOW

N
W E
S

THOR'S CAVE

LADY LOW

BLORE CHURCH

STATELY HOME CAMP

UTTOXETER

RIVER DOVE

BAGOT FOREST

BIVVY CAMP

~NOT TO SCALE~

20

CAVEMAN

As I tramped past the remains of Throwley Old Hall, a rather impressive fortified manor house up on the moors, before coming down to the Manifold Valley, I saw a youngish couple walking into the ruins. Maybe for a snog or even covert sex. Yet my thoughts were not engaged. I couldn't care less. In fact, I only said hello because they acknowledged me first . . .

The long road up the Manifold Valley, gated off to road traffic, was a rather dim, damp and claustrophobic hike. It was grotty, edgelands-type of walking – littered with plenty of discarded things that would not biodegrade fast – washing machine gaskets, traffic cones, ancient car seats showing their damp yellow foam, bins stuffed and overflowing with rupturing bin bags. The mysterious dried-up river was a depressing fact in the middle of a lengthy period of rainfall. Nothing was propitious. I even doubted the map coordinates from the dry-as-dust *Penguin Guide to Prehistoric England and Wales* which had been accurate to the nearest 100m with nary a blip so far, but still I doubted. And still I walked. I even got Thor's Cave wrong at first, mistaking it for a different cave, smaller, high up and impossible to get to. Then I saw the cave, the real one. It was unmistakably huge and obviously meant for dwelling in.

And staying here changed everything. Or rather, it changed one important thing. It built on my vague rebellion of the night before. The answer did not lie in being tamer. It lay in becoming more wild.

Everything was different; I was sleeping in a prehistoric cave.

Spending a night in a cave should be mandatory for children, like work experience. Not necessarily alone. I am not a sadist. They can sleep *en masse*, with pals from school, but overseen by a stern teacher;

no scallywagging off, no phoning big soft Mum or big soft Dad to come to pick you up at 3 a.m., tearful for your shabby suburban bunk.

This was Thor's Cave, the mighty hammer-wielding god. I was glad of that. Sites with mythological names that set the mind imagining have always appealed to me. It's a journey I now see that started with Wayland's Smithy, a smithy for the soul all right, that has led me here, to Thor's Cave, high up on a bank that rises into a cliff face. Below is the wide, stone-laden River Manifold, although manifold it is not. I still cannot work out why it should be dry. Later, I talk to a woman selling coffee near Ashbourne and she says it's always been dry. But dry it wasn't in the past, the scoured rocks in the river's bed tell me that. It's easy to cross the river and scramble the steep slope up to the cave.

Something I've learnt from visiting primitive peoples in jungles faraway from modernity is that they are much more nimble than us because they don't have steps and stairways and safety rails; they leave slopes muddy, log bridges *sans* handrails, rough-hewn ladders to the log house – high stepping and positively scary. And so they adapt. And Thor's Cave reminds me of this. It is perfectly situated, with a view across the river and far away; but to get to it is a scramble, an easy one, yet still a scramble.

The entrance is enormous: maybe twenty metres across by fifteen high. There is a hewn 'altar' at one side. To me, it looks like a useful table and place to hang out. Why should it be an altar? The cave is filled in a bit with earth and slopes rapidly to a halt, though there are half-buried side entrances. It would probably go back further if excavated; a Bronze Age burial happened here, the bones now removed. But Thor's Cave is way older than that. Stone Age people came here, bang on the Line, 5000 years ago, maybe more. There is evidence that Thor's Cave has been occupied from the Upper Palaeolithic Age, 40,000 to 10,000 BC, on and off to the later Roman Period around AD 300. And after that, given that it became a tourist attraction in the nineteenth century, there was probably someone living here at various times.

Let's face it, caves are very useful places. They certainly beat tents: a decent cave is warm, dry and airy, with a constant temperature when you go below ground. They lack windows, of course, but then you should be outside during daylight hours, not loitering indoors. Caves are easy to defend against both man and beast, especially when, like here, the entrance is halfway up a substantial slope.

Modern humans may like to think they are special, especially when they embrace 'civilised' behaviour like avoiding meat they have not personally caught and cooked, or becoming neurotic when they can't take a shower. Yet there is increasing and contradictory evidence about how 'nasty, brutish and short' Stone Age life really was. Kennewick Man, a 13,000-year-old skeleton found in a bank of the Columbia River in Kennewick, Washington, was seventy-five years old with all his own teeth (and he had a stone spear tip lodged in his thigh bone). We also know from looking at San Bushmen in Namibia that even existing in a harsh desert climate involves fewer hours' work per week than those carried out by the average European employee.

However, when I've given talks to the executives of leading multi-nationals and tried to push the advantages of primitive or tribal life, they push back with: if it's so good, how come everyone wants to live like a rich American now?

But not everyone does. The American Daniel Suelo, who exists in a moneyless world of gift-giving and foraging, and has spent time in caves, is an example to many who don't want to be 'modern'. He's our version of the hermits and cave-dwelling Christians and Buddhists who pull away from sophisticated but corrupting urban culture to get real.

Hermits often live in caves. As we've seen, the poet Stephen Duck was made warden of Merlin's Cave at Kew by Queen Caroline. I've even been a Hermit in Residence at Wigtown Book Festival, though, like many hermits, I had plenty of visitors . . .

Caves were our homes for thousands of years. We've only been in houses for a fraction of that time.

Thor's Cave had none of the evil vibe of Notgrove. Here it felt good. I don't think this was purely because of my desire to find a good billet at last, but of course you can't rule that out. The walk along the Manifold had been damp and doleful, past dodgy-looking campsites with semi-permanent caravans, dogs and discarded tractors. So the cave was certainly a nice contrast.

This was almost the midpoint of the Line. It felt for the first time like a real achievement to have come this far. Then it started to rain, heavily, but of course I was bone dry, like the leaves on the cave floor. The high ceiling protected everything. Drips fell in a solid curtain from the lip of the entrance arch. It was like hiding behind a waterfall, invisible behind a sheen of falling water. The landscape took on a punctuated clarity from behind the water curtain. I felt I could see an infinite distance, right to the end of the Line. Further. The smell of damp earth, the baked smell of dry earth newly wet with fresh rain, came from around me. There was very little wind.

The altar was perfect for cooking on. I set up my stove, stretched out my legs and got a brew on. An evening jogger came along the track that ran parallel to the river on the other side. He didn't look my way. Then I saw a couple coming towards me. The girl, I think, saw my semi-camouflaged outline but said nothing; there was that too-long pause when she looked my way. Then they both turned off along another path. I could hear the bell of Wetton Church faintly ringing out the hours. A woodpecker was noisier, hammering on the dry, tall stump of a pine. Hollowing his way with his routine drills. I realised the altar allowed me to see each way up the valley – the best possible lookout point.

When the railway ran along the Manifold Valley, Thor's Cave was actually a station where you could stop and have a cup of tea and a Bakewell tart, take a quick look at the cave and hop onto the train again. Now there is only the track where the old railway line used to be.

I lay out my sleeping bag (perfectly warm and a decent size) on the groundsheet, towards the back of the cave where it was dry. There were low, small entrances to further parts of the cave that looked good for a badger or fox. Fuck it. If I got gnawed, I got gnawed – I'd just ignaw it . . .

Now the rain had gone, the sky had cleared and I could see stars beyond the entrance archway of knuckly and knobbly limestone. My view was half stone, half sky. There were a few ancient constellations I could recognise: Cassiopeia and the Great Bear and, looking up, the Pole Star.

The Pole Star is, of course, how they made the Line; knew where the next stop should be. The Great Bear with his tail (there is no bear with a tail, the Great Bear is clearly mythological) is the shamanic beast par excellence. Deep in the caves of the Pyrenees, bear statues have been found, and bear skulls and bear teeth. There is a connection between bears and shamans. Partly, it is to do with the Pole Star and partly it is the revered strength of the bear. It used to be thought that in the older chthonic religions, with their supposedly simple worship of animal spirits, animal strength was believed by the practitioners to be absorbed by a shaman and used for his or her own purposes. But the more recent interpretation is less unsophisticated. The shaman enters a dream world where animals have a different significance, mean different things. They are a part of a language that is beyond words and communicates knowledge we could never arrive at by trial and error. When he returns to this world he shows his enlightenment by making these new and unsuspected connections.

At about 1 a.m., I was awakened by a noise at the back of the cave. Something was coming out of its hole. Normally I'd be feeling nervous, fearing some unspecified form of attack, but today, in my cave home, I feel easy-going and generous. I turn over, let it sniff around my sleeping bag and discover it has company. Fox or badger, I don't know. No big deal.

When a group is aligned, there is no need of a leader. The 1930s Everest expeditions under Shipton and Tilman relied on the alignment of the group to the objective. This required each person to possess a certain level of skill and flexibility of action – no specialists. Specialists and unskilled porters don't make for an aligned operation. Similarly, in primitive tribes everyone is multiskilled, capable of doing any task, should the role fall necessarily vacant. Big groups need leaders, unaligned groups need leaders; and leaders need followers, people who have switched off. The whole thing is suboptimal. At one point in my life I only wanted to do expeditions; it was the closest I could get to living an aligned life.

MORE SITES ON THE LINE...

MAM TOR - ITS NAME MEANS HEIGHTS OF THE MOTHER.

A KEY ANCIENT SITE IN MID-ENGLAND

TWELVE APOSTLES OF ILKLEY MOOR. TWO OTHER STONE CIRCLES ARE WITHIN A MILE.

CUP AND RING ENGRAVING ON THE ROMBALDS MOOR STONE. ECHOING THE SHAPE OF EARTHWORKS, CUP AND RING ARE ESOTERIC SYMBOLS.

FIVE WELLS
- NEOLITHIC BURIAL SITE - THE PEAKS. LOOKS LIKE A MAN LYING DOWN.

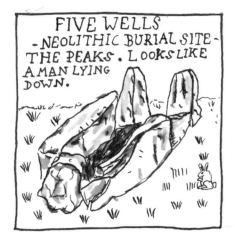

WEST KENNET LONG BARROW. ONE OF THE LARGEST.

ARBOR LOW - A FLATTENED STONE CIRCLE.

FIGSBURY RING - WITH ITS STRANGE CENTRAL HOLE.

21

ARBOR LOW AND FIVE WELLS

If Thor's Cave was a revelation, Arbor Low and Five Wells confirmed it. I was a new man, in terms of mood, though traces of timidity remained. Instead of yomping across a field being ploughed, I went the long way round, walking along a nasty A-road. Official writers of guides to ancient monuments often spend all winter writing to landowners to get 'per' – and I hadn't done that. Instead, my winter had been spent in prolonged gloom as I pondered the state of the world from a shamanic point of view. Also, it's funny how cautious you become when you have kids and try to set a civic example. And, if that weren't enough, I had another excuse, since earlier that day I'd been told off by an angry farmer's wife – but more of that later.

I was once a fearless trespasser. Aged thirteen or so, I remember sneaking along a ditch that separated two large properties on Boars Hill, a wealthy hamlet on the outskirts of Oxford where the archaeologist Arthur Evans once lived in a substantial country house. In fact, most of the houses were big, built in the nineteenth century for wealthy dons and poets; Matthew Arnold had a field named after him and John Masefield and Robert Graves both spent time here. But I was in a ditch, crawling like a commando between two big houses, one shielded by a compact line of cypresses, the other open to an expansive lawn. And on that lawn a large family were eating a late lunch in the sunshine. Equidistant from me and the table was the barbed wire fence, beyond which was a field of wheat, fully grown but not yet ripe. I could, of course, have crawled back up the ditch but I knew I was heading for the field. Like Peter Rabbit, I just had to make it across the garden . . .

Up and running, I was halfway across the lawn before anyone took notice; I was closing on the fence before I saw the dad stand to his full height and boom: 'Excuse me! Excuse me!' But I had already prepared myself for any interruption: nothing was going to stop me, nothing. I cleared the barbed wire in one leap and was ploughing through the cornfield. I looked back and the dad had given chase but he didn't jump the fence; laboriously, he stepped over, careful not to snag his tweeds. And he did, to his credit, make headway into the field – but I was over the slight hill and heading down fast to the hedge at the bottom, and free.

I do recall the punishing sense of guilt, though; how I crept home almost shaking along the roads of Boars Hill, absolutely sure the family would be driving around looking to 'get me'. This was my only excursion into garden hopping; friends who lived in nearby Abingdon would go out at night and cross a whole estate by jumping from one small backyard to another.

Back to that farmer's wife who I'd met earlier ... The path from Thorpe to Ashbourne had followed a road, or enhanced track, to a farm. It then swerved left so I followed it. I knew at the time that this was not what the map had led me to expect, but I assumed the map was 'wrong', even though OS maps are almost never wrong in this way. Soon I came upon an electric fence strung across the track, obviously the work of the farmer squatting in his stone farmhouse down below. Damn him! I took to the fields, noting with contempt that the lush silage grass was without a single weed; obviously this bastard was a fully paid-up member of the Monsanto death cult ...

I could see the road I wanted to get to. But two drystone walls topped with barbed wire stood in my way. I cleared the first with minimal trouser snagging. The second I surmounted and watched from this elevated position as an estate car pulled into a layby down below, where there was a gate from the field. I had an obvious presentiment that this was Farmer Giles intent on telling me off. As if to justify his suspicion of interlopers, I knocked a stone off the wall as I jumped down. I put it back but like rebuilding a damaged sandcastle, it didn't look quite the same ...

Still, I had my excuse – that bastard fence; so I yomped down through the thick, wet grass ready for a confrontation. Sure enough, once over the fence, a woman of about thirty-five quickly got out of the 4WD Subaru. At the same moment, wishing to play my 'oldster' card, I pulled off my cap (which could, I suppose, be construed by the generous as a form of doffing politeness) to reveal my greying poll in all its glory.

She started politely: 'Do you need any help?'

'No, I'm fine, thank you. I . . .'

'It's just that you're crossing private land.' A determined set to the face now. Hers, I mean. Ready for battle.

'I know but that's because the path had an electric fence across it.'

'That's not the path, that's a private road.'

'Well, on my map that's a path. Here, I can show you.' After a bit of pointing and looking, I realised she was right and that the real path departed the track just ahead of the wild swing left. 'OK,' I conceded. 'But it's confusing up there. If you'd put up a sign then people wouldn't go the wrong way.' (I'd already suspected this was her hobby, catching people, and I was being punished . . .)

She blurted, 'We had people steal our sign. There are thieves out here. We're not going to help them. You should read your map better. You . . . walkers!' She was properly angry now, which made me feel rather superior.

'Even so, if people often make this mistake, you could save yourself a lot of bother with a better sign,' I continued in a reasonable tone. 'I've walked through farms before where the path is not just signposted but there is a fence either side to keep people on track.'

'With due respect to your age [here I had to smile inside], people should KEEP to the path.' She glared, and then as I started to speak again (I was going to suggest a homemade cheap sign could be easily fabricated; indeed in a fantasy of involvement, I imagined myself helping her make one like something out of *Blue Peter*), she turned away, shaking with fury, jumped back in the car, slammed the door and then did an angry wheelspin getaway.

What was she so annoyed about? The thieves. And now anyone who trespassed was in the same category. I was, in fact, an immigrant on their land . . .

Afterwards, I felt nervous about field hopping. Or getting caught. What about 'the right to roam'? I wasn't sure. Probably should have read up all the legal detail on it before embarking on this journey. Nah . . .

Somewhat chastened, I'd headed up the Tissington Trail towards Arbor Low. There had been rain in the morning and I was glad of the bridges left standing over the old railway line. I crouched in the entrance of one, out of the rain, and brewed up a morning coffee. Walkers went by. Cyclists winged by. It was a popular recreation trail. I debated if I had enough time to take a piss without being surprised. I did and I didn't, buttoning up just as a middle-aged man and his wife appeared in his and hers *Guardian* sweatshirts, visible under their Rohan walking jackets. My kit lay spread out very untidily under the bridge entrance.

'Just having a brew,' I said, feeling the pressure to explain myself. Never apologise, never explain, my grandfather always told me (and he never, well hardly ever, did).

'Are you camping?'

'Not here,' I said, as if to initiate laughter at the absurdity of the idea – even though I had thought a minute earlier how convenient it would be to kip out under just such a bridge. 'But I alternate between campsites and some wild camping.'

They nodded benign and interested approval. I was glad that wild camping was now the socially acceptable term for dossing out. When they were out of sight, I'd spent ten minutes climbing out of the deep cutting I was in. Though grass clad, the steepness of the cutting was deceptive. I had to hang on to grass to haul my way up, being very careful not to slip. It was thirty feet down to tarmac: no thanks. But at the top my nerve left me. Enough of dealing with irate farmers – there was a tractor busy in the next field I would have to cross – so I went the long way round by road.

*

Arbor Low was another of the high points of the Line, a stone circle of generous dimensions but laid flat, as if a bomb had exploded and knocked the giant menhirs down, or as if wind had flattened corn into a crop circle. (It is worth noting that crop circles mimic the circles seen from the air in corn that tell us a henge lies beneath them. The faking of crop circles seems driven by a desire to connect to the ancient world by mimicking in some way the evidence for it.)

This was an oval-shaped henge, vastly impressive, 83m by 75m, with entrances north-north-west and south-south-east; oddly enough, facing the same direction as the mouth of Thor's Cave. Within the curving high bank is a small mound barrow that contained a cremation. It's a typical mother and baby formation. Inside the banked henge area, the inner ring of upright stones (now flattened to the ground) would have also been oval shaped and about the same diameter as the main standing stone ring of Stonehenge.

The fifty or so stones lay all about in interesting confusion. For some reason I decided to find 'my spot'. This is a Carlos Castaneda exercise that is quite interesting to do when you enter a restaurant, especially with a group. The idea is that within any enclosed or defined space there are some privileged spots; it's like the feng shui of sitting down. And there is a spot with your name on it that is the best one for you at that moment. You trust your intuition to guide you to the 'right spot'. And do it quickly. I've found it works surprisingly well, especially when you fear getting stuck down the wrong end of the table . . .

So I cast around for my 'spot' among the stones. It was easy to find. A long scoop-shaped stone on its side. It had been lunchtime when I arrived, and warm; I ate a quick meal of bread and cheese and fell asleep on the fallen stone.

When I woke, a youngish man dressed in jeans and a blue wind jacket was standing with a woman clad in purple waterproofs, whom I took to be his mother (they had that us-against-the-world niggling intimacy that single mums and their sons maintain long into adulthood), and looking at me from about two metres away. Obviously they thought there was something wrong with me. There was a moment of pure English embarrassment as I immediately fiddled with my rucksack, as if there was some very important business to be had there, and the woman gave a high pitched laugh while continuing a sweep of her pointing finger, as if she had all along been explaining the stones to her son.

I wished now that I had camped the night here, having spent the previous night by the old railway track that is now part of the Tissington Trail, a good enough spot if slightly windy. Arbor Low feels like a castle, though it is just earth and fallen stones. Like the Rollright Stones, the place seems saturated in narrative; there is a complexity not just in the look of the place but in the vibe. Imagination? Of course, but then why should some places excite the imagination one way and not another? Why do some places feel dead and others profoundly alive? It couldn't just be the fact that I ate cheese for lunch . . .

Next stop after Arbor Low was Five Wells – and again no path to the chambered cairn. Just to get started around the boulder-strewn hill where the cairn lay required a delicate manoeuvre over the now familiar but highly irritating combination of knackered drystone wall improved with enough barbed wire to please a trench inspection in the First World War. (By avoiding the loose stones you get snagged; then, untangling yourself, your footing starts to go . . .)

But I went all the same. Well, actually I waited as an obvious father–son walking team went by. Dad, aged about sixty-five, son, thirty-five. Dad: 'We're off to get some lunch somewhere. I reckon there might be a pub down in the valley.' The son wanted to check; he had the fearless, unprepared look of someone used to organising his life by phone. He held the thing out in front of him like a divining rod or holy book – searching for a signal.

The name 'Five Wells' told me that the old connection between a sacred spring and standing stones was again at work. The magic of the place intensified as I contoured round the egg-shaped hill and into the wooded valley where the springs arose. Ancient terraces and the remains of walls, a hawthorn hundreds of years old, soggy underfoot from rising water; it had a very similar feel to the Kennet spring near Avebury.

I only had the grid coordinates to go on. Up another hill expecting to hove into view of the big farmhouse I'd seen only a little while back. I crouched low along the wall and kept going until the slab-sided chamber took me by surprise.

Two upright portal stones marked the gateway. The tomb itself was open to the sky. Slab walls around the first chamber, about chest height. A dozen skeletons managed to rest here undisturbed from Neolithic times until 1846. Five more lasted another year or so. Pottery, arrowheads and a flint knife had lain here just as long. The second chamber behind it also had portal stones, but this was semi ruined with moss over the stones. It was like a small version of West Kennet Long Barrow but stripped of all covering.

Chambered barrows are my favourite. It's the Wayland Smithy thing again; an artificial cave, ancient and beguiling even if bodies were once buried here. The bubbling happiness I felt at Thor's Cave and Arbor Low were here too. The views down and across Chee Dale were immense and satisfying; the old places endure, they will always endure.

Boys, really; I'd clocked them entering the pub in Miller's Dale, they'd seen my silly walking poles, my brightly coloured rucksack and Buffalo walking shirt. Another walker, another wanker. They were brothers, it turned out; the younger one shyer, dyslexic ('not that he's thick or anything'); the other a year or so older and sharp as whatever makes paper sharp when it cuts . . . But nice lads.

Luke and Fraser Marshall. Luke works in a factory – 'dead boring' – and Fraser works in construction. He's whip thin and strong and interested in a newcomer in their local. They praised my taste in lager (Stella) and were impressed that I was a real writer of books. Were they taking the piss? Didn't appear to be. Being impressed by a writer, is, in my experience, an increasingly rare reaction. When I started being published in the late 1990s, being a writer meant you at least had a typewriter; most people didn't. Now being a writer is very likely to meet with 'I'm a bit of a writer myself'. Blogs, Kindle direct publishing, *Fifty Shades of Grey* – and all jolly good things too – the brief, and let's face it, largely undeserved status the maker of doorstops used to get is gawn forever.

But not in Miller's Dale. I tell the brothers I'll namecheck them in my book. This tickles them pink. Both lads are great anglers; when I tell them I'm wild camping, Fraser nods his approval and cautions it's only poachers they are after along the River Wye. I had planned another spot in any case. As they leave, Fraser hands me a loo roll he's taken from the pub toilets. 'You'll be needing this,' he quips as they go to their car.

For a brief lager-sozzled, paranoid moment I wonder if the bog roll is an ironic comment; that these lads think I'm making it all up and that I'm really a Class A bullshitter . . . But then it dawns. This is their contribution, a jokey parting shot from the princes of banter. (And it should be noted that this confirms my experience of previous visits: Derbyshire is the banter capital of Britain – they're all at it.)

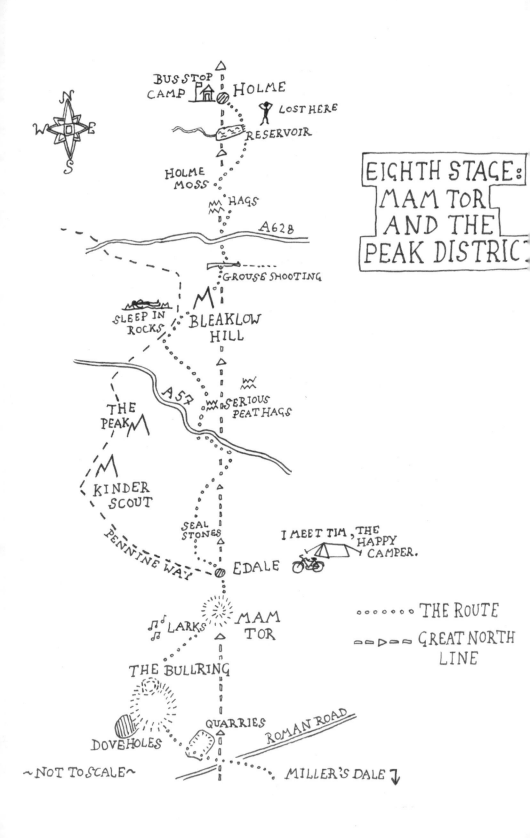

22

BULL BURIALS AND THE MOTHER

'Excuse me, are there any shops open near by?'

'*Absolutely none.*' He was lean, grey-haired and trim, walking his dog. He had just emerged from a neat house on the busy A-road, and clarified his point with an ironic smile.

No shops in Dove Holes. From the near distance came the clanking sound of a mining bucket, excavating the huge quarry next to the town with no shops; well, that was not strictly true: there was Dove Tyre and Exhaust, a place selling signs, a fence supply shop and two pubs that looked shut. Nothing else, but a lot of houses. For the quarry workers. And a really busy road through the middle.

Dove Holes probably started as lots of little holes. The entrance to the town is pockmarked with them. Then, finally, the big limestone quarry took over. It was deep and covered hundreds of acres with its own rail link. A goods train started up with the yelp and squeal of sticking train wheels like a dog that's been trodden upon. Every so often there was the avalanche sound of falling crushed rock, along with the clank of buckets swinging on huge chains. Even the grass had the faint white hue of dust.

Later, people I met would look askance when I said I'd been to Dove Holes. It was more like the arsehole of the Peak District, they implied. But as in all such places of universal disregard I felt the people I saw were good people, the school full of cavorting, cheerful kiddies in the playground; it felt like a good place. A good town with no shops. I wasn't here for the shopping, though; it was the Bull Ring henge that drew me.

The Bull Ring is a big henge (75m across), 'badly damaged by quarrying' according to the guidebook. There was once a ring of stones in the middle, but by 1789 all but one had been removed. The temptation, given that quarrying was going on all around the area, must have proved too great. The back of the Bull Ring abuts a steep drop on to land owned by ICI, and the back of another quarry.

So in a way it's remarkable that the henge has survived at all. And its name put me in mind of that other Bull Ring – in Birmingham, which now seemed like another world. I linked it in my mind to bull worship throughout the ancient world. What if the main purpose of a henge was a religious ritual involving bulls? We might be seeing a remnant form all over Spain and parts of southern France. Just as for Amerindians, wild cattle must have been a primary food source for early man. Perhaps in a missing step towards domestication the wild bulls were rounded up and kept in a henge; this would explain, for example, the curious fact of a ditch on the inside rather than the outside: the henge was for keeping things in, not out. And the different entrances echo the various entrances to a modern Iberian bullring.

And maybe it had something to do with that most mysterious of things: the sudden and widespread domestication of animals. Farming forces transitions, a distortion of the natural way of things: this needed a ritual to balance it. Alignment in various dimensions of living was thus maintained.

Both at South Cadbury Castle in Somerset and a subterranean shrine in Cambridge, where a complete bull was interred, we see evidence of the pit burial of cattle. Wearing a bull's hide or cow hide was a common shamanic garb. Even as late as the eleventh century there are accounts of medieval Irish seers sitting on a bull's hide to scry the future.

Behind the graveyard and the noisy primary school the park-like Bull Ring remains. You can walk your dog along the top of the curving ridge. There is a barrow off to one side, rather similar to the one at Arbor Low. And close by, an ancient sacred spring in boggy ground next to the A623. Springs and stones, always together. Derbyshire, like Wiltshire, has a lot of springs. As late as the 1940s, out of a 100 Derbyshire villages, 60 relied for all their water on a combination of rainwater and a local spring. Well dressing, a ritual whose origins are lost, still takes place in Derbyshire. It must be one of the most ancient traditions still going.

Now I had to brave the ICI notices that said the edgelands between the quarry and the Bull Ring were off limits and dangerous. The dry mud path cut through wild woodland along a cliff edge where old fridges, beds and other crap were dumped in convenient corries. Once through, there was an old disused rail track I could follow. It would have made an incredible playground for kids. And probably still was. No one seemed to be paying attention to the 'Keep Out' signs. At the same time, it had that slightly ominous feel of potential urban violence (a feeling you never get in the deep countryside); it was very easy to imagine a body being dumped, a pointless mugging.

In one damp and sheltered rock cleft was a dew-hung spider's web. The droplets were even sized and caught the light. About twelve strands radiated out (I wondered if it was always that number for this species) and the encircling spiral was evenly spaced, but by no means perfectly even. Where the filaments crossed over each other, they made an elongated 'X' shape drooping under the weight of droplets. At the end of a filament, just as it joined the rock, a bigger blob of water hung; the rest were like tiny, identical pearls. The combination of light, water, almost invisible threads and an absent weaver made it seem especially magical. I stared long and hard, trying to utilise the method that Goethe recommended for naturalists: just looking, but looking without preformed thought, theory or prejudice. It's hard work, with the mind scraping its own barrel just to register stuff and concentrate. But it does serve to burn the image into your memory.

Mam Tor via Thor's Cave was almost the dead centre of my walk, and rightly so: the Mother Hill, the mother of all forts, was part of a striking hog-back ridgeline one valley up from the Pennine Way. The ridgeline had other forts or visible camp-like constructions; it was a ridge of true magnificence; there is nothing like it in the South.

Ridge walking is a special satisfaction all of its own, akin to, but different from, contour walking. For the lazy or meditative, nothing beats hogging a contour, ideally one etched with a path that runs the full length of a line of hills. You want to be close enough to the top to get the views and the sense of grandeur, but not right on the top where it's windy and the going is up and down – i.e. the definition of a ridge walk.

Yet a ridge walk has its own satisfactions. A series of challenges that come into view. The feeling of true command of the valleys on both sides. Summits and cairns. Coming up to Mam Tor is like this, though there's a horrible dip down and a steep climb necessitated by the winding pass.

But larks! All along the ridge, I can hear larks on either side rising and singing, invisible. I pass a signpost, solitary and surrounded by a consternation of deep, dry rutted paths. Its concrete base is exposed like rock after ice has long retreated; I half-expect it to have the mileage to Land's End on it. A woman, svelte in Lycra garb, wired for sound and Fitbit clamped to her arm – a robo-runner – unplugs an earbud and shouts at me: 'Is that a sign?' In keeping with this aurally challenged landscape, I simply nod like a moron. After all, what can one add? It is so patently obvious even from thirty yards away that it is indeed a sign. Only after a few steps do I realise why she asked; to read it means a few extra steps' deviation from the path. Lazy robot!

This route along the ridgeline is truly ancient. There is a path off it that connects to the Bull Ring too. I meet my first foreign walker, she is far too friendly and polite to be English. Or rather, to be an English walker. English walkers are never lost even when they are. They hate asking directions except obliquely – as if tendering a view, an opinion. This Polish woman was lost and quite happy about it. She wanted to get to Edale and I told her about the sign a way back. I hope she found it. Even if she didn't, she'd be happy to ask another walker.

For many years, the naff hobby of hillwalking was intensely British and middle-class in the South but across all classes further north. And by British, I mean that recent immigrants were usually loath to get in on the game. But times are changing. You often see whole families of middle-class Indians out in their walking boots and Gore-Tex. Not many Afro-Caribbeans and Chinese. I expect it will change over time.

The Tor proved popular. Foot traffic increased immensely owing to the small car park near by. There was a stone-slabbed path to the top, but the hillocks and revetments of the fort were all still grassy and rabbit burrowed. I looked for flint tools as I tend to at such places, but found none.

On the very top, where it was most windy, so windy I had to clamp my cap hard down to my head with both hands, two men and a young woman were trying to put up a tent. They looked like university students on their first camping trip. Except they had chosen the most insane place and conditions to try out their skills.

The gale ripped at the nylon as the lad in charge vainly got the other two to sit on various bits of viciously flapping tent. It was like a challenge for a reality TV show. Other walkers gathered to watch. His commands to his team couldn't be heard. Someone had dropped the tent pegs. The bag, momentarily not sat upon, inflated in an instant and lofted high and away, as if being reeled in on a cosmic fishing line. All three watched it until it was gone forever . . .

Like most hillforts, Mam Tor is a composite construction ranging over different ages. The defences, ditch and rampart spread gracefully around the steep hill. A Bronze Age axe and urn have been found, and carbon dating of interior occupation layers have given the early date of 1180 BC, but instinct suggests it is far older. Mam Tor is bang on the Line, a pivot point: from here on things will be different, and they are.

Its name is very ancient. The Mother. I remember that one of the oldest continuously inhabited places on earth is Mut, a town in Dakhla Oasis, Egypt, that has been occupied for 13,000 years. Mut means mother there, too. Ma, mam, mut: easy first words for an infant to pronounce, and evidence of the ancient proto-languages that predate the split into Semitic and Indo-European. The mother language.

The wind gives me earache. It is time to descend from the mother, downhill all the way to Edale. I foolishly set out on the direct route, which is too steep in places. But nothing is stopping me now . . .

23

EDALE BLUES

Nothing is stopping me, except rain. It is raining hard and I am in my tent. This is my second day of being marooned in Edale, a day in which I do very little, except lie in my sleeping bag and watch the rain run off the tent's edge, wobbling down in silver rivulets across the gap to the wet grass. The rain sounds like a monsoon on the drum-tight Cuben Fiber, an ominous sound that has kept me abed even longer than I would normally. It's just heavy drizzle really.

The night before I had stayed at a local pub and suffered terrible cramps. Both legs strung out like I was being tortured on the rack. Salt loss from the day before – walking fast in sunny, windy weather and replenishing water but not electrolytes. It's the worst cramp I've ever had, probably not helped by the fact that I simply crashed out after my pub meal of mainly chips and onion rings (there was a burger in there too, but it was way out-carbed).

I should have made use of that lovely, spotless, shining white bath which perhaps had held the celebrity bodies of Ben Fogle and Davina McCall (at different times, I imagine) since their photos adorned the downstairs. The landlady was helpful and hardworking; up early the next morning, she got me breakfast and told me about the much cheaper campsite down the road, which is where I am now.

Edale village is strung out along a road. The road ends and the Pennine Way begins (or ends if you have come down from Scotland). There are a fair number of walkers about even though it is midweek. For me, Edale is a place of romance owing to this Pennine Way connection. It was the first long-distance path in Britain, and is still the most famous. It follows a zigzag route north along the top of the backbone of England. For some of the way I would be following it from here, but when it veered west I'd continue due north, directly over moors if need be.

This was both the blessing and the problem with the Pennine Way. It was a veritable motorway; in parts, flagstones had been laid to stop erosion of the peat below. You'd be hard pressed to get lost on it, though people do in fog and white outs. Walking a route like this is restful, almost meditative. There is none of the constant worry about what path to take, what field to skip across. And camping on the path is allowed pretty much everywhere. There is also the camaraderie of the trail, and always something to natter about with people you meet.

But it wasn't for me. Doing a few miles would be enough. I'd start tomorrow. Crack of dawn. For sure . . .

For now, I cook in the tent, brew up tea and coffee, still gleeful that the special burner on the stove does not lick and flicker like a usual gas flame. Even so, I half unzip the door to let the fumes out. Through the opening, I make out a newcomer to my patch at the Edale campsite. The owner said only backpackers are allowed here. No car campers. Privilege indeed.

The new camper, dripping in his poncho, is a bikepacker. He's about forty, tubby with blonde hair swept in a lick across his forehead; he's wet through too. His mountain bike is set up for touring, laden with camping gear, panniers front and rear. He wheels the bike about the site, sizing up different spots. I greet him through the tent entrance and he says hello and then goes back to the difficult task of picking his spot. It's as if he's been reading Carlos Castaneda too and must select the best place. I like the fact he's taking his time about it. I did, and I really *do* have the best spot (he gets second best).

The next day, I could tell that the bikepacker was in his tent too. We were about fifteen feet apart and I'd heard him snoring in the night. Maybe he heard me.

During the morning, I went as far as the shop near the start of the Pennine Way. They had gas bottles and tinned mackerel and everything else I needed. I bought some beer too. Then back to the tent.

Towards evening, the rain abated and I met the bikerpacker coming back from the toilet block. He told me his name was Tim, asked me about my tent and then walked round it, finding different angles from which to look at it. I wasn't surprised when he told me he was an architect.

He explained that he lived in Manchester but needed to get out for three or four days every month just to keep it together. Living in the city and doing his job drove him nuts over time. He liked to camp in places like Edale and then go on walks and bike rides. He was intrigued by the lightness of my tent and its pyramid shape.

'I can almost stand up inside,' I said and showed him. He nodded with sad acquiescence; his own tent was a one-man sock, about big enough to sit up in if you happened to have no head.

Tim had a chuntering, educated, northern way of speaking. He chose his words carefully. He spoke his mind but not in a way that lacked awareness of others. The year before he'd split from his long-term girlfriend. There was no one else on the horizon.

'She just didn't like camping,' he said. 'She was holding me back. She was holding us both back. Now she's going on cruises all the time. Incredibly cheap they are now. Couldn't stand one myself, could you?'

'No,' I said. 'Though they are good for when you have a book to write. So I've heard.'

Tim was happy to hear I was a writer. He was a great reader. We bonded over a joint love of *The Songlines* by Bruce Chatwin. He even wrote my name down. Maybe he is reading this book right now. I hope so. I felt I was providing support to Tim's growing philosophy of travel. He was evolving, becoming.

'I'd never even camped until two years ago,' he admitted. 'I was blown away. I couldn't get over how you can just walk out your front door and get moving. Go anywhere, almost. I started just with the bike and then I got the tent.'

I told him about wild camping and he said that was his next

priority. Camp anywhere. It was the logical conclusion, the ultimate freedom gig.

'You see,' said Tim, 'I work from home. I mainly design office space. Repurposed interiors. I hardly need to go anywhere except up the road to get a pint of milk. Without this I'd have more . . . problems.'

Tim told me in a circuitous fashion that he'd been depressed around the time he split from his long-time girlfriend, and had been on meds for 'quite a while'. But he'd been determined to get off them. 'I mean, it must be wrong if the only way you can do a job is to take drugs to make it seem less awful than it really is?'

I had to agree. Tim had found his ever-more adventurous cycling and camping trips were enough to keep him 'up'. He was looking forward to even more adventures. There was something both endearing and very heartening about Tim. I felt he was solving something very important to mankind. We both were.

It starts raining again and we retire again to our respective tents, me basking in the greater size and comfort of my own dwelling. I am childishly glad that Tim has recognised its value and not assumed that because my tent is an odd shade of green and looks a bit strange (like Scott's tent in fact) it is a dud.

Tents humming with the drum beat of rain are good places to read for hours. I am wading through notes on the origin of ancient Britons, the people who actually built the Line. The theories change all the time and DNA studies often contradict each other. The written record starts around 400 BC with comments made by the Greek traveller Pytheas; he refers to the ancient British as 'great wheat farmers', which, along with the tin, was something that drew later Roman interest. All empires are hungry for corn, and later, of course, slaves.

Wheat of Middle Eastern genetic origin has been found on the Isle of Wight dating back to around 6000 BC, so we've been wheat farming a long while. The old idea that there was a sharp Neolithic farming revolution around 4500 BC has been quietly dropped. Nothing about that period requires us to impute discontinuities; hunting, farming, religious practices – they stretch out and meld into each other. Even the concept of a pure hunter-gatherer is now suspect: many of the most primitive forest tribes of Indonesia and the Amazon effectively 'farm' the rainforest with forest gardens of deliberately planted trees and shrubs at different points of a migratory cycle. These are people, who, because they don't practise slash and burn agriculture, were wrongly assumed to have no knowledge of plant husbandry.

Most of Britain was covered by ice until 11,000 or so years ago. Successive Ice Ages had wiped out earlier inhabitants – or, more likely, encouraged them to leave. Connected by the area known as Doggerland to northern Europe, the first post-Ice Age arrivals were dark skinned and blue eyed, and carried the haplogroup U5 gene, as do many Finns, Laplanders and Estonians today.

'Cheddar Man', dating from 7150 BC and unearthed in 1903 from Gough's Cave, a deep cavern near the village of Cheddar in south-west England, was of this type and shares a common ancestor with a teacher called Adrian Targett from the area. Indeed, when the face of Cheddar Man was reconstructed, he was found to bear a strong resemblance to his 9000-year younger heir, although he was darker skinned. Light skin came sometime later from the Middle East, it seems, probably mixed in with the people known as the Beaker Folk, with those who came before them from Central Europe.

One recent study suggests that we are 90 per cent descended from the later Beaker folk (who arrived after Stonehenge and other major monuments were built). In other words, the majority of the UK population is only 10 per cent ancient British. The small, dark British type, which is fairly common and just as much a native as the red head or a blonde, predates these later more Germanic types.

But one study does not the whole story make. Given the sense of continuity, the way we imitated ancient sites and built on them, it makes sense that there was no clear-cut ending of one culture and sudden shift into another. Tacitus tells us very clearly that the ancient Britons encountered by the Romans after 55 BC were similar to the Gauls, but more warlike, less interested in an easy life ... He suggests that Britain was only conquered by the Romans because the tribes could never unite . . . He surmises: 'On a general estimate, however, it is likely that Gauls took possession of the neighbouring island (Britain). In both lands you find the same rituals, the same superstitious beliefs, the language does not differ much; there is the same boldness in courting danger, and, when it has come, the same cowardice in avoiding it . . .'

With respect to religion, Tacitus wrote of the Celts: 'They do not, however, deem it consistent with the divine majesty to imprison their gods within walls, or to represent them with anything like human features. Their holy places are the woods and groves, and they call by name of god that hidden presence which is only seen by the eye of reverence.'[13] The Celtic religion of the Gauls was shamanistic; in this it had continuity with the earlier inhabitants of Britain from Lapland, who still practise elements of shamanism to this day. The Roman gods and the Romanised Christianity they eventually brought with them to England and Ireland represented more of a change than the slow amalgamation of Celtic people into the ancient British landscape.

Again, you'll find angry professors who refuse to even call Brits, Celts; but the battle lines are constantly being redrawn. Swathes of Wikipedia can rise and fall in a day on this subject. The important point for the Line is the continuity of shamanic-based religion from the earliest times to its slow withering away into witchcraft and herbalism. (And from the stub end of those two practices it has staged a mighty recovery in the last 100 years.)

The continuity of the use of ancient monuments, the building of new ones in sympathy with those already there, even to the point of siting Christian churches on ancient sacred mounds, all this indicates the ancient origin of the Line. I was beginning to think it was like a key that ran down the backbone of Britain; no wonder it took a parallel course to much of the Pennines. Knowledge of the key only died away gradually. Why was Lindisfarne the first settlement sacked by the Vikings in AD 753? Because they wanted to turn the key, attack the heart of this land.

*

It is still raining when I pack up to leave. Tim's off too, his bike comically laden with a large rolled mat bungee-corded to the big bag on his rear rack, somehow emphasising amateur enthusiasm and too much gear.

There's some emotion in our parting, Tim and I, in our own way, have had a meeting of minds, the kind that happens more often when you are travelling than stuck at home. I wonder where he is now?

24

THE MOORS

The surface of the Earth is mainly cracked. Nature is happier with a crack. Even when you have the simulacrum of smoothness – a Saharan sand plain or a cold desert like the Antarctic – you get cracks in the form of wadis and crevasse fields. All the contrasting tensions between inner and outer manifest as cracks in the surface of our world. Away from the wilderness we smooth over things; the cracks left are the very widest only: the rivers we cannot turn into drains, the valleys; or the very smallest: the myriad cracks in a tarmac road, a dry earth field.

On the moors, the cracks in the heather-clad surface cleave the underlying peat into micro river systems. These are called peat hags. You know them by the overhanging corniche of undercut heather that resembles the unkempt hair of . . . an old hag. These overhangs disguise the fall into the peaty water that awaits you below and of course they make climbing out difficult. Usually you have to follow a feeder stream out from the main ditch.

There's a whole advanced mathematics of cracks: how they prop-agate, the number of branches, whether they are 'forked lightning' style cracks or more like a capillary, the relative width of crack trunk to crack branch . . . Ecologists want to fill in the cracks, while en-gineers want to over-engineer them out of existence. Only artists appreciate cracks; I know one whose project is planting seeds in tiny cracks in walls and buildings and nurturing them into life . . .

The peat hag seems anomalous. The moor looks fine as it is, clothed in lovely springy heather. But then you start walking through the heather and your foot goes down a full leg length into nothing-ness. The surface underneath is not level! It brings home to you like nothing else the first rule of real wilderness: nothing is level. Go into virgin forest and it's crammed with rotting and fallen wood, and it can be almost impossible to make decent progress.

The same with the moor. When there's no path it's for a good reason: don't go there. Don't do what I did!

All the same, at first I was disdainful of the other walkers. Amateurs. I would soon be leaving the trail that led to the Pennine Way and going north across open moorland. At last I had reached the freedom offered by real wilderness. The other walkers, and there were a lot, were more nimble footed than I with day packs rather than the heavy ungainly one I carried, which didn't help my skipping around boulders that jutted out into the path. People came up behind me, wanting to get by. I started to hurry and in turn, I came up behind others, such as the kids on a Duke of Edinburgh scheme, scheming how to get to the shops. It was a veritable log jam. Time to break free.

My route led uphill, dead north, following a line of fence posts. In the end, it was so steep I had to cling on to them to get traction. At the top, the purple heather of the moor spread out to the horizon. I checked my compass due north again. I was aiming for a line of grouse butts on the other side of this, my first bit of moorland. I had never seen a grouse butt before, but I assumed it was a bit like a shooting butt on a range – a mini-bunker for the convenient slaughter of birds.

My intended direction was thwarted almost immediately by regular peat hags. Some were fifteen feet deep. In fog, it would be a nightmare to tumble into one. At the bottom, there was sometimes gooey, black peat mud, sometimes dry and often with a piddling stream carving its own slack tangle of oxbow curves down the middle.

Until this moment I had thought it utterly laughable that anyone could describe this place, which was no more than three or four miles from a major road, as potentially dangerous. And as long as you stayed on the path, it probably was completely safe. But wading through thigh-high heather, wary of sudden drops, skidding my way down and then hauling up the peat hags, I grew a sneaking respect for the troublesome nature of the place.

Long years of getting lost had taught me to be careful and precise with compass work; I popped out exactly where I needed to be, in front of the line of butts. But it had taken hours to get there, and I was knackered. As I went downhill, past the semi-ruined butts, they looked like small machine gun emplacements, a stone semicircle you could hide behind: you'd train by mowing down vast numbers of birds, then move on to people.

Cracks in people's faces. The single deep worry line that perhaps reflects some inner disquiet of the skull. Angry people often have two cracks in a 'V' sign lodged at the top of the nose. I knew a mild mannered sociopath who had a single horizontal crack running across his forehead, as if he'd just been unfolded. As a general rule, faces have vertical cracks for tense emotions and horizontal for decadent ones ... while some people have none, like the performer Harry Belafonte, looking like he's only sixty-five when he's actually a singing 92-year-old.

The man in The Snake Inn on the Snake Pass – the A-road I briefly drop down and over – has a face with two little anger cracks, chubby little 'Vs' each side of the bridge of his nose. The rest is smooth. He is a thin, young man but he has a loud voice (northern, articulate, well-off) and considerable authority. He's bubbling with something, though. You feel he's about to punch someone. Maybe he's a former fighter who's bought this pub. He makes a big deal of bringing me my sandwich and it is a good sandwich – but he sets it down with such finality I think I'm lucky he didn't fling it in my face. He bellows back to the kitchen, fills the whole pub with his voice. I like to see people owning their own space but this seems a little too much ...

I ask for water and the slack, fat, friendly girl (yin to his yang) tells me there's a tap outside. They get lots of walkers and this is a good solution. But still, as I fill up I see the angry boss staring at me as I switch water bottles and spill a little, before I'm done (it's hot now, I want a full 2 litres). I feel for him, maybe the pub is losing money, maybe my spilt water is running into all the cracks in the earth ...

I realise my last pathless excursion was relatively easy. Now I'm back in deep hag country and I'm going uphill, having to cross line after line of these deep incursions. I'm an exhausted soldier invading the enemy trenches, long deserted by fleeing grouse, larks and even lizards. Before I headed up to the moors again I passed an information sign that told me the moors were created 7000 years ago by ancient man chopping all the trees down. What nonsense! Most research now suggests these patches of moorland formed after the retreat of the Ice Age, an anaerobic blanket rolling out from under the craven shrinking ice.

I haven't been counting paces or timing myself so I don't know how far I've come. Fighting my way up and down over countless peaty ditches means no average speed is possible. The path I am aiming for should be substantial, though: it's the looped return of a section of the Pennine Way. I'm thinking about this national trail with affection and happy expectation. It's only a path but in my mind it's truly a benign motorway of the moors complete with service stations (camping spots) and fuel pumps (water).

When I finally drop through a heather bush and land on stone I have found the Pennine Way at last. Here it forms a flagged path across the moor, following a hilly scarp dotted with boulder outcrops. It's very windy and raining now, and I shelter in a narrow fissure between two large, low boulders. The gap is only about two feet wide, just enough to wedge my sleeping mat in. I cover myself with the loose tent and sleep in this rocky crevice, wind whipping over the top of the boulders above me. It's not a bad place to sleep. Around 1 a.m. I wake and find a sliver of star-massed blackness above me, all I can see from my crack in the earth. The air is so clear the stars looks gaseous, cloudy with light.

A new day, a new challenge. I've arranged to meet John Zada, a writer friend, at Holmfirth, which is a day's moor/more walking from here. This time, I need to avoid the nightmare traversing of the serried ranks of hags; I need to go with them, follow the flow, and use paths as much as I can. The moors, being private, don't have comforting green-marked public rights of way. Footpaths appear on the map as an archaic-looking, thin, dashed line in black – as if drawn with a mapping pen in a past century, perhaps when these moors were carved up for shooting purposes.

As a natural nomad, I'm naturally opposed to any privatisation of land or its usurpation by any group, including blunderbuss-wielding grouse lords. On the other hand, as long as there is access (as there is now in the Peak District, thanks to the mass trespass incidents in the 1930s on Kinder Scout, which I lolloped over yesterday without giving thanks to my cloth-capped, tramping forebears), grouse hunting probably keeps these places free of something worse. I like to think there is a balance of power at work: the private gamekeeper kept in check by the publicly employed park ranger. If it was all national parkland, we might suffer the tyranny of the government standing unopposed; and governments build roads, whereas gamekeepers and hunters don't.

For it's the roads that kill wilderness in the end. The ornery, un-grateful but brilliant American writer Edward Abbey liked to chuck his empty beer cans out of the window as he drove along roads. When eco-minded friends protested, Abbey would growl back, 'Beer cans aren't the problem, roads are.'

I'm up and off a bit later than usual, revelling for the first time in knowing I have a perfect right to be here, a man in a crack asserting himself at last . . . Wearing my boots again, I pace very carefully back to where the path north is supposed to lead. There is nothing but a confusion of heather patches, boulders and rough clumpy grass. Sheep and rabbit paths further confuse things. Fine rain angles side-ways, covering my glasses in droplets every few minutes.

Pacing, along with contouring, is one skill every walker needs to master. (Contouring means using a marked contour on a map like a path, while trusting your own sense of remaining level to keep you on track.) Pacing is made unnecessarily hard by trying to count every pace, left and right. Instead, you just count every right step; so a pace is actually two steps, usually around 4 to 5 feet, 1.2 to 1.5 metres. When you next get a chance, measure how many paces it takes on flat ground for you to walk a kilometre. This will be your inalienable number, as per-sonal as a fingerprint. By knowing your average pace length, it's amaz-ing how accurate you can be. Too cocky and then too discombobulated to pace yesterday, I am pacing with a vengeance today. Trusting the OS map 100 per cent, I find my mark and follow stream-cut hags north off the moor. These grow at last into the expected path and with the sun out I enjoy some of my best walking so far.

I pick up a gently descending path on the left side of a widening valley, a stream far below. As I descend, the first tree is a mountain ash. It's an outlier, but eventually I'm in the woodland that clusters around the end of the valley. This is the best moment of my day: following a peat hag that becomes a stream bed that becomes a path with the mountain ash at the end of it, and now a place to fill water bottles from the river and have a brew on a flat rock – all in the sun. My face is warm; I lie back, eyes scrunched shut, light everywhere.

And then it all changes. I am in the worst shithole imaginable (at least from the First World perspective of hillwalking). A field of reeds and tough moorland grass sprouting from hummocks with streamlets in between. From the edge of it, not a problem. A vista of emptiness. Not even a pylon on the skyline. In fact, when I look back there isn't even a fence post to be seen. There is nothing in view that wasn't here 200 years ago, only a ruined shepherd's hut and a stone sheepfold. So it should be a cause for celebration.

But the going is like wading through mud. At least mud allows regular pacing. Here it's a hop, a tumble, a wet foot, a forcing through. There is no rhythm and no let up. And it's uphill, up a valley now with only a faint sheep path, which disappears into bracken. I'm complaining: I chose this pathless route. I chose true north and now I'm paying for it.

A lamb is separated from a group of sheep. It's on one side of the stream, having got down there via a vertiginous route. It can't cross and it can't get back up. I think of rescuing it but watch instead. In the end, the group, after bleating and dithering and making forays to the edge of their side of the stream, give up. The persistent heartrending cries of the lamb get greater as it runs back and forth on the narrow ledge by the water's edge. Finally, its mother (I assume) appears and comes skittering down into the ravine and onto the ledge. Then, with moments of skidding and rockfall that reminds me of a 4WD going up a cliff, it leads the lamb out, a few feet at a time, showing how it can be done. If you want to help someone you have to get in that hole with them; doesn't do to just offer advice from the sidelines . . .

Bracken'd out (and bracken is no pal these days, accused of being carcinogenic and harbouring ticks), I launch myself across the stream and up. More clumpy grasses but the ridge scarp is ahead, and there's almost always a natural path along the top of a scarp made by animals unable to descend. Below me, there's a marsh and a patch of open water. Two Canada geese have made it their home and think I'm attacking them. They squawk and honk and do dummy runs at me, both wings flapping, neck stuck straight out. I can't see it but they must have a nest to protect. One of them attempts to draw me away from the lake and perhaps thinks it's succeeding, but that is the direction I want to go in anyway.

It is now a long and winding path around the scarp edge, eventually leading past dammed reservoirs to the town of Holme. This is grouse butt country again but these ones are on the cheap and cheerful side, made from sleepers piled up into a wooden bunkerette.

The thing about grouse butts is that they are often near a road. Shooters are lazy. Each butt here has a white number whose significance I try to work out, since they aren't in an obvious order. A friend's father started doing this with telegraph poles once, decoding the code left by the Post Office on a strip of metal around the pole's base. On country walks he'd note these down. He made a map of their location and each pole's code, spreading out from his home. (This was pre-internet.) He was slowly amassing examples and cracking the code when he died. You'd think he'd just ring up and ask someone. It probably wasn't even secret.

There's probably a DSM disorder here: the belief that everything is encoded. And that cracking any code is, by the doctrine of signatures, equivalent to cracking all codes, i.e. enlightenment.

Cracking the code. I'm walking along the Line and there is a buried assumption that I'm making which is that these stone ruins all mean something when added up. The sum of them is more than the parts. The Line is the code I've cracked in theory. Walking it is a kind of proof by involvement, like a PhD that nobody reads or cites but still ensures you get tenure . . .

It turns out that I can't crack the grouse butt code, but like a dream where a bad pun or a double meaning signals a path through the labyrinth of the unconscious, I am brought back to cracks again. A crack is a failed line, one that went off half-cocked, or met stiff resistance. The shorter the crack, the stronger the material under pressure. Lightning is a crack in the sky caused by electricity: it never goes straight down because nature abhors a straight line. A crack is its best shot at straightness: lots of short straight bursts linked together in a zigzag.

When nature wants to do continuous, it prefers a curve; a Riemann surface, the delicate sag of the horizon at each end when viewed from on high. The whole of the martial art of aikido is based on curves: even supposedly short straight grabs and throws are slightly or tightly curved. And when using a sword, you put a curve into it so that the blade cuts and doesn't chop. On an anecdotal level, I've even found that keeping a beat on conga drums or a tabla is easier if you sweep the skin in a kind of curve, rather than tapping in a straight, direct hit.

We see straight, or, rather, we imagine straight lines. Then we try to build them. 'The man of reason,' wrote Le Corbusier, 'walks in a straight line because he has a goal and knows where he is going, he has made up his mind to reach some particular place and goes straight to it.' The man of reason, presumably, also makes buildings with straight walls. Yet only a small amount of time spent in a circular building, a ger for example, makes it clear that Turanian steppe dwellers are correct: bad thoughts lodge in corners. The Turanian, from whom we can trace the most continuous flowering of shamanism, abhors a straight line in his house; he is not a man of reason. He'd have laughed at Le Corbusier.

And at me too. Surely I was confusing metaphors with reality, something static – a line, with the ever-changing, ever-forming and re-forming world. Lines were metaphors, or could be; there was nothing wrong with that, no sort of contradiction. The important thing was that if a line indicated an escape route, was an arrow pointing towards the exit, was a crack in the surface of a hatching egg, the straighter the better.

My problem now, though, is I can't follow a straight line down off the moor. I can't use my compass except to make short, sharp, straight treks in a widening circle around the heads of each feeder valley. But scale solves every problem in the end: I am large enough to leap across the smaller feeders.

Nevertheless, I'm lost, while all the time knowing where I am. More or less. Sometimes more or less is enough, but sometimes it puts you in the wrong valley, which leads the wrong way a long way. On the map a nearby village is marked: Netherthong. A distraction, but I am sorely tempted to investigate. Are the residents sick of the joke? I once made a pilgrimage to Bognor Regis expecting it to be heaving with ironic travellers sharing . . . it wasn't.

OK, I know what I'm looking at: a couple of large reservoirs, so I must be within sight of them – but where exactly? The only thing is to keep going. I change my boots into trainers, slippery ones, but it's worth it to feel light footed again.

But now I'm sloppy. Climbing drystone walls with abandon (fuck it, it'll be getting dark soon), I make a wrong turn along the reservoir wall. Suddenly I'm across from a bunch of cool-looking school kids larking about and plunging off the slipway into the dank coldness of the reservoir. It's like a scene from that coming-of-age movie *Breaking Away*. I feel I've stumbled into some high school drama so alien from my own upbringing – where the highpoint of an outdoor social gathering was a cider party in a disused pill box by the Thames.

These kids are not interested in me, and I walk over the dam and into the woods. And go wrong again! Finally I surface in the village of Holme, hoping for the pub to be open. It's shut, bank holiday Monday . . . again. I spend the first part of the night in a bus shelter, cooking my meal; good shelter from the light drizzling rain. And then, desiring more privacy, behind a pile of rocks in a disused quarry up the road.

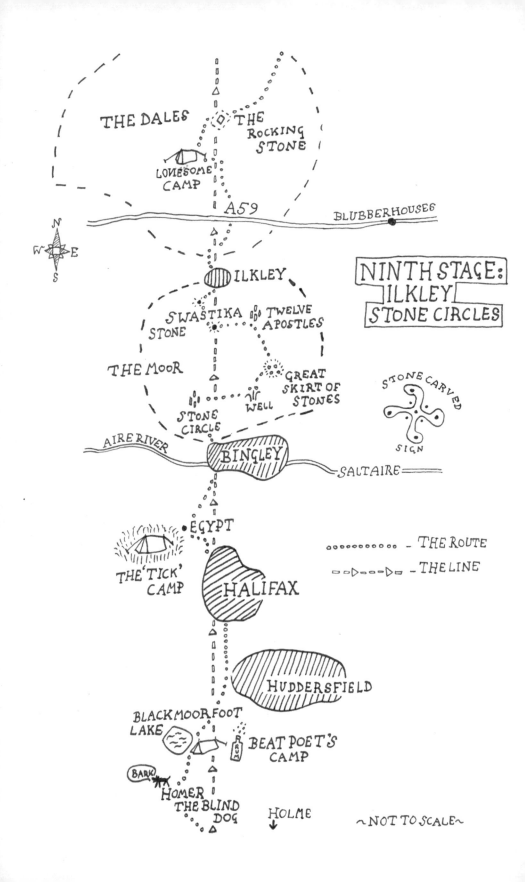

25

BEAT POETS AND THE BINGLEY BYRON

'The light that winked out—
was it a distant empire
or just a firefly?'

Jorge Luis Borges

You tend to rise early after a night in a quarry, especially one close enough to a road to experience the sweep of late-night headlights over your own personal rock pile. I had few complaints apart from the mosquito bites on my face; it had been a pretty dry night and I'd used the sleeping bag inside the tent cover, using the cover as a bivvy bag not a tent. Back in the bus shelter for breakfast. A sticker, half-peeled off: 'It is against the law to smoke in this bus shelter.' Come on, where are the kids going to go? Having passed a fair few bus shelters in rural spots, I think this sign is a first. In the village, another sign by the public loos which are open 24 hours and very handy I must say: 'These toilets are cleaned and maintained by the residents of Holme Village for the benefit of all, donations are gratefully received.' That's weird too, understandable but still daffy – the public toilet as hero . . .

I was now in Yorkshire, and I would be for a long while yet. Yorkshire is the Texas of England: it goes on forever, from the North Midlands to only a county away from the Scottish border; the people think they're special, cut from different cloth to other Englanders; it's the only county I know of where an introduction is preceded by 'I'm from Yorkshire . . .' Being settled by Danish Vikings and harassed heavily by various kings intent on destroying their county may have been a contributory factor. I was expecting something different, but I wasn't sure what yet.

On eBay, I had bought a selection of work by Yorkshire dialect poets. I was hoping at one point to write the whole Yorkshire section in cod dialect, but dialect always has something a bit fake and hobby horse-ish about it, even work by Hardy's favourite, Dorset poet William Barnes. And everyone I ran this past thought it a terrible idea. Dialect is not popular. The idea is, perhaps, but faced with the reality most people would rather eat a ketty[14] sandwich.

I have several hours in hand before John arrives on the bus from Leeds. Walking four miles to Holmfirth to get supplies: mackerel, pasta, a bottle of rum, some vegetables seems a good idea. The road is long but I anticipate getting a flat white somewhere along it. There are signs of gentrification.

The Holme valley was mill country. Gritstone factories and mill buildings. An odd gateway with a sad dedication: 'Doorway from Yateholme farmhouse mentioned in the Domesday Book of 1086, demolished in 1936, placed here in 2012.' The maths is interesting. A building stands for 850 years, gets knocked down, then another seventy-six years pass and regret starts creeping in . . . too late! But the mill buildings are being saved, even if they are repurposed as fancy OAP apartments.

I pass a fenced-off roadside site. A knackered deep fat chip fryer stands on cracked lino flooring – no walls, or roof, or anything else. The lonely fryer is all shiny and slightly technical looking, as if the shop was vaporised by aliens from outer space with a deep longing for chips.

Everyone I buy things from is friendly, but the Indian lady running a small grocery is the only one interested in my walk. She tells me her daughter is about to do her Duke of Edinburgh Award hike and can't wait. We agree that the warm weather will change and I gear up for the usual moaning but she says, 'It's better, isn't it? Walking in mist and rain.' And she's right. An umbrella really helps, though.

Flat white secured, I turn back and walk four miles in reverse. It's a sign of increased fitness that I just think this is normal, no problem with adding eight miles to whatever John and I manage during the day. Suddenly a bus goes by and I know John is on it. That's a good sign. Even better, the bus swerves to a halt and he gets off – an even better sign. 'Wow, that bus driver was almost too helpful,' said John.

John Zada had been a good friend for some years. He was a former TV news documentary maker who had worked in Afghanistan and Iraq. Of blue-eyed Syrian origin, his parents had moved from Egypt to Canada where he grew up. He was also the author of a marvellous quest for the cultural and mythic origin of the North American Sasquatch in British Columbia.[15]

When you walk with someone else, when you travel with someone else, you enter a new shared reality. With this comes the exciting possibility of having experiences you never usually have on your own. Conversely there are some people you travel with who seem full of promise and yet mysteriously usher in a more boring time than you'd ever think possible. It isn't always obvious at first, but over time the quality of experience you have becomes indicative of the shared reality. Have you harmonised and are therefore generating better-than-usual experiences or are you cancelling each other out, like waves out of sync, leaving pretty much a flat nothing, barely a ripple? It's not simply about travelling with an extrovert who talks to people, though that helps. There is some inner magic at work; but you have to be aligned with the person you are travelling with. There's an Arab saying: 'Two doves tied together do not make a perfect flying machine.' Well, you can't be like that. I hadn't really travelled with John before so this was a test.

Within a couple of hours of walking round fields and past reservoirs, we met an old man with a blind dog. I think this was the first time I had ever encountered a blind animal. The man who owned him encouraged us to mock punch the dog on the nose. The wire-haired terrier was grey muzzled but otherwise looked fine. But sure enough, though his eyes were open, he never flinched: he was completely blind.

The man was tall, somewhat stooped and wearing a grey suit in the summer heat. His white collar was open at his saggy, grey, stubbly neck; he peered down over rolled lower lids, as if his own eyesight were none too good, but his eyes were bright and not a little beady. The dog was called Homer. John gave me a look when the man called for Homer to sit. This was gold dust indeed. The man reached into the saggy pocket of his suit jacket and pulled out a carrot that was partially gnawed at one end.

'Homer loves carrots,' he said, thrusting the vegetable right under the dog's nose. Sure enough Homer began gnawing softly on the carrot as if it were a bone. We all looked on approvingly as if Homer was an OAP who had discovered a new hobby that would keep him busy.

'Wow,' said John, as we walked away. 'A carrot-eating blind dog, and not a dog for a blind person, an actual blind dog.'

'Called Homer.'

'Called Homer.'

The stars were in alignment.

Which is an odd phrase that comes from astrology. A good omen was when certain stars and planets appeared in a line. And the Line we were on was aligned with the Pole Star. It felt charged with meaning, but a meaning that was still hard to grasp successfully. Luckily we had Homer to remind us. Homer was living proof of the connection between incongruity, which forces you to look more closely, and truth. Humourists and a certain kind of travel writer make a living out of spotting incongruities, but they tend to focus only on the funny ones. There are unfunny incongruities too, or simply less funny ones.

Incongruity spotting is a nice temptation to deviate from straight-line thinking. You get to leave behind dull expectations, the straight line from assumption A to event B. And the stronger the expectation, the blinder you become to everything which doesn't follow this formula.

Japan and India are travel heaven, partly I am sure, because they deliver so well on the incongruities, usually a mix of the ancient and the modern in some bizarre new form. If you always stay at home everything is familiar, nothing seems odd or strange. But what has this to do with truth? I mean dynamic truth here, not some kind of static sentence or insight or lofty pronouncement; dynamic truth is when, in the midst of life, in the midst of some kind of experience, you realise you're *really* seeing what is there. You are aware of what you're looking at, but more than that, it feels like truth. So the experience is obviously open to a huge amount of delusional thinking . . . unless you practise looking for incongruity.

That feeling of seeing something incongruous, which very often produces laughter, is the truth feeling. Or at least it is training for it. Zen koans are frozen snippets of incongruity, maybe fossilised, but you can get the idea from them. Sufi stories and Mulla Nasrudin jokes similarly deliver incongruous punchlines. And you are encouraged by some authors, I suspect the enlightened ones, to seek as many non-trivial interpretations as you can to each story. The incongruous gives food for thought. Real food.

Both John and I were into Nasrudin stories. There are hundreds of them out there, from Greece and Russia to Turkey, Iran, Egypt and China. There are several woven into *Don Quixote* and wanderer and nomad par excellence George Borrows translated a book of them in the nineteenth century. For a good modern selection in English, try Idries Shah's versions. Quite a few feature walking and being destitute so they have an added appropriateness to an endeavour like ours.

We were walking now across a deep valley; there was no path to be seen, but John was game. When you're with a foreigner England seems delightfully bizarre. We passed a place called Royd, then another called Royd Ash, then Royd Farm, Sun Royd and finally a road simply called Rawroyds. 'Kind of painful to even think about,' said John. We still managed to miss the earthworks we were looking for (Royd Edge).

It was hot now, really hot; so much for mist and rain. John was in shorts but I stuck to my tick-proof trews, despite sweating heavily in them. I managed to scare John a fraction about the dangers of ticks but still he didn't exchange his shorts for long trousers. So far I had been lucky and not encountered a single tick. It was almost certainly due to always laying out kit on a plastic sheet and never sitting on grass or heather without laying down the sheet first.

The map was getting greyer by the inch. Huddersfield was only a few miles to the right. It was a job to sliver our way through the lines of greenery in between all the building. We had passed one ancient site near Oldfield Farm: 'a large quadrangular settlement' in a field, thought to be Roman but found now to be Iron Age, perhaps earlier. But it had been eclipsed in interest, I have to say, by Homer and his master. We were now passing the impressive stand-alone hill Meltham Cop, a gritstone knob of a hill that just had to be a place of ancient interest. Though it is often mentioned alongside other sites in the area, it has never been excavated. I was quite pleased that there was anything so near to the creeping metropolis of Huddersfield; tomorrow it would get even greyer: Halifax and Bradford were on our route. To John, these places had a romantic resonance; Halifax is the capital of Nova Scotia in eastern Canada and Bradford's a place in Ontario; now he'd be seeing the originals. I was less enthusiastic.

And where to camp?

We wandered round a large reservoir. On one side it was planted with rhododendrons and cedars and pines with lots of space beneath them, a long stone wall and a straight driveway, which reminded me somewhat of the road to a crematorium or large cemetery. But there was a narrow strip of pine-needly ground between the road and a sloping stone beach and the lapping waves of the lake.

The sun was on its downward path and would set in an hour. We settled on the low wall at the top of the 'beach', feet dangling, watching the sun set while passing the bottle of Lamb's Navy Rum back and forth.

Swigging and passing. And rum being the 'truth teller' of alcohols (gin stimulates a reverie, red wine conviviality etc.) we were soon revved up and soaring – yes, soaring!

The sun, low on the horizon, arrowing and glinting shards of sunlight across the lake, did purpose as a fire. You need a fire to stare into and kick from time to time when you are swigging, but the sun setting over the lake, sending long, blinding shafts of gold our way, warming us not quite in the way a fire warmed but better, was more summery even though the day's weather had not really been summery. John and I were rambling around now in our conversation, talking about Sufism and Sasquatch, when out of the blue John announced that this place was the Monte Carlo of the Beat Poets. I immediately knew what he meant, this beautiful setting, the fact that we were walking and camping, the euphoria brought on by the rum, which usually only happens when you are meeting someone for the first time for a while (for example, I knew we could never replicate the same euphoria the following night, however good it may be).

Monte Carlo – the fabulous health resort and casino of yesteryear, somewhat tarnished in modern times by its association with tax dodging – but still, when considered in the timeframe of the Beats, an appropriate measure of luxury. And yet, the Beat Poets would naturally have had their own definition of absolute luxury, which would, as John had intuited, be *exactly* where we were right now, with this light and these drooping cedar trees and this warm breeze and lapping lake waves. Another swig was called for.

Now we were naturally allowed to think of ourselves as bona fide Beat Poets. It mattered not a bit that the Beats were mostly miserable, screwy individuals who all fell out or committed suicide or drank themselves to death (well, apart from Gary Snyder); it was the concept that mattered, the idea of them in their heyday. Nor did it really matter that I hadn't published any poetry for ages and neither had John. I was reminded of the Italian idea that you could be a poet even if your day job was being a tax collector; at night, you put on your cape, went out to dinner and you were 'The Poet', and of course you never needed to write a thing.

I now went into a long exegesis of what I think is Kerouac's most intriguing work, *Big Sur*, in which he writes about a pathetic attempt to walk fourteen miles to Monterey from Big Sur, but he's wearing the wrong boots, and no one will pick him up when he finally concedes it was a bad idea that went off half-cocked. But he captures all the tragedy and self-pity that occurs when hobbling along in too-tight boots on an asphalt-melting day as stupid tourists drive by in their big-ass Fifties cars. A 'travel' writer would miss this part out (and again I voiced my perennial distrust of those books where the technicalities of hiking are omitted) or make it humorous, essentially downplaying the sheer painful significance of making foolish decisions on the trail.

There are other wonderful images in *Big Sur*: Neal Cassady flipping tyres on and off at a late-night tyre repair garage; a hot spring colonised by gays where Kerouac coolly notes semen floating on the surface of the water; an argument between Kerouac and a bossy local at an amateur theatrical event. The small and ordinary are somehow made heroic and interesting . . . Anyway, I was at the end of my Beat rap when John took up the running and talked about roaming and the sheer outstanding beauty of never knowing where you were going to sleep that night; and how in Canada it's all one kind of wilderness or another, there just isn't that chop and change you get in the UK: fields, woods, streams, village, hill, ancient site. 'It might be manicured,' he said, 'but it's more interesting in a way.' High praise indeed. We swigged some more, determined to scrape this Beat barrel clean.

In a surge of inspiration I suggested we start an organisation called The Beat Poets of America. There was no good reason for this except I very quickly became attached to the sound of it, the idea of it, the picture of me in a some kind of jaunty cap and leather jacket somewhere in Mexico or Madagascar. John had the fantastic good sense to not point out that he was Canadian and at least North American – and I was neither. It mattered not a jot. The Beat Poets of America (BPA) would storm the world. There'd be a magazine, an annual gathering somewhere in Texas or Wisconsin (there were reasons for this that now escape me); we would have lots of members. We would roam around. I had once heard an Indian tell me how he enjoyed 'roaming around' and I had taken to using the word myself.

When you're drunk you put up the tent and go to sleep like contented babies. And we did. All day John had said he'd brought a pillow and I'd thought he meant an inflatable Thermarest but it was actually a full-sized pillow straight off his bed. It took up maybe a third of his pack. He told me it was the sleeping equivalent of me carrying an umbrella.

Ah, but the next day was a hard one. We kept up the Beat Poet banter for as long as we could, though the obvious holes in the project were hard to ignore in the cold light of sobriety and a chill dawn. This day was another 'grey day', we would be storming straight through Halifax and skirting Bradford, touching on Brontë country, though the bit that had been built over. There would be no more urban walking after this, I told myself, which didn't really help much.

We got lost on a golf course (golf courses abound up here, right next to the poor areas). A lone worker on a little tractor had stopped to fiddle with a watering device. He could see us, we could see him, but we ignored each other. It was better to wander around without permission than to ask and have it denied.

We walked along the canal for a while and finally, after long miles in the suburbs, reached the centre of Halifax. It was run down and lacking fancy shops. Plenty of charity shops, card outlets, betting shops, discount Poundland-type shops, pubs, non-chain coffee shops, pie shops (pie shops? Well, places that sold pies and sausage rolls). The people walking around looked beat, in the bad sense. Lots of crutches and mobility carts. We followed two young dads pushing pushchairs, two kids apiece. They were young and thin in grey trackie pants and football shirts, with razored haircuts, no beards. They walked slowly. Everyone was sort of meandering. There was no hostility, though John felt we were being eyed by the tough-looking lurkers at betting-shop doors (well, he said so later) but at the time he said, 'My God, Rob, this is like the *Night of the Living Dead!*'

'Yeah, and to think this is the home of the famous Halifax Building Society!' I added, though John had no idea what I was talking about.

I think that having been to the thriving capital of Newfoundland that is Halifax, Nova Scotia, John was all the more disappointed by the obviously colossal downturn the original town had taken. It was here that I began to notice the widening gap between places. Rich and poor had their own environs further south, but as you went north the extremes were greater. In Halifax, it felt as if people had given up.

I asked a gentle-looking man and his wife if there was a bookshop, maybe a Waterstones in town. 'Oh, no, you'd need to go to Hudders-field, I think, for a Waterstones; there's a WHSmith though.' Water-stones will no doubt be proud to know their name was uttered as if it were a rare and exotic place, an opera house or a botanic garden rather than a chain book store. I have to say, though, the WHSmith in Halifax had a very good selection of true war experience books, which at the time I was consuming at a rapid rate. They also had maps for the next section of the walk and after coffee served by cheery girls in Costa Coffee, Halifax was really just another town, another place you have to walk out of.

Now the walking was harsher still and perhaps ill-considered, but we needed to break free, possibly into Brontë country, which owing to suburban sprawl is no real distance from Bradford and Keighley. We heave-hoed our way highwaywards along an A-road with big semis (as John called them) and numerous zoomy little cars windbusting our chops. At the back of both our minds was a plan involving a pub and then oblivion, or relative oblivion, making the choice of sleeping quarters less crucial. In spitting rain, I pointed on the map to various quarries. There were no promising woods. One hamlet was mysteri-ously called Egypt. For sentimental reasons we decided to kip as near as we could to Egypt.

This decision settled, we uphumped our packs again and slogged on. One town straddled the road. It had two pubs and an armoured liquor store where we stocked up on a few bottles. The pubs looked very uninviting and not the kind that did food in any form you'd particularly want. People vaping and smoking on the pub doorsteps returned our gazes with blank incuriosity. All of which drove us onward like dogs in a hailstorm.

In the car park of an Iceland a simple youth of friendly demeanour in charge of the 'Trolley Pen' (it had a homemade sign over it) gave us detailed instructions for reaching a fantastic pub for food. He had been there on his birthday. Within a mile we were already lost, even with the 25,000 scale map which is quite an achievement.

Hailing into sight were two hot-looking chicks who, as we got closer and the viewing conditions more harshly revealing, turned out to be middle-aged cougars (said John; I felt I could not apply this term, being over fifty myself) who were tipsy and off to find a pub themselves. They knew our pub and strongly commended it but said we were on the wrong road. One wore white trousers of a tightness and whiteness you could only admire. The other had a glittery gold top that was like a Mercator's projection of a live disco ball. Around her neck, a chunky chain, also gold, on bronzed puckered skin; and an ineffable softness, a knowing of the score without a trace of bitterness.

They said they'd show us the right way, but we knew the pace would be high-heeled wobbly slow and garrulous and quite possibly wrong. (Later, it turned out they were right after all.) We thanked them roundly and like the true troopers they were, in the long war of attrition that involves dating past the age when it is quite possible you have grandchildren hidden away somewhere, they cheerily waved us off and wished us luck.

'One of them was pretty good looking,' said John when we were about a mile on from them and already suspecting we were lost again. Which we weren't. We were off course, for sure, but now I could identify our position on the map, as we were walking under a dripping double viaduct that was long disused but made of such hard and sturdy blue brick it would never fall down unless bombed by a Stuka or subject to an earthquake. So far, Brontë country was not much to look at.

We were also in grooming country, the edge of Bradford, our senses razor alert. Sure enough, a mixed gang of teenaged girls and boys, tended by a fat Asian lad older than the rest, eyed us with an interest we returned with brisk-striding hostility. A boarded-up pub had several posters stuck to the metalclad windows: 'Behold!!! The Tory Economic Recovery.' A street we passed was called Crack Lane and merited a picture.

Onward, onward, past a pub that would do but wasn't the one. Now it was all about faith. We had been walking since dawn. Our feet were sore. It was nearly night. It was night. And then we found the pub and had our snug meal with roast potatoes and wine and a couple of brandies and everything was a lot brighter even though of course it was a lot darker, when we emerged with head torches at 11 p.m., looking for Egypt. Another homemade sign, 'Egypt 0.1km, World's End 0.5km, Yew Trees 1km', was pasted over a genuine walking sign and at first glance you couldn't tell the difference. Looking at it with my wavering head torch, I felt the sign had been put there to sum up my life at this very moment . . .

We found a field next to Egypt over a gate. The grass was long and John, in his cargo shorts, was concerned he might pick up a tick – the result of my unceasing propaganda about the danger of them, the horror of Lyme disease, all the people I knew who had it (four). I assured him with all the confidence of a night's drinking that we'd be fine. The tent was pitched over the high grass which filled the interior almost to the roof. It had to be stamped and rolled down by me kneeling and patting the plastic groundsheet. A dog barked in the farm next door. It sounded close but still we slept easily.

I suspected that John's mind was elsewhere the next morning, when we reached the democratic portal of a cemetery, which was our place for a breakfast brew. The stonework was granite and grey, damp in the morning dew, and we were cheery. But John's comments about what the next days held were more circumspect and I understood he was wearying of the walk when he told me his knee was giving him trouble.

People out walking their dogs were miffed to see down and outs up earlier than they, the efficient Guernsey-sweater-wearing, Jag/Beamer driving elite of Yorkshire walking hounds post-shower-pre-drive to the office. Well, we hadn't showered. Ah yes, we'd clocked the greater difference up here between the haves and have nots. There is a kind of hauteur the northern wealthy types reserve for their less fortunate brethren. It confuses southerners because both types talk northern, but one is hard-edged scorn, the other an easy-going whinge. Our interest, though, was purely anthropological: both types are alien to a Beat Poet of America.

Though John's knee was playing up, he kept a brave face on it. He even expressed a modicum of interest when we crossed the River Aire not a mile from where the Yorkshire poet John Nicholson drowned in 1843 after a heavy night of drinking (he slipped and fell off the stepping stones across the river). The 'Bingley Byron' wrote plays and a good amount of poetry, much of it interesting: 'The Poacher' is definitely worth a read. On a rare visit to London he was arrested for drunkenly addressing a bust of Shakespeare in Drury Lane Theatre. Next day in court he complained of the overzealous handling he'd received from the arresting bailiff. The magistrate, Sir Richard Birnie, as a form of recompense, allowed Nicholson to roughly drag the arresting officer around the court to demonstrate how he had been treated; Sir Richard, 'on hearing all the circumstances and laughing heartily, then discharged him.'[16]

Nicholson, who had taken the pledge in his youth, now drank more and more. It was a theme he drew upon in his poetry. In 'Genius and Intemperance', he wrote with something like premonition:

> 'O! drink no more – stop, ere the hour come soon
> 'Which makes your morning sun go down at noon!'
> [. . .]
> O! could I write that I myself could save
> From this one curse, this sure untimely grave,
> This endless want, that soon must stop my breath

Perhaps it was the sombre effect of contemplating the drunken end of a man who was surely the equal of any Beat Poet, but some of the sparkle had left our happy caravan. John was flagging a bit owing to the excessive yomping along hard roads the day before. When we limped into Bingley, he called it a day. I didn't blame him. His girlfriend was in Leeds, a short train ride away. I said goodbye and heaved myself onto Ilkley Moor, always the sadder for seeing a friend go, but determined and interested in the stone circles that lay ahead of me.

26

LAND OF STONES

I t was only midday when I pitched my tent in rain-laden mist on Ilkley Moor. It was with a certain reluctance, but I told myself it was wet enough and windy enough to merit the decision. And misty enough. I wanted a brew and my jacket was slick with rain; I needed to be undercover. Once inside the tent, which was still damp from the night before, the light was translucent green and it was like being underwater.

After the brew I lay down, fell asleep and then heard voices all around me. I peeked out through the entrance, unzipped it a fraction. Well-equipped walkers were streaming by, a rambling club of some sort; this was their local patch. The rain had almost stopped, the mist lay lower, time to push on.

The trick with a moor is never trust to luck, never take your eye off the ball. Know your direction, how fast you are going, what you should be looking out for. But my rest-stop had zapped my mindfulness. A bit out of it, I went on, hoping for a path to the Twelve Apostles.

The mist was the sort that it would be dangerous to drive in. You could hardly see the path ahead; you could get no sense of the line of it the way you can see the faint line of path in the dew of an early morning stretch across a playing field, say – an illicit path of dog walkers only visible in the dew-soaked, dawn-rayed early hours. Mist obliterates all that; you're reduced to looking for crude signs, marker stones, footprints, cycle tracks, cobbles, fences, real signposts. On a moor, the heather has gaps that make it harder to gauge what is the path and what is simply a haphazard progress of gaps. Then there are sheep tracks that start promisingly wide and then falter, turn back on themselves; you wonder what the hell happened to the sheep that followed this track – were they transported, teleported, abducted by sheep freak aliens?

But mist has its good side. The smell of mist, always a little coaly even up here. The dampness on the nose, condensing on the scarf by your face. The shapes it distorts and conceals. Mist and mystery. The Gaelic word *neul*, derived from the Old Irish *nel*, has its primary meaning as mist. The word *neuladaireachd* originally meant cloud gazing, an acknowledged divinatory practice; the word now refers to astrology. The phrase *neul a bhais* meant literally 'in the mist of death' although it referred to being in a trance state. The adjective *neulach* can mean both cloudy and sickly, pale like the moon, the paleness associated with pale lovers who are quite possibly sha-mans in a trance, scrying the future like the *nechung* living oracle of Tibetan Buddhism.

Mist gazing is not the same experience that cloud gazing is, lying on your back on a summer's day, watching the scud of high-up cu-mulus, looking for meaningful shapes, faces of the devil or a loved one. Then there is the curiously relaxing experience of being on top of the clouds – in a plane, say, or on top of a high peak – and all below being carpeted in cotton wool. Above the clouds; above the petty cares of the world.

Mist swirls; even when there is no wind, you hit solid patches where visibility is almost nothing, and then it dilutes, wafts away. Mist has no rhyme or reason; it acts like the dry ice on a pantomime stage – there to conceal and confuse. You can walk 100 yards from a road in mist and think you're on another planet. The lost planet of sheep.

Things loom out of the mist. And you can't walk too fast, you might end up over a cliff. Even walking a contour, trying to remain level, is not easy. Using the compass kind of works, but you have nothing to steer by so you're reduced to staring at the needle and trying to keep it steady. A GPS makes mist travel easy, supposedly, but it cannot eradicate the minutiae of a walk. You may have the general direction down pat, but the problems of the trail remain; you can still take a tumble, clutching your Garmin to your chest.

In a place only a few miles wide, the notion of 'being lost', even on a moor, is relative. But the feeling of being lost is magnified by the homogeneity of the landscape, multiplied greatly by fog and mist. Fog and mist make everywhere equal and new, like snow but in an obscure way. Mist symbolises our path to enlightenment, say the Celtic shamans; a path requiring faith and persistence and the ability to deal with boredom.

In the end I settled for another camp among rocks, the crags above Ilkley being buried in thick mist, with damp on my cooking pot, damp on the tent outer the following morning.

With a full day ahead, I was determined to criss-cross the moor through all its mysteries – from the stone circles to the enigmatic swastika stone. Probably of Celtic origin, the swastika stone is unique in England for its swirly Bronze or Iron Age design. That there is only one, when we have so many cup and ring marks, is something that deserves thought. Were the Celts simply less interested in carving stone?

My first stop though was the Grubstones, a circle said to be formed by the destroyed kerb stones of a former cairn. It is just one of at least eight stone circles on the moor. There was something haphazard about it: a stone circle, yes, but without gravitas.

Stone circles, like henges, camps and forts, form a shifting continuum. From the remains of a hut or a cairn, to a marked-out area, to a potential astronomical observatory, stones lend themselves to being arranged in circles and it seems appropriate to arrange them thus.

Next was the Horncliffe stone circle, which is next to a well. A stone, perhaps removed from the circle, has the name of the well carved into it. This stone circle has forty-six stones in a ring, close to each other if not touching. In the middle stands another smaller circle, perhaps marking a burial. It was overgrown with grass and not so impressive.

Circles seem so obvious, so why did we stop using them and move to squares? One thinks of yurts and gers and wigwams and igloos and other dwellings of nomadic, shamanic people. All of them prefer living in a circular space. I once worked in an octagonal office that felt like a circle – albeit a compromise circle. I did some of my best work in that place. (The octagon, a symbol of mystical Islam and much used in architecture, also appears in the odd octagonal church tower in England, including that of Uffington, below the White Horse in old Berkshire.)

Nomads move in a line and live in a circle; settlers prefer building with straight lines. Straight lines in a building look good, as if you have really made a difference, imposed your will. When I had an allotment, one of my favourite tools was the measuring line wrapped round an old stick. I'd stretch it out to make perfectly straight seed rows and edges of my growing area. It was a statement against the chaos of the overgrown verge, the encroaching wilderness.

Circles play to a different tune or melody, a different harmonic of thought. Instead of the fight against chaos, the circle blends in instantly – and yet is instantly noticeable as something 'made'. A circle seals its own energy; by this I mean it is aesthetically complete, you never want it to be bigger in the way a small square building always wants to be bigger.

Today was a sunny day, all the mist burnt off, though very few people were about. Most of my encounters were runners in Lycra, wired for data and sound, toiling along the scarp above Ilkley. With earplugs in, the world is at arm's length; it's like wearing wonderful waterproofs on top of down clothing. You are in the wild world but delightfully insulated. The transition from outside to inside is not nearly so painful. Some never give up the cocoon, but for many I've noticed this is the way they dip a toe in and get used to the strangeness of being outdoors, before giving up their protective gear along the way. You have to start somewhere.

Finally, the most famous circle on Ilkley, the Twelve Apostles. Some say there were once twenty stones, but not any more. Sandy moorland reveals this to be a well-visited site. Other stone circles are just about visible from here, only a mile or so distant. And the stand-alone boulders with rock carvings are visible from each other too (some boulders are devoid of carvings but these are out of the eye-line of the others).

Next, I walked to the carved Badger Stone and then to the Swastika Stone. Actually, the Badger Stone has a proto-swastika on it, though not so finely carved as that on the Swastika Stone. It is hard to tell when the symbol was carved in relation to the other cup and ring marks, concentric circles connected in places to small ladder-type engravings. I had seen these before in the Egyptian desert. Ladders symbolise our ascent to the heavens, to a higher consciousness, to a greater understanding. The symbolic connection of ladder and concentric circles are the connected ideas of ascending in insight, allowing penetration of greater mysteries; getting to the core, the greater connectedness of things. More pronounced ladder marks are also to be found on the transplanted Panorama Rocks, which lie behind metal railings in Ilkley town.

The Swastika Stone is also behind railings. I was admiring the clarity of the carving, its aesthetic beauty, how different it was from the cruder cup and ring carvings – when I realised I was looking at a Victorian copy. The flatter, much less distinct and, it has to be admitted in comparison, more ancient and weathered-looking original is behind it on a larger chunk of rock. But the copy is instructive. First, it looks real and it looks old; without the other to compare it with, I think anybody would be taken in (perhaps not if a microscopic examination of hammer marks were made). Rather as the cover of a pop song enables you to realise its perhaps hidden potential, a copy of an ancient artwork releases something too. There is a strange completeness about the design and yet the copy better encourages one to notice the odd 'moon' it has dangling off one limb, that exactly mirrors the moon barrows we see in so many camps and henges.

But enough of bloody stones!

I tramped down into Ilkley ('baht t'at' – as in the old song; ask if you don't know it), down a winding, narrow road so steep my feet rammed into the ends of my boots. I passed another group of walkers, well-off and retired ladies, still talking as they went uphill, so no lack of fitness here. I was already rekindling my nomadic/homeless person's disdain for the settler. Sure enough, on entering the town, there was road after road of large dark stone houses with drives and well-tended gardens . . .

But too many! Ilkley is obviously a top retirement hub for wealthy Yorkshire folk, very different to Halifax. Well, there is no comparison. Yorkshire is a painfully divided county and I see no solution and offer none either. I walk on, that's all I do.

Through the town, past the well-hidden Panorama Stone outside St Margaret's Church (worth a look); in and out of Café Nero, flat white sipped and supped down to its frothy foundations and cup reluctantly discarded in a too-full urban dog-poo bin (that's Ilkley!); and up and out of town again to another moor.

This one was called Middleton Moor. A Roman road petered out somewhere in the middle of it. I followed the road a while and wondered if that Roman road had been something older. Lots of cup-marked stones and fallen stones but I was hurrying on now. Crossed a quiet A-road in what was becoming a pattern (lonely A-roads are the only ones that traverse many of the moors) and was now on Rocking Moor, a much more sullen and creepy place than any of the others. Not helped by there being no path.

Getting cocky, I assumed that at least one side of a drystone wall would have a semblance of a path (sheep tend to run along walls, scarps and ditches, and usually leave a trail) but there was none. I walked a while in a dry, stony streambed and then plodded through knee-high hummocks of thick matted grass, cursing in an unimaginative fashion. All in by 6 p.m., I refrained from entering the austere and forbidding Rocking Hall – which was, I saw from the map, some kind of dwelling – and camped in the corner of two intersecting drystone walls, both leaning my way as if blown by the constant gales. It was a dry corner of sheep-shorn grass (I kicked away the few nodules of dung as part of housekeeping before laying out the tent), the grass so minutely short and evenly cut it would have made a good bowling green. Look over the drystone parapet – get your head blown off by the wind. Below: all comfy and nice and secure.

*

The next morning I was emboldened to walk the short trackway to the Rocking Hall, expecting to find the dismembered remains of some old lord there, his blunderbuss twisted around his stringy aristocratic neck. It was shooting lodge straight out of Sherlock Holmes, built to look like a stately home but in disconcerting miniature, about the size of a suburban bungalow. And maintained by someone who rode a quadbike, by the look of things. The windows curtained, it appeared draughty, damp, musty and windy as all bloody hell, without a spot of cover except its irrelevant square wall around it. Some kind of barn for the ponies, perhaps, and the lodge, really too small; no shooting party would care to spend much time here. Built around the conceit of the Rocking Stone. Which I was too numb fingered and early-morning feeble to make rock.

Always stones. The Rocking Stone was as big as a Mini (a new one) and rested on two points on another, larger, stone. I could imagine the shooters, pissed or bored, coming out periodically in the wind to test it out. All of them eventually leaning their tweed-clad weight against its gritstone bulk to make it rock. A cheer goes up, another round of whisky chasers!

But there was something too desolate about the place. It would have to be one hell of a sunrise or sunset to make it all look beautiful.

I had set out looking for stones, but the stones again drew me to water. I was crossing a fast stream, or about to, and it gave me the greatest of pleasure. First it was raining, then not. I set up the Wind-Burner in the lee of boulders above the stream. I filled the pot direct, no mucking about – it was fast flowing straight off the moor, cleaner than anything I usually drank. Oh, what about those dead sheep? people always ask. I think in years of walking I've only ever seen one dead animal (a horse) actually lying in moving water. But even if the dead abound, the swiftness of the stream is decisive. The kind where water sweeps over just-showing boulders, giving them the look of a glass helmet, shining and ringed with splashing, dark, utterly clear waters; have I described it well enough? That kind of water is always pure to drink. In the end, you have to learn to trust yourself. People suckling on plastic water bottles from supermarkets must learn to trust.

I drank my tea all the while bothered by gnats. The first real biters on the journey so far. Seen no grasshoppers either, come to think of it. Insects are down everywhere, and I am not sure what it will mean. But, here, under warm grey skies, being bitten on the wrists, I am happy.

Now, loaded up again, I have to cross the water. The St Christopher moment: do I leap or look for a stone to step on? Or perhaps a half-submerged log just buoyant enough for a quick step over? This stream is deep enough and fast enough to be troublesome if I fell in – all the better, I have to think about it, focus the mind and feel real. Then I opt for something I don't usually do: throw my pack and poles across onto tussocky grass and take a running . . .

. . . jump. Water, black, white, mysterious flows under me.

27

LEAVING HARROGATE

You find your identity walking. You have the leisure to reflect . . . But that is not really it. You untangle. The tangled lines of living can be separated. In everyday life, each section, each spurt of life, is a thread that overlaps another, births it and nurtures it awhile; except all too easily they get tangled, feed back on each other, become incestuous and repetitive. Think of a rat king, or the ouroboros . . . Ideally we run these parallel life-threads two at a time max; then one is gone and you're on your own riding clear and clean – you can see the way. Later, you may be joined by a new impulse, idea, person and you find you are teaching yourself in preparation for a new thread, a new growth spurt, based upon an old thread that has ended. But this happens rarely. Usually, to take a third (mixed) metaphor of tangledness, it is a Gordian knot of messed-up yarns.

But then you start walking and something miraculous happens. The threads get teased out, they separate. The overlap occurs without a tangle ensuing: one thread teaches another, as it should . . .

I teach myself about this walk, how to proceed based on the dead thread of two years of doing photography and drawing, and suffering from chronic unfitness, until one day I knew I had to go back to walking and writing again. God knows, I wanted to continue with the art, but my body wouldn't let me.

I have mentioned my great-grandfather Harry who had been a photographer, one of the earliest in Warwick. An even earlier relative, also called Robert Twigger, had been an illustrator, church decorator and teacher of writing in Suffolk in the early nineteenth century. It was in the genes! Like many discontented folk, I yearned for some kind of artistic outlet; a visual creative outlet, not a wordy one. Of course I could write poems, as I still did from time to time, but poetry was still words and words were too left brain. I found inspiration from the classic *Drawing on the Right Side of the Brain* and found I could make a good likeness with a 2B pencil and a putty rubber as long as I just *looked* and didn't think too much. I'd been thinking too much, analysing too much, writing too much for too many years. One day, the words that had been my escape became my prison.

I'm not sure how it happened exactly, but part of the blame lay in accepting long commissions to write historical pieces that really were interesting only as ideas. My writing, from being a poetically inspired endeavour, became workaday and mechanical. If you use a fine talent as a hammer, don't be surprised if you blunt all your edges.

Drawing and photography were a great release. I even fantasised about a change of career. People older than me had managed it, squeaked by. But though my photography improved with nights spent in the darkroom and my drawing was good enough to illustrate a book (though one critic unkindly called them 'itty little cartoon things'), I found I was slowing up, getting overweight, more fearful, more of an indoors person looking out and cursing the bad weather.

You follow the wrong path long enough and it will kill you. The thing is I didn't *know* it was the wrong path, apart from general physical decline. Walks had saved me in the past, and this walk would save me now. With only about ten days to go, I had found my way again.

All those tangled lines become clear again when you're walking; you can see clearly how you walked a while with someone or some idea and then let it go or it let you go. You may *want* to do something, but wanting is not enough. It has to be in your stars, up there with the Pole Star, a guiding light, leading you along that old straight line.

I had a brief sojourn there and back to Harrogate to post stuff home, restock and get the maps for the last stage: the final big push north to Lindisfarne. I would have to walk further than I had before, with only so many days left for this journey, but I was fitter now; I looked forward to it. I knew at last that I needed to alternate boots and trainers. Boots for early morning, secure-feeling, traipsing across wet boggy grass and moorland. Trainers for the track and tarmac slogging in the afternoon; for that is how it seemed to work out. Both my Achilles tendons were inflamed, I would just have to walk on and massage them each night into some kind of repose. I had yet to suffer a single blister after my disastrous start: the one-and-half sizes too big trainers and single thin sock method was triumphant. Though I'd rather have blisters any day than a strained Achilles heel . . .

Harrogate is a prosperous town with an efficient post office and a well-stocked Waterstones for maps, and the famous hotel where crime writers gather in memory of Agatha Christie each year. I got a taxi from the town centre, and a nice man called Phil drove me back into the wild. It was raining quite hard and Phil felt a bit sorry for me. He thought I was retired as it was a weekday. I guess it was the grey poll, but I didn't bother explaining. It felt novel to be thought seriously old (up to a point). He was only cab driving, he explained, because his car valeting company had gone bust. He was actually only a few years older than me but he'd owned a business, lived and worked abroad, seen attack ships on fire off the shoulder of Orion;[17] it had all taken its toll. But he was still positive about the future; he acknowledged that some might think he was on the scrap heap but he didn't feel that way. He kept fit. He'd like to do a walk like mine but he didn't have the time. He was happy to help me. I gave him a tip.

And then *splat*, I was on the roadside in the pissing rain, messing with my brolly. Thank God for the brolly. By *splat*, I don't mean I'd fallen, just that the harsh wet-tarmac reality, with water streaming off my rucksack every time it nudged out from under the brolly, had just struck me. *Splat*: a car went by and drenched my leg from the streamer-like puddle along the dark roadside. A car with new tyres, new rims, low profile: *splat*. Wet through, despite dragging the rain kilt down too late of course. Rain kilt down FOR GOOD now.

Pull yourself together. Have a laugh. I did laugh. It was so silly to be there. But I had my trusty Pacerpoles, heavy, a bit gritted up,[18] but you could still push off them. (What's more, research showed a Pacerpole race team went 10 per cent faster than teams using normal poles. I clung to that statistic and repeated it so often even my dad bought Pacerpoles.)

And I had a new brolly with an extendable handle, which could be stuffed down my waistband so I could walk *Hands Frei* – appropriate because it was a German brolly, designed for serious outdoorsfolk.

And it rained on. And harder. I was walking along a straight B-road north. That was all. North. Along the Line. Didn't care that it was dead straight tarmac. Middle of nowhere, and only in the middle of nowhere: a house a short way down a track flying a Union Jack and at the road entrance, a post that reads: 'Notice of removal of implied Right of Access.' Screwed to the top of the post was a small video camera. Why?

Rain. Very few cars. And then ahead, a church. Ah, an empty porch, a covered porch. I was soon in it and dripping over the flags, happy; a windy porch but dry and a good place to make a brew.

I looked around inside. Always the same: dark glistening pews, faint smell of wax, the table with prayer books and pamphlets about the church. The visitors' book which I sometimes signed, sometimes didn't. Silence. Calm. The ticking of the church clock above the font was reassuring. A single bell rope with its stripy plush grip; but I'd never have the nerve to ring a church bell. I absorbed what I could, as I always did, but a brew beckoned.

Suggestively there was an empty Costa Coffee cup in the porch. Just bare washed wood benches fitted into the walls, sagging stone flags on the floor. Nothing else except a left-behind umbrella. There was always one, sometimes more than one. A few times there'd also be a traffic cone, maybe a crocheted hat on a wooden peg next to the notices and a piece about the church, an orientation and introduction. Sometimes there would be a donation box, gunmetal grey and set in stone with its simple small keyhole.

These places always welcomed me, never turned me away. No one bothered me, helped or hindered me. I was no longer even of the same faith but I valued them ever more highly as I walked north; a pilgrimage whether I liked it or not.

That evening in a pub called the Shepherd's Arms, I had a very unusual experience, unique actually. I will write it down exactly as it happened, with no embroidering, though I expect few to believe it.

After ordering my pint from the beardy, friendly publican and my meal from his flirty wife, I sat down about ten feet from the bar with nothing to do except read. And make notes. I started to muse on titles for this book and one I had considered a year or more ago suddenly from nowhere came back to me: Uppards! I was in Yorkshire too, and that made it more resonant. The title comes from a poetic monologue about a northern lad who goes out in the snow with a strange banner and keeps walking on and on when everyone else is safe indoors. And on the banner is written 'Uppards'. And on his dying lips, he mutters the word, 'Uppards.' It's a comic piece, but rather mysterious, and I tried to remember who'd performed it on the ancient LP record that my parents still had.

Anyway, as I was thinking about this, I became aware of a conversation at the bar. The flirty wife had mentioned that only meat, not fish, was 'well hung'. Of course a double-entendre like that is never going to go unappreciated in the lounge bar, so a regular quipped something unintelligible that ended with 'hung by a Prince Albert'. And then I had a powerful intuition of knowing something important would come next, but it took a second or two. There was even a request to explain what a Prince Albert was.[19] And then it came. Beardy the landlord, a man about sixty, rumbled into conversation to the effect that 'Albert got eaten by a lion', and then, another explanation (people are *so* ignorant): 'It's from a monologue by Stanley Holloway.' *Then it struck home.*

Stanley Holloway was the man who performed 'Uppards'.

Like lots of psi phenomena it is strangely pointless. But . . .

I've had many seemingly telepathic experiences with my wife, in-laws and close friends, in the form of thinking something and someone else saying it. But it could always be explained by us already being in some kind of connection. Some kind of alignment maybe. Perhaps the apparent communication was just both of us having a similar response to something said earlier or a common stimulus.

But this was completely different. The sequence went: I think, 'Uppards,' and briefly, 'What was the performer's name again?' Wife says,

'Well hung.' Customer says: 'Prince Albert'. Landlord says, 'Albert and the Lion,' and finally, 'Stanley Holloway.' The answer.

Bona fide evidence of telepathy. I was surprised that I was not more moved. It didn't seem like a miracle, even though it defied current scientific thinking. Maybe in 200 years they'll find a new super-subtle form of communication we are currently unaware of. And all the telepathy in the world wouldn't change my life that much. Unless it became a stage act. There was something slightly depressing about telepathy being both real and not very important. I finished my bangers and mash and slipped out without even taking my pint glass to the bar.

The day was still damp outside. I rang home from a still-working phone box, a nostalgic and pleasurable experience. Even the urinous, fag-ash smell of the box, the grey-pitted, butt-strewn concrete floor, the single smashed pane – none of that spoilt the cosy feeling of using a proper phone, with a proper mouthpiece and earpiece smelling faintly of perfume, as I also remembered they often did. Maybe it was the drizzling damp outside but I made a resolution to call home every day from such a box, if I could find them.

I walked past old lead mines and quarries to a wood that promised good camping. Along an unfenced road, under a bruised sky – overcast, rain-heavy but not raining – and a shaft of evening sunlight finding its way through the dark cloud, making daffodils very yellow and grass very green; one big rabbit bolts and a scatter of baby rabbits, more reluctant to run, ten or twenty everywhere across the tarmac and the wide, well-cut verges.

Camping near water was what I wanted and the stream could be seen far below through the sloping woodland. It was an ancient wood, I could tell; big beeches widely spread, their long branches dipping down into the ravine of the stream glimmering blackly, black rounded pebbles and dolorous pools good for filling a water bottle if you could balance on a fallen slimy branch. A great fallen root plate, like the door to a hobbit hole, reared up ahead. It made a gravelly indentation into the hillside large enough for a tent. But all the twigletty root ends, bendy and tough as cable, stuck out and made tent pitching a bind.

In the end, I slept upside of a small tree to stop me rolling downhill into the stream. I could hear the water and it reminded me, for no real reason, of an old clock ticking in a church.

Time. Walking and time are linked. Walking alters one's perception of time, the way we experience it. When I was walking, say plodding through the rain past the caravan sites along the windy hillside road, as I was today, I could hold on to time for several steps. It's like a meditation. Your focus is solely on the experience of walking, step, step, step, aided by the soft fall of rain (not too hard, but there, constantly present, an aid to focus as it shuts you in under the hood, under the umbrella). You hold on to the singleness of the experience for as long as you can and that means no thought of past or present. You feel as if you are in a perpetual present. But as soon as you reflect on any of this, you lose the thread, and the only way to make sense of it is to fall back on the tired old distinctions between past and future and the whole crappy bag of associations that go along with that.

After all, who doesn't strain after some new understanding of time, some new way of looking at it so that we escape the doom-laden feeling of moving inexorably towards death, or at least an indistinct future and a growing garbage pile of past events?

The Hungarian-American psychologist Mihaly Csikszentmihalyi (to spell his name, you only have to remember the middle bit is 'six cent', while the front and back are both mihali (-ish)), anyway, him – the author of *Flow* and inheritor of the French philosopher Bergson in the modern age – Mihaly's six cents' worth is that we are at our best when we are engaged in 'flow' activities; that is, activities which nestle between the stressful and the boring. Too mechanical an activity (e.g. a production line) and we find it boring; too demanding and chaotic (having to lead soldiers in a losing battle, crossing a busy motorway on foot) and we become anxious and suffer from stress. But in the sweet spot between these extremes, we prosper and flourish – and most importantly our sense of time, the way we experience it, dramatically changes.

When we're bored, time creeps in scratchity hops, tiny jerks from past to future; the present doesn't exist really. We're either looking ahead or thinking how much we've done, and wishing we had done more. Boredom is one place where time and space meet: when we are bored our greatest desire is to move, to be somewhere else.

And when we are stressed by something beyond our competence (if we can get breathing space to even be able to reflect for a moment), we also want to be elsewhere. But the desire is not so strong; stronger is the feeling of *make it stop*. How does time pass when we are stressed? Like the slow scratching of fingernails across a blackboard . . . a melange of past, present and future, where past and future constantly stab present in the back.

But in a 'flow' situation – such as dancing, making model train dioramas, shelling peas on the back porch, driving a 4x4 over a desert landscape – in these situations, time is a deliciously expanded present, like the single lung of a snake that extends the length of its body, that precludes even self-reflection beyond 'this is good', 'keep it going' and 'don't stop yet'. And time passes in a way that contradicts usual experience. Four hours can go by in a flash. We can be shocked that we missed lunch and aren't even hungry.

Some people are naturally drawn to the theories put forward by Henri Bergson (who thought time is about duration, not the instant), while others incline towards a more atomistic view. I think people who are happier in their lives are more likely to want the moment to be prolonged. Duration becomes their unit of choice. Nervy discontent leads to an eager desire for the moment to be supplanted, for change and revolution. As with many things, philosophy is more a matter of temperament than argument. Wittgenstein, who went from being an unhappy atomist to a less unhappy 'natural-unitist'[20] (or even soaring above both), wrote: 'The world of those who are happy is different from the world of those who are not.'

Happy people like flow as an idea, whereas 'splitters' tend not to. Christopher Hitchens, not the happiest of men, famously described himself as a 'splitter', apt to emphasise differences rather than similarities. The atomistic tendency has proved enormously powerful – divide and conquer; and yet has left us bereft, alone, alienated, unhappy. The drop of water wants to be part of the ocean, but it also wants to retain a certain amount of 'dropness' . . .

And many splitters arrive at their conclusions out of a legitimate horror of false 'flow', sentimental or coercive group mindedness.

But even this, walking solves. The pace, the one-two, one-two of making progress satisfies our atomising needs. The numbers are also satisfying. The best time of the day can be laying a string on the map and calculating the kilometres walked (I prefer kilometres as there are always more to the day than miles). And then there's the timing, walking so many hours, having a break for so many minutes. All this seems counter to the essence of a *wandervogel* appreciation of duration and flow, but are in fact necessary conditions, just as a hard glass container is needed to hold wine and an even tougher one needed for champagne.

I was scribbling these thoughts in my after-walking diary, which was different from the tiny flip-top notebook I carried in my top pocket for instant observations, momentary insights, as I walked. Breaks, no doubt, in the flow experience of simple plodding.

For that is the big heart of walking, the real deal, and why it attracts so many different kinds of people, from the gregarious to the loner, from the laidback to the military stickler, from the lazy to the motivated: walking alters our perception of time. Sometimes subtly, sometimes drastically.

It alters time; it untangles thoughts. Why did I have to continually relearn that thoughts proceed in an orderly line when we walk? Like rubber bands, they tangle the moment we stop; and the tangle gets even worse if we sit at a desk.

That is the connection: pilgrimage, labyrinths, walking and thought. Why walking a labyrinth – a mimicking of the confusion of the unstretched mind – should be the equivalent of a straight-line pilgrimage. By some kind of alchemy, to solve an external tangle works also to untangle an inner mess; and walking in a dead straight line does the same. Both are derived from the mystical necessity of a pilgrimage.

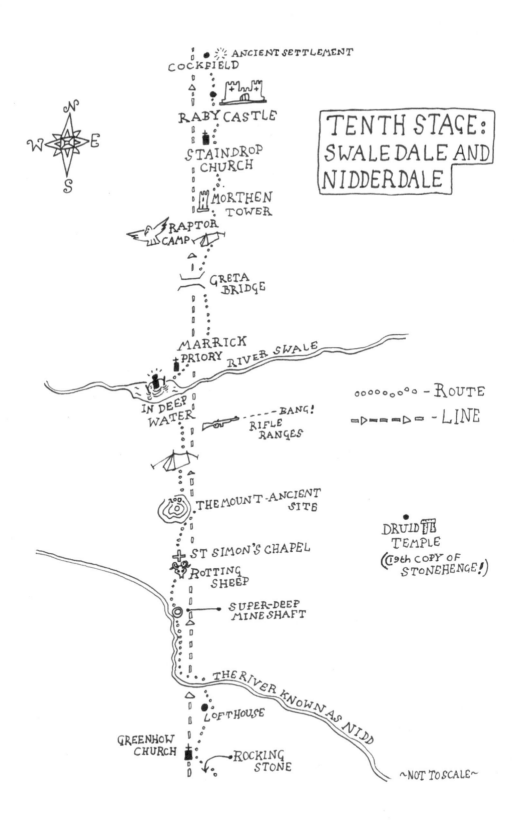

28

SHAFT

'Aye, you'll be heading up t'scar, will you? There are actually two paths up thar.' The young man hoisting bales effortlessly over a fence grinned almost to himself at the superfluity of exits from his green valley up on to the moor. 'Both will get you to t'scar.' I could tell he liked saying the word. I would too. It was what he called the scarp edge, but scar is the older Viking term. And Yorkshire is Viking territory still.

When you walk alone, a single encounter like this can have a profound effect on mood. A good one, a cheery one, can set you up for the day. To be scorned or cursed, well, you get over it, but the mood becomes grimly resolute, narrow focus, blinkers on. All that airy-fairy looking around, scampering as with a butterfly net up the hill of possibility – forget it, put your miner's lamp on and shoulder that pick axe . . .

But this lad had left me thinking only good thoughts, which, in its relaxing effect, led me to stray from the direct route while looking for something marked 'shaft' on the map.

To one side of the path, some thirty feet away across bouncy heather, I saw a hummock about ten feet above the rest with a rude wooden enclosure, a fence of sorts. And bushes up against the fence and loosely strung barbed wire to deter sheep.

Any diversion is welcome to the man with an open mind. This fenced-off area hid a mysterious deep hole. Apart from the overhanging bush, some sort of evergreen with small bright delicate leaves, when I looked down the shaft, there was nothing but black and a palpable drop in temperature. My face was cooled by an upflow of dark, dank air.

I love all holes dug into planet Earth; always have done, the deeper the better. After reading *The Thirty-Nine Steps* as a twelve-year-old, I planned to become a mining engineer like Richard Hannay. And one of the few things I have used regularly from schoolroom physics is the formula for finding the depth of a hole by dropping a stone and timing its fall.

To paraphrase somewhat: S=0.5at.t where S=distance, à=9.8 (metres per second per second – the rate at which things accelerate when dropped to earth) and t is squared, t being the time in seconds recorded for the drop. Simple stuff. Galileo worked it all out first.

A one-second stone drop is roughly 4.4 metres. Two seconds is roughly 19 metres. And fractions thereof. Any reasonable sized stone will do, i.e. bigger than an egg and big enough to not be blown about by wind.

Sheep had grazed the turf down to sandy soil and exposed rock on one side of the hummock. I found a biggish stone, the size of a shoe, and lobbed it into the hole. And started counting.

One-barra-barra, two-barra-barra (was that a faint noise? Not sure), three-barra-barra, four-barra-barra. Barra-barra is a good counting method as it allows a subdivision of a second to be counted too.

Crash. A far-off echo of landing. Very far, deep away down, far down in muffled damp blackness; was it a sort of splash, even? A quick calculation: I had never found a deeper hole. It must be 75 metres! That was over 150 feet! Impossible.

I found another stone, did it all again. Same result. The hole looked too ordinary to be that deep. I knew there were lead mines all around here. This must be an old one. They often dug in horizontally from the hillside lower down via an adit, and then vertical shafts were dug down from above. This must be such a shaft. Throw a body down it and no one would ever find it.

But still I was sceptical. One last stone. Yes, a small sound at two seconds, where it must have hit the shaft wall or some blockage. This changed the formula into an addition of two two-second drops (an assumption that the rock had slowed to something approaching zero when it hit) – so 40 metres. Still a great depth, and more than a 100 feet.

There was something amazing about the unpretentiousness of the deep shaft. If you didn't have the map, you'd miss it for sure. I fantasised about all the things you could hide down that shaft. There is a Middle Eastern saying that 'you find out who your friends are when you ask them to help you get rid of a dead body'. In countries with corrupt or non-existent police forces, this saying has slightly more middle-class appeal than here. One Englishman I know told me his test of a friend was the opposite: someone who *would* turn him in rather than collaborate on a cover up . . .

The Beat Poets put friendship above the law. And, typically, Jack Kerouac really did help a friend who had a dead body to deal with.

Kerouac's young friend Lucien Carr was nineteen at the time. During a moonlight walk by the Hudson River, he was sexually assaulted by David Kammerer, fourteen years his senior, a strongly built PE teacher who had known and been sexually obsessed by Carr since the younger man was eleven years old. To fend off the attack, Carr stabbed him twice with the small penknife he carried. Kammerer died and Carr panicked, rolling his body into the Hudson.

He then asked his Beat Poet pals Burroughs and Kerouac what to do. Burroughs told him to tell his family and get a lawyer. Kerouac took him to an art gallery to talk it over. The result was he helped Carr dispose of the knife down a drain hole. In the end, Carr got ten years for manslaughter and Kerouac only just missed a sentence for aiding and abetting a criminal.

I crossed Steel House Moor, falling several times into ditches concealed by reeds, slow, squelchy going in windy and wet conditions. Lunch was a damp huddle in a grouse butt, a three-sided stone-built shooting hide, out of the wind but not the rain. Far off I could hear the snap, crackle and pop (it really did sound like that at a distance) of grouse shooters elsewhere on the moor. Then, much closer, a gun went off like a car door slammed, but I couldn't see anyone. There is something final and wayward and stupid about a gunshot. Time to hurry on before becoming a target.

Time to hurry on when I didn't know exactly where I was . . . due to hurrying on. Heisenberg's rule of navigation: you either know where you are or you know which direction you should be going in but knowing both is somehow impossible . . . or at least exponentially much harder than it should be.[21]

But everywhere in England, however wrong you are, as long as you keep going in a straight line you'll hit a road. And I was going in a straight line. And when I found that road, I followed it downhill for a while until I found myself crossing the river at the site of a ruined church, St Simon's Chapel. In among the flinty, crumbling walls there was an appalling stench: the rotting carcass of a sheep lay as if sacrificed in what looked like the altar enclave of the medieval ruin.

It had been a fine and busy church and mini-monastery in 1200; now it was way off the beaten track. They had brewed beer here and made bread, depending on the stream for water and power. Now ivy swarmed over the crumbling walls. The smell of the dead sheep carried for 100 yards or more.

Ups and downs, tracks and roads, another abandoned mill; however rural the situation, industrial remains make a place dank, lonesome. Climbing again as dusk fell. Between a drystone wall and a rabbit fence was a six-foot gap, perfectly flat. On the wall side, a recently harvested wheat field. On the fence side, another ancient wood. The tent was hidden by the wall. It all felt good.

29

RIVER CROSSINGS

I am woken by the loud sound of a tractor driving by. And judging by the bounce and crash accompanying the chugga-chugga engine noise, it's towing a big trailer. Like the trained vagabond I am, I observe all this through the gaps in the upright stones topping the drystone wall. There is a wooden walkover to climb this wall and my coffee is brewing on the lower step. The tent, my gear and me are all invisible but as the tractor rumbles by about ten feet from the wall there is a curious rush of adrenaline – it's the closest I've come to being 'discovered' since the infamous stately home/lawn camping episode in Derbyshire, which seems another century ago.

The strip I slept in betwixt wall and fence was surprisingly congenial. All night long, in the ancient oak wood behind the fence, I heard bird and animal noises, fox squeals and badger grunts and once, swooping overhead, a tawny owl in flight almost low enough to brush my tent – *twoh, twoh* – using the strip as a hunting lane. Three-quarters of Britain's bird species are of forest origin; and it's no surprise that oak woods have more wild birds to the acre than any other kind of natural habitat.

When you get to compare the different levels of nocturnal activity, you realise in an experiential rather than merely intellectual sense, the depth of ecology in an ancient wood; not just the interconnections but the sheer pleasure of living in a place with so much history. I mean pleasure for the animals themselves. The variety of different species means a wealth of interconnection and activity. Knowledge of this kind builds up over the centuries, passed on from one generation to the next through instruction, but also epigenetically. In a new plantation, there just isn't the same foundation of skills.

The human version also exists. I was reminded of what an engineer told me about the old Jaguar factory in Coventry versus a new one near Liverpool. In Coventry, there was a century of automotive engineering skill to build on; in Liverpool, there was none. Not surprisingly, the Liverpool factory found it hard to compete. We overlook such things, think we can build new towns, shift populations around to do the bidding of multinational companies. But where you live is always about more than just a way of earning money. People should feel connected in more ways than one with their environment. The idea that you can just up and shift to find new work only succeeds if you can integrate in a richly contextual way with the new place. The resistance seen in the North to the free movement of labour is a crude refraction of this idea. To have dormitory workers shipped in to service an Amazon warehouse because no one else will do such dogsbody work for £7 an hour is like a planting a Sitka spruce plantation with the view to clearcutting it in a few years. Nothing grows in such a monoculture. Which doesn't mean you can't integrate Sitka spruce into a deciduous forest; after all we've been growing it here for one hundred and fifty years.

Peeping through my embrasure in the wall, I observe that there are actually two tractors and trailers working in relay. They roar and rattle to transfer earth from a digger hard at work in the corner of the field. In fact, I espied that digger the night before, parked on the side of a huge mound of dirt, dumb and inert, but caught by the setting sun so brighter than normal, suggesting a life it did not have; a vitality contradicted by the dead hang of its metal arm. Now it was hard at work, crafting and shudder-bucketing, sunlight glinting off its tiny, aggressively working pump rams.

It was all about timing. Tent down, gear packed, pack on back, ready on the lowest rung of the step-over, I warmed to the idea that I was like a man on the fire step of a front-line trench. Then I was faintly embarrassed that the possibility of being discovered seemed such a big deal.

But still, the game was on. One tractor rattled by. I saw it start its trek across the field to the digger. At the precise moment the tractor and trailer blocked the digger's line of sight, I was over the wall. Then, to switch wars, I was like some Colditz escapee assuming the nonchalance of a local worker, I slowed my pace to an amble, as if I had been all morning on that track. After a hundred yards or so the second tractor came into view. The driver, a youngish guy, did not hesitate. He waved cheerfully at me as he went past. Hadn't seen me earlier and didn't give a toss who I was anyway. I waved back, and yes it felt satisfyingly like: Settlers 0, Supertramp 1.

It seems appropriate, then, that the day's second obstacle was a moorland military firing range. Flags down, it was safe to roam past flinty shell-shocked holes, overgrown but still hurting. There were one or two stunted survivor trees, some yellow gorse. Bits of frag and rusted rounds, signage:

DANGER! MILITARY DEBRIS MAY EXPLODE AND KILL YOU.

NO ENTRY LIVE FIRING KEEP OUT!

ARMY LIMIT (this one posted on the wall between farmland and the range, presumably aimed at trespassing soldiers rather than the grazing sheep next to it.)

On a loose pile of grey gravel the detached jaw bones of a fox, very white, lay side by side with impossible-to-ignore symmetry. There was not another bone in sight. I took a photograph and pondered what happened to the rest of the animal. Blown to bits?

The crater holes were old; I guessed nothing seriously explosive had happened here for years. I was becoming a connoisseur of the way land is reclaimed by the Earth and I could not help comparing the craters to the ditches and earthworks of several thousand years ago. One thing is for sure, holes don't fill themselves in. They remain. All that happens is a subtle rounding of the edges. New holes are raw and, as I noted earlier, distinctly lumpy. Old ones: smooth, grass covered, urbane after the manner of a golf course, but still very much a hole. We leave traces far more permanent than we believe when we dig into Mother Earth.

I reach a road that runs through the range, and I follow it north. It's not busy but I see mainly military contractor vehicles and buses running squaddies up to the rifle range. Far more talking than firing, it seems, from my distant position. No doubt they have restrictions on how much ammo each one can fire off.

From the dry moor there is, in half a mile, a drastic change into a verdant valley with trees; the valley of the River Swale. I saw a new sign that made my day: 'Marrick Priory 1/3 mile with a difficult river crossing.' Then, nailed under it with some desperation: 'Stepping stones difficult in wet weather.'

Off and on rain for days, dripping now. We'd certainly had wet weather. The river will be high. This was the challenge I was looking for after the false danger of the morning evasions.

'Difficult' was music to my too-long-on-the-tarmac feet. A challenge clouded with a certain anticipatory smugness – all those rivers in Canada I crossed, some of them wading shoulder high. This'd be easy.

For a walker on a pilgrimage, crossing a river is something like a sacred act. Even by bridge, there is some significance to it. When you cross the vast, empty ditch that is the drained North Loch in Edinburgh you feel misled; there's no water in it, the journey is a cheat.

Religion and water: we've seen how essential the sacred spring is to standing stones. Recently, archaeologists in Wiltshire have dated remains found at a spring near Stonehenge to 8000 years ago. Things we do to survive: breathing, drinking water, eating bread, do double service in ritual. Ritual is a way to see things for the first time, feel their true significance.

River crossing is a ritual act I feel almost every time I cross even a piddling ditch. I feel a tiny fraction of that mythological weight. St Christopher, carrying an unknown child across a river; the child was Christ. John the Baptist helping people ford into dry different clothes. Hades found after crossing the Styx. Rivers make borders, but they are more than that. You can't step in the same one twice.

I had changed over the years. I knew more about how a river could be those two things: its symbolic self and the ordinary run of water. All great cities are based on copious water. Failed or lumpen ones – Birmingham, perhaps – just don't have enough. Their rivers are mean and off-centre. It impacts the people, for sure. Less energy, less élan. They turn to the enemy of the shaman: the working of metal, the grumpiest of professions; the hammering of a thousand anvils; Birmingham, the world's first engineering capital and the birthplace of heavy metal rock music; the monstrous inheritance of the biblical Tubal-cain.

This river was wide and full and I was excited; I'd show it who was boss. A light drizzle was falling, pitting the ripples with a definite pattern. At a wide curve of the river was a field with a high zip wire crossing. I thought it would be even easier just to zip over, but the pulley on the wire was locked up; property, I surmised, of an outdoor centre on the other side which was run out of the old priory. Whose square church tower beckoned most insistently.

I pushed through weeds and verdant riverside vegetation to get a closer look at the water. No stepping stones were apparent. I walked on, now on the boulders at the river's edge. No question about it, and a certain frisson: I'd have to wade across, and this was not a slow or especially shallow river. The stepping stones were so far submerged I couldn't even see them. I would have to make my own way.

There are many rules to wading and I was about to transgress one: you wade in trainers, not in boots. However, in my favour, there was the catastrophe I'd experienced in the Pyrenees, when I removed my boots and hung them round my neck by their laces so that I could wade across a mountain stream in bare feet. It was ice cold and full of sharp rocks; I made slow progress. Halfway across, an idiotic urge to divest myself of my boots came over me. One boot made it to the far bank. The other fell short and was swept away . . .

Never let go of your boots.

So, keeping mine on, and using my walking poles as aids to balance,

I headed out across the raging torrent. Of course it looked all benign and friendly when it was shallow, but midstream, as the water crept up my thighs, I realised it was almost too powerful to resist. Each step became a nightmare balancing act, made far worse by the streaming weed and algae on the smooth pebbles under foot. My boots were so big they offered significant resistance to the river's flow. When I lifted up a foot I could feel a sudden power threatening to over-balance me. I realised too, too late of course, that a single 'leaning pole' as I had used before crossing rivers in British Columbia, was far better than my trusty Pacerpoles. A big, thick pole six or more feet high creates a sturdy triangle with both your feet. If those feet are in low-drag trainers covered in socks (socks grip algae way better than plastic does) then you have the optimum crossing combination. But even using this, if you trespass in water that sweeps above the knee, you can be in trouble. Some rivers are simply too powerful to resist. You have no choice but to scout along the bank for another method of crossing.

Every river has its deep bit. I was crossing at the widest part (usually the shallowest, i.e. has the least deep, deepest bit). You build up to the deep bit which will often be on the outside part of a curve, where the water runs faster and erodes deeper. Crossing on a straight wide bit between curves is usually a good tactic; and that was mine now, but as I approached the far bank, which was tantalisingly close, a mere six feet or so, I saw how the channel suddenly dropped away into darkness. The deep bit. Turn back? I prepared instead for disaster, transferring my camera, notebook and wallet into a waterproof bag. Which I put in my waist-pack, which now hung round my neck. I loosed off the belt of the rucksack. If you topple into a fast flowing stream, a rucksack can drown you. I'd once experimented with swimming in very fast river in Indonesia while wearing full clothes and jungle boots: it was possible but only just; a rucksack was out of the question.

Edge forward, don't step. Position pole one, edge forward again. Position pole two. Feel for slipperiness. Lock the soles into the river bed. Facing upstream seemed no different to being side-on to the current, one leg taking the strain off the leg behind it. Inching forward, being careful, a bit trepidatious. Not fun, but still, it was something. *You need a challenge*, I would have told myself, if I wasn't focusing so hard on not falling over.

Step, step, deeper step, reach for the grass of the bank. And then it's over. Sitting on a grassy bank with a few bullocks nosing around, drying my feet off, pouring water out of my boots, putting on dry socks over blue-white feet.

Sheer relief is hurried away as it was spitting with rain again. I hadn't exactly enjoyed it as much as I had anticipated. Too many scares for that. I only felt I had triumphed over something small – yet such a triumph was valuable, necessary, worth risking a dunking for. Yes, worth that.

You cross a river and the accent changes. Now I was edging out of Yorkshire and into County Durham, the unmistakeable tones of the North East would soon become apparent. For anyone of a certain age, these were the tones of James Bolam in the TV series *The Likely Lads* and *When the Boat Comes In*. Whereas speaking Yorkshire is just a version of northern, North-East speak is more exotic, as far from Scottish as it is from English.

Marrick Priory, next to the river crossing, still looked medieval except there was a child's BMX bike leant against the church tower. I strode quickly away, up a path, an ancient one, padded with giant flagstones like paths in the Himalayas, steeply rising up the hillside. It was a joy to walk along. A giant oak had split and fallen across the path. It was so massively split and so hugely fallen (it blocked the path completely) as to command respect, reverence even. A strong wind? Lightning?

Resting amidst moorland. A tough-looking, bullet-headed man of aged appearance accosted me as I brewed up at a confluence of paths on the windy moor. 'Where you bin'?' he asked with admirable directness.

I told him I'd come from Marrick, crossed the river there.

'Oh aye, I know that river. That's on one of my routes. Got about five or eight routes myself. I work through 'em. Just been doing a circuit of t'moor right now myself – about ten mile, ten mile'll suit me. Ten mile is about all I can manage. Haven't had a kneecap since '77.'

I showed friendly concern and glanced over-quickly at the stubby knee below his shorts. He grinned a warrior's grin.

'Had a heart attack in '85. Type 2 diabetes in 2004.'

'Golly!'

'Yep, ten mile is all I can manage at my age. Too much wrong with me.' To his credit, the almost boastful way he listed his infirmities gave a lustre to his ten miles that outshone my own efforts by far.

'I've been retired seventeen years,' he added. But for some reason (possibly because he seemed to be inviting the question too needily) I didn't ask his age. Seventy-five? Eighty? Older? And how did his lose that kneecap?

'Kicked by a horse in Heckmondwike.'

More moorland. A woman at a farm who served teas in her sunny garden waved at me to come in, but I rushed on, regretting it and not regretting it at the same time. On the map, the blue tankard sign indicating a pub in a village was flashing at me.

The village had been upgraded. It was posh. A suburb for well-off folk who worked in York or other places that employ middle-class people with Mercs and Audis. One such man, looking like he had just finished a game of squash – unlined face, Clark Kent specs, well-groomed hair, a shirt that had football in its DNA but as interpreted by some designer – was clipping his privet hedge, I kid you not.

I trolleyed up and asked if the pub was still open. He rather thought it was closed for good. You know you're a commuter when you don't know if the only pub in your village has closed for good or not. However, be that as it may, he remarked that there was a much better pub by Greta Bridge, which – did I know? – was famously painted by John Sell Cotman, and I really ought to see the interior of the pub, which for some reason in his enthusiasm he suggested was decorated by Cotman himself. While I agreed it sounded extraordinary and well worth a visit, it also seemed implausible as I believe he only did watercolours – which would be far too valuable to have on its public bar walls, surely?

But by now my time was up, and he was back on schedule, clipping some more. Professional courtesy had been extended; he had passed on what he knew. It was like an email, a communication of optimum length containing one and only one piece of useful information. It was the new model of communication, superseding the rambling face-to-face conversation or the phone call that can go anywhere.

He said the pub was hardly any distance, about two miles, but I could see he had never walked there and never would. How bitter I sound! Envy, of course, the envy of the nomad for the settler's wealth, just as the nomad is envied his freedom. Did he envy me as he clipped that privet? Not by the look of it . . .

It was getting dark and almost dangerous as I walked through the wood that ran alongside the Greta gorge; and it really feels like a gorge: the river is way down below. Cotman fails utterly to convey that sense of height and wildness, though he does capture the bridge well. Greta Bridge, he famously painted twice; in the later, 1810 picture, Cotman puts mountains in, although there are none really visible.[22] I think I know why: it is an attempt to symbolise the wildness anyone feels while crossing that bridge and looking down stream at the gravel islands and boulders in the stream and the flood borne tree trunks. Cotman, who along with John White Abbott (what was it with artists' names in those days?) generally understood the Lawrentian grandeur of England, its weirdness and fecundity, much better than the sea-obsessed Turner.

Yes, I was entering a world where rivers had islands with gravel beaches. Wild rivers are like this, as are French rivers even when they aren't wild. What's the use of a river without islands? you may very reasonably ask; and now I was heading to a place where they did have islands. It was something to do with being closer to the end of the Ice Age up here.

What was the allure of those gravel islands? I think it has something to do with breaking the river up into different channels. One of the several wonders of Cairo and also Paris is the way a midstream island divides the river, making two rivers and four river banks – doubling the riverine energy of the place instantly. London is quite plodding by comparison: you always know which bank you are on. The multiple streams of the river mimic the threads we live, the paths that we braid together, sometimes apart, sometimes together, a complexity we can't escape.

My feet were ever so tired but the lure of a beer and pub meal drew me on inexorably. It was dark now and the public bar was not too busy. There were three regulars, one with a greyhound lying on its own blanket, provided by the pub it seemed. The regulars were about sixty and well seasoned by drink, smoking and now by surreptitious vaping. One had a half pint on the go – a sure sign of an alky. They were all in cahoots with the black-clad bar staff.

It was a chain pub, pseudo gastro, and the promised Cotman murals were simply decorated wallpaper. The bar itself was a dark little hole, all the small tables bereft of chairs, and all the chairs congregating like babies round one empty table of no discernible difference to the rest. The black-trousered bar girls, though all cheeky and cheery, clearly saw no merit in redistributing the chairs, which showed me they had no subtle knowledge of pubcraft: a room full of tables with no chairs round them is a lonely sight.

So I took my meal instead in the dining area with people who had paid for a weekend break; they were only allowed certain items on the menu and the subdued couple next to me kept unerringly choosing prohibited dishes. I had my book so I was not really lonely but I did not overly like the people I was dining with. Maybe a mood thing, maybe not, but sometimes you feel a kind of bond with your fellow diners. Sometimes it can even change halfway through a meal; yes, these are *good* people. But not here.

Maybe it had to do with the pub having a spa attached. Why go to a spa? I have never understood the concept except in the snobby, old-style form dished up by Milan Kundera and the one in the film *Last Year in Marienbad*. English spas of the modern kind seem a dumb extension of luxury bathroom culture. Towel-happy places to pamper plumpness and be lazy in a stupid way, a TV celebrity and footballer's wife way; spa people all drive jelly-mould cars too.

I shuddered out into the bracing dark, and made my way through a long tunnel under the A-road. I was walking by head torch alone, not a good time to fall in the river, which I was alongside for a while. Too late to find an oak plantation, these were all sheep-cropped fields. But I was wrong again: a half-fallen wall let me into a place of ancient trees. Careful to avoid 'widow makers' (oaks are notorious for dropping a heavy extended limb for no reason), I pitched camp and fell into deep and dreamless sleep.

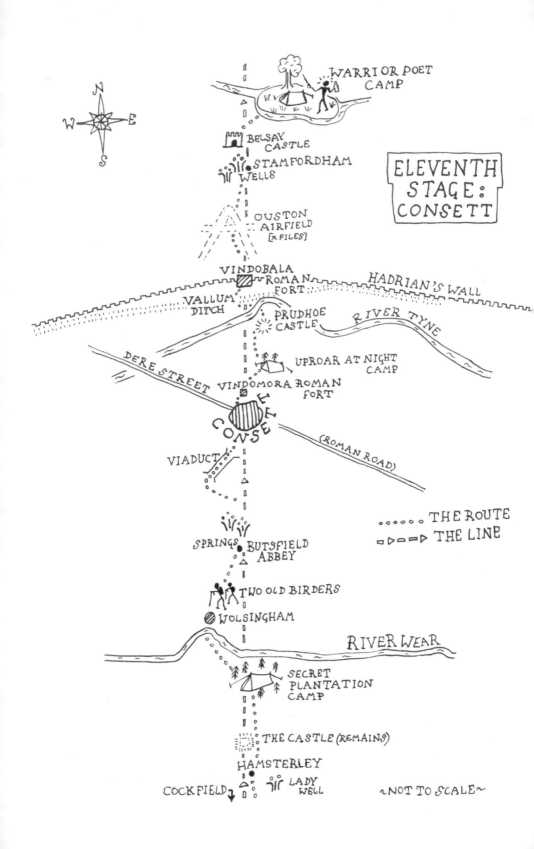

WARRIOR POET CAMP

N W E S

BELSAY CASTLE

STAMFORDHAM WELLS

OUSTON AIRFIELD [X-FILES]

ELEVENTH STAGE: CONSETT

VINDOBALA ROMAN FORT

HADRIAN'S WALL

VALLUM DITCH

PRUDHOE CASTLE

RIVER TYNE

UPROAR AT NIGHT CAMP

DERE STREET

VINDOMORA ROMAN FORT

CONSETT

(ROMAN ROAD)

VIADUCT

THE ROUTE
THE LINE

SPRINGS BUTSFIELD ABBEY

TWO OLD BIRDERS

WOLSINGHAM

RIVER WEAR

SECRET PLANTATION CAMP

THE CASTLE (REMAINS)

HAMSTERLEY

COCKFIELD   LADY WELL

~NOT TO SCALE~

30

STAINDROP AND ONWARDS

With a name like that you don't expect much. Imagine the jokes: I come from Staindrop; I come, therefore I am . . . a staindrop. The place is a stain on the map, but only a little stain, more like a Staindrop. Yet Staindrop has at least two good things going for it. Simon's, a marvellous butchers that sells pulled-pork sandwiches for a very reasonable price, and an ancient church full of ancient royalty. It restored my good mood after I'd managed to electrocute myself on the edge of town on a cow fence (most unusually it was actually switched on). And a further treat after the sandwich: a Taylor's of Darlington Pork Pie, far superior to Melton Mowbray.

Staindrop's church, St Mary's – 'the cathedral of the Dales' – is, in parts, more than 1000 years old. As the guide I picked up from among the prayer books puts it, 'The magnificence of Staindrop's church owes much to the beneficence of the incumbents of Raby Castle.' There the mighty Neville family lived for centuries. The Nevilles were a cunning lot, Anglo-Saxon aristocrats, though they married into Norman blood and took a Norman name, Neville, in the thirteenth century. Their line can be traced back to Anglo-Saxon royalty and Raby Castle (which is an impressive pile) is raised on an obviously ancient site; previously one of King Canute's castles stood there. King Canute – one of my favourite kings!

The mighty Nevilles became Earls of Westmorland and then of Warwick. Richard Neville, known as Warwick the Kingmaker, is buried here and in the Wars of the Roses the family's star was at its zenith. After backing the wrong monarch a few years later and opposing Elizabeth the First's new English prayer book, their last earl, Charles Neville, died abroad, disgraced, stripped of lands and titles, and without issue. The Nevilles were no more. A junior branch survived through a zigzag line of marriage, and though not originally entitled to be Earls of Westmoreland, they petitioned hard and got the title and some land back. The current lot are descended from them.

And the obscure and rather remote church at Staindrop is full of their giant bedlike tombs, carved with medieval grandeur. Rock-hard in every way, they look. St Mary's in Staindrop is the last English parish church to celebrate the Roman Mass in Latin.

I went through the forest behind Raby Castle, where they were cutting down one of the huge grey-trunked sycamores. I was walking somewhat on tenterhooks, expectant of the next burst of chainsaw noise; that waiting feeling of the humble rumbling of the chainsaw as it idles, and then flares up with a biting roar, almost a scream. White sawdust everywhere on the forest floor. A man in an orange helmet gestured with clumsy friendliness.

And out from the trees to Cockfield, where there is a St Mary's Church too. Oh yes, Cockfield, it was a day of funny names all right. Made a different impression to ancient Staindrop, being the site of one the oldest coal-mining villages in England. Since medieval times, just as the Nevilles were riding high, the proles have been digging up coal in Cockfield. The last mine closed in 1962. Though even before the coal there were Iron Age settlements here.

Though Cockfield is as working-class as Staindrop is aristocratic, it has had its share of famous sons. Appropriately for the Great North Line, Jeremiah Dixon, though buried in Staindrop, was born in Cockfield. He became an astronomer and went to the United States, where he worked on a survey with Charles Mason to resolve the border dispute between British colonies in America for which the Mason–Dixon Line is named. A line you crossed at one time to escape slavery.

The lands of Cockfield Fell are pitted with lumpy filled-in workings. All grassy now, innocuous. And round them all kinds of odd one- and two-storey sheds containing pigeons. As its name suggests, Cockfield is a bird lover's paradise, if pigeons are your pigeon.

Because of the coal digging, the fell was not seized by land-hungry gentry during the enclosures. Unusually for an area of lowland fields, it remained in common ownership. The land was used for mining and to keep pigeons – and remains so to this day.

Past the pigeons and the disused railway, I got lost in the steeply wooded valley, which reeked of dope as I found myself inadvertently trailing some youthful smokers. They were ambling slowly and didn't hear me coming. I wanted to hang back but kept catching them up. When they suddenly realised I was behind them they bolted on, in silence, leaving a slipstream of exhaled hash smoke.

On and on now, back into deep countryside and a vast plantation of firs that reminded me of the Canadian North Woods. I left the track and blundered deep into the forest, pushing through pine trees and sure, for the first time, that no one could possibly accidently find me. The pine needles were soft and brown and though I was no more than five miles from the town of Wolsingham, I felt as though I was in true wilderness. When you earn your place in the wild through physical exertion, you're rewarded with a greater sensation of wildness. In a car you'd have to go much further to feel the same thing.

Such was the felt isolation of my camp spot, I sat around next morning drinking several cups of coffee, reading and making notes before I left. I even whittled a new spoonette for shovelling noodles down. I'd lost my spoon a few days before and the rough carved sticks had been just as good really. Now I upped my game by some neater finishing. I'd missed the luxury of pottering in my stealthy campsites, always eager to be away before The Man arrives . . .

Now I am walking along the River Wear and I pass a hipster on a horse that he can't really control. Beard, specs, a sort of army battledress, he gives me a friendly 'what the hell am I doing' look which is very endearing and not at all the normal self-satisfied, tight-arsed grimace you get from most horse folk (OK apart from the younger ones who are still in training). I watch a heron glide for ages. It's a good fast river with islands upstream visible as I cross into Wolsingham.

Here I find a marvellous coffee shop called Number 10. The

owner, a cheerful man with a camp style, goes out specially to buy some Worcester sauce (because I asked and they have none) for my ordered bacon sarnie. I ask a chortling elderly couple what his name is; 'Mark,' they say. 'He's a lovely bloke; he'll do anything to help, will Mark,' says the man, and then as if embarrassed by his warm-heartedness, adds in a mischievous undertone, 'Though I do have another name for him.' His wife punches him playfully. 'But rather not say with kids about!'

There are all sorts of interesting books too in Mark's shop, rare Bloodaxe poetry and photo books. Mark has taste and the coffee was excellent. In fact, everyone I meet in Wolsingham is very helpful – from the postman who directs me to the supermarket, to the man in the supermarket who tells me where I can get something cheaper. But you never know if it's you or the place. Sometimes you arrive with a special vibe that people all respond positively too. And other times it's the reverse. But still. Wolsingham is special.

And very, very different to Consett.

I had been somewhat dreading Consett, just as I dreaded the other bigger towns I'd crossed. I wanted to walk in wilderness, not along pavements and through shopping centres. But Consett was slap bang on the Line, and the way in was along the old railway line, which is now a recreational cycle and running track.

I walked in along this track half-expecting to be mugged. The prejudice was deep: Consett is an old steel town. Steel was just about all it made. Then they closed everything. In my imagination, unem-ployed youths lay waiting for unsuspecting ramblers. This old railway line was how the coal and lime was brought in to town. As a kind of Exhibit A, I passed an old railway truck once used for carrying some-thing very hot and essential to steel making, by the look of it. There was a plaque too. And graffiti sprayed in both English and Polish.

I passed people out for a bit of exercise. On a mountain bike, a lad, aged fifteen or so, with a skinhead haircut and broken nose, skidded to a halt in front of me. But this was just bravado to cover his embarrassment at being out with his entire extended family, who soon appeared. Everyone was overweight and his fat mum was gamely riding a tricycle. Which takes courage, I have to say. Grandad (not much older than me I suspect) was on an old postman's bike. Dad, wheezingly bloated, was on a brand new Boardman racer, his wide track-suited arse enveloping the tiny saddle. He grinned at me, knowing he looked silly. 'Ay up,' he said. Two more nippers: a young kid with a big grin on a BMX and his tubby snaggle-toothed sister on a pink bike with tassels on the handlebars. The family was good humoured, even ironic about their exercise. I felt this should be a government health broadcast: all that scaremongering about fitness being essential has finally paid off. This was a poster-family for the twenty-first century!

Then I passed a couple of kids, late teens, out on a romantic walk. They were emo types, intellectuals. He had a satchel; maybe it had a notebook in it like I used to carry at his age. I had a caricature image of a dead steel town – and this isn't it.

What came next surprised me too: Hownsgill Viaduct. The railway track suddenly launched out on a long bridge over a beautiful wide wooded valley, Howns Gill. I expected to see a river down there but there was only a thin stream, a hundred and fifty feet or more below. Huge brick supports hold up a viaduct spanning a gap of 700 feet.

I like viaducts but this one was different. It was partly caged over with wire fencing, the fences curled inward to make them very hard but not impossible to climb. Then I see the first sign: *Samaritans, call us if you are in despair.* Then another sign saying: *Please do not leave things attached to the railings.* What's that all about?

Then I see the bunch of dead flowers and some waterlogged notes. And a bit further on another bunch. It's a suicide bridge. The only way into town – well not really, but my way into town.

What was chilling for me was remembering a good friend, close to despair, who described a vision of crossing a bridge to the other side, to what he dreamt of doing with his life, except when he imagined the scene he always fell off the bridge while crossing. Google Hownsgill Bridge if you want some truly depressing reading.

You take things from the ground, you take stone, you crush it to make metal: there is a price to pay. Most of us escape, the price is paid by others. I had always thought the aborigine indignation about mining a bit crazy. Not any more. The Earth is sacred. Sacred stones come up from the Earth. Mining must be paid for by sacrifice. This is, of course, the meaning behind human sacrifice in gold cultures like the Incas. We make our human sacrifices too, here on bridges like this. Everything has to be paid for if it is out of alignment.

Humans can't face up to the price of technology. We haven't even worked out how to dispose of nuclear waste yet – and we're building more nuclear power stations. Someone will pay, not us of course, but someone down the line. Maybe in a hundred years, on an old bridge like this.

Moving on, more odd cyclists and joggers. The track is well used. Then I'm suddenly in a bright new business park with flags and car showrooms and even a giant Costa Coffee. There are closely mowed roundabouts, padded with grey bricks; everything looks new and like a thousand other out-of-town business parks in the UK. Except this one was built on the old steel works. There's a huge Further Education College and lots of car parking alongside the chain businesses. Grants and easy loans to the right people – and why not? Heal the scars.

Into Costa and the vibe is like Halifax: a bit stunned, overweight and at a loose end. This is a town on medication. Oh fine, they have an active bowls club; later, I'll walk past a great gaggle of determined seniors measuring whose bowl is nearest. There are lots of churches (all locked – the ones I tried, anyway). Row upon row of rather nice steel-town terraced houses now probably for retirees. I mean, where are the jobs here?

The entertainment district is a single street of barnlike clubs with signs – first three shots free, all you can drink and curry too – the tarmac grease-stained after a thousand too many Saturday night throw-ups. The pubs are takeaways and the takeaways are pubs . . . Most common roadside can: Red Bull.

Consett is hilly with nice views, but who would live here except the damaged, the old, the one that never got away? These towns are our sacrifice, the sacrifice we make even now to the Earth gods we violated for so many centuries. And we'll be paying for a hundred years to come . . .

Such are my thoughts, which are interrupted by some truly wonderful shop names. They say a symptom of schizophrenia is a fondness for bad puns:

Jugga's Plaice: fish and chips
Butt Licious – more than a Beauty Salon
Shauna's Hair: unintentional?

And my favourite, the utterly brazen: '*Tanfastic: we have the most powerful tanning units in Europe.*' I peek through the sticker laden windows to glimpse the copper-coloured staff operating some truly monstrous machines . . .

I also like: *Kutz and Colourz, Wok 'n' Go* and *Gypsy's Kitchen*: '*Bringing good food and fortune to your table.*'

And then, a pub down by the river that's now an Indian restaurant, not a late-night barfhouse but rather a decent-looking establishment called Rumi's, after the Sufi poet; my spirit soars: I am sure Rumi would have seen the joke too. But maybe there is no joke. Consett is being remade, as much of England is, in hopeful and also depressing ways. Stunted but trying very hard. One thing is certain, though: as long as we deny the shamanic and truly mysterious inheritance that runs through our distant past and extends to the present, we will fail to remake England – except as an adjunct to a pathetic business park, all flags flying, all souls fled.

I wasn't far from Consett when the light started to fade. I ignored some semi-public woods that looked ideal for leaving a dead body wrapped in bin liners, and pushed on into real countryside. In the end, the best option was a dense plantation at the side of a road, with farms both sides.

Dense? It was truly close packed to the point of being almost impossible to navigate. There were no paths through the low aspens and firs and hawthorns – a hodge podge of trees and dense undergrowth, suggesting a random experiment in forestry. I suspected a replanted clear cut: the ground was bumpy and uneven where trees may once have stood. I followed animal trails to get away from the A-road, though it was not hugely busy. I had to push my rucksack in front of me, like the fugitives in *The Great Escape* shoving their suitcases down the tunnel in front of them. Snag-scratched by thorns, stung royally by rogue but hopped up nettles, I gave up pushing deeper into the glade when the flash of passing car lights seemed almost invisible. But not quite. I wondered if my own powerful head torch would be seen in return. No, surely not.

Tent pitched over a mossy hole, air mat lodged between two root clusters that broke the surface like aged knuckles, it was not the comfiest of spots. I distracted myself by reading in my sleeping bag and sipping a coffee.

I was startled out of my reading by sudden barking. Fox or dog? Shouldn't it be obvious? But I wasn't sure. A car slowing. Stopped. Now its lights were off. Ker-thunk of a door shutting. Talking? None I can hear. I check my watch: 8.45 p.m. Then a very loud shout: 'Oi!' Then running, then something indistinct.

I had doused my light at the 'Oi!' Surely I was impossible to find? Perhaps my light had been mistaken for that of a poacher? I lay with held breath, taut diaphragm, a hare set to run – except I had nowhere to run to.

And of course nothing transpired, nothing happened except the return of a hooting owl criss-crossing the plantation, huge eyes alert for dormice and worms and slow-moving black-jacketed beetles.

31

WARRIOR POET ISLAND

Gliding clubs can be dangerous places. In the *Yorkshire Post* I read of a walker on the Cleveland Way who was killed while walking across the end of the runway. The gentle swish of air was not noise enough to penetrate his woolly balaclava. And the pilot had nowhere to turn . . . Smacked on the back of the head by the descending glider, the walker died without knowing what had hit him. So I'm cautious when crossing the Prudhoe gliding club landing strip, though it's only 6.30 in the morning.

On the way into Prudhoe, I meet a man out walking his dog who tells me his wife is from town and he has lived here forty years. His name is Roger Newman and he tells me Prudhoe is the kind of town where, if you are born here, you know everyone. He is retired and walks to the top of the valley hill most mornings, and I feel very much the better for meeting him at this early hour.

Into Prudhoe for a bacon sandwich and a chat with another friendly fellow, who gives me lots of tiny salt and sugar sachets from the back of his café. He tells me he'd like to take up walking but his girlfriend, who he emphasises is highly educated, would likely be against it as she does not approve of anything except holidays abroad.

Across the Tyne: the rivers get better and better the further north you go.

And now with due solemnity, I approached Hadrian's Wall, to be ritually crossed at right angles if possible. Hadrian's Wall is like the Pennine Way in that it occupies an iconic place for anyone who grew up walking in the 1970s. 'Doing Hadrian's Wall' might even be a precursor to 'doing' the Pennine Way. It is a mythical transection, our own Great Wall – so naturally I assumed I would be disappointed. But I was not, and not because of the wall per se, but because of the Vallum.

The mysterious Vallum is a ditch that runs just south of the Wall. Sometimes it is right below the wall, and sometimes it is a hundred metres away. Most of the time, it is as close as it can be. The purpose is mysterious because of something mostly overlooked by mainstream commentators: the Vallum is almost dead straight. Unlike the wall.

The old antiquarians believed the Vallum predated the Wall. But now we know better – perhaps. Why build a ditch that varies in distance from the Wall? Was it symbolic in some way?

We know that the Celts pioneered straight road building, and it is increasingly suspected that the Romans simply added their exquisite road *finishing* quality to already existing lines. Could it be that Hadrian's Wall is simply another exercise in copying, that the Vallum was some kind of symbolic dividing line betwixt the tribes of England and those of Scotland? One is reminded of the way colonial Britons were drawn into supporting warring tribes in the countries they conquered: did the Romans, too, build the Wall to appease a tribe they wanted support from?

Once over the A-road that follows fairly exactly the route of the Wall, I looked for people 'doing the Wall'. A man hammered by, wearing an Eagles sweatshirt. Another runner, catching him up, had 'No Boundaries on Hadrian's Wall' on his shirt. Obviously running is the new walking. Still, I walked it until I was bored, which was quite quickly. Then north again, past some sunny old quarries.

There was something not quite right, something almost sinister as I circled a supposedly disused airfield, Ouston, still ringed with fencing topped with razor wire, guard dogs patrolling and 'civilians' jogging round the service road that parallels the fence. An ideal rendition site, I'd say . . . and the old RAF housing is still in use.

In one garden glimpsed through the fence, I saw the same kiddies' red-and-yellow plastic car that I spotted on a military lawn way back at the Larkhill barracks near Stonehenge. Despite this very domestic detail, I am sure there is something fishy going on . . . Though some of the runways are slowly becoming overgrown with grass and trees, I'm sure you could still land a Hercules here at midnight.

I have a morbid love of such places and, possibly due to their resemblance to an old set for *Doctor Who*, I half-expected to see the Brigadier and a group of UNIT soldiers Land Rovering out to intercept me. At one gate, locked with a passcode panel, swivelling CCTV gave me the evil eye. I shook the gate and then moved on. A man in civvies was hurrying towards the gate as I disappeared out of sight.

And into another dimension, across ploughed fields steaming in the midday sun, the steam rising from recently cut curved and shiny brown slabs of compacted earth. Then I was down to Stamfordham village, where they were holding a fire-brigade cycle race. Apparently it was won by a man aged sixty-eight! (Who won the previous year too.)

I wanted water from the pub but it was shut. A fat man loafing at his door kindly gave me some and told me about the health-giving Stamfordham well in the middle of the village green. Next to the village lock-up: room for only one prisoner by the look of it. I sampled the well water – and it tasted wonderful. On the way out, I noticed a faded Barclays sign over a fine Victorian residence: this one-pub village had once had its own bank as well as its own gaol![23]

The road was hard and the way hot. Past two giant puffballs poking up through long grass in the verge. Both as big as footballs. One would be enough to feed me for several days.

Fields, paths, burns, brooks; most fields are grass with nothing else in them. Roughly 40 per cent of English land is grass, as opposed to 17 per cent used for crops, say the stats; but it feels different when walking the Line. Perhaps I'm repeating myself but only because the experience repeated itself so often, along with the same reflection: if we just grew vegetables in these fields we wouldn't need to import any food at all.

Again, it was hard walking along stony tracks to Bitchfield (yes, appropriate) and its neighbour Beechfield. Bitchfield was some kind of fortified manor with a pele tower designed to honour Brazilian football. Such towers have recently become popular owing to the spread of top Brazilian players in the Premier League ... No, in fact pele towers were fortified to resist the constant raiding and warring that characterised the Borders up until the sixteenth century. Bitchfield was flying its own self-aggrandising flag, whereas the euphemistic Beechfield looked to be a solid working farm. But then I was past 'em both and dog tired and flaking when I found the farm shop.

A proper posh farm shop! With all kinds of fayre but mainly ice-cold Italian Moretti beer. While I am aware that this brand is widely advertised and routinely also sold in service stations, in this case it was accompanied by game pie with cranberries and the smoked mussel pate I also purchased with glee from the friendly lad in charge.

There was a bench outside where I installed myself and watched rich folk in Audis buy expensive comestibles on the way home from work. One BMW manoeuvred back and forth, as close as possible to the letter box, back and forth as if this was masterclass in bone idleness before the driver leant over to post the letter. I observed this but not in a bitter way. As the beer enriched my perspective, I tipped my cap at a few of these wealthy locals like a half-cut labourer, yet one who was also furiously at his tablets. I wrote:

> *A sudden, superior excitement*
> *Poetry matters.*
> *People out there, a few, a lot*
> *Are tired of the prosaic*
> *Or even the filmic*
> *They want the direct truth*
> *Which poets, duty bound, must needs supply*
> *All poetry is love poetry*
> *A love of poetry and a poetic rendering*
> *Of love.*

Another bottle later: *Poet Warriors have No Fear. Poet Warriors aim to Perceive the real truth of any Situation. Poet Warriors are generous and strive to help all who are oppressed. A Poet Warrior knows no home except the Road and the Battlefield.*

The Poet Warrior in me popped in for a parting purchase, a small flagon of rum, and was off down the road ecstatic about the possibilities ahead.

And I was rewarded completely. Following my inner truth pilot, I soon left the road to wander the fields, off-piste for sure. The map indicated a barrow or tumulus of some kind but this was only the MacGuffin and I was damned if I could find it. Instead, I drew inspiration from a small, fast brook which I crossed by hanging on to a fallen log, using the slimy, spike-like branches as handholds. Quite impressed with myself, I then climbed a single venomous strand of sheep's-wool-tufted barbed wire at the water's marshy edge.

Looking downstream, I saw a little hidden valley. And there I found the island with a single small oak. The 15-metre-long micro-island was ringed by two halves of the brook. No sheep could get on the island and one fallen tree made for a great seat, a regal seat, a *Poet Warrrior's* seat.

I surprised myself at how quickly I pitched the tent and then luxuriated in the setting sun seen from my island home.

Next morning, dry mouthed but not much the worse for wear, I also caught the sunrise from another glorious angle. The Truth, illimitable, undeniable: everywhere you camp is more than a reflection of your state of mind; it is absolutely the creation of your inner state.

HOLY ISLAND

CASTLE

N
W E
S

BELFORD

STONE CIRCLE

HILL FORT

BEANLEY MOOR HILL FORT CAMP

········· — ROUTE
— ◁ □ ◁ □ ◁ □ ◁ ▷ — LINE

ST NINIAN'S WELL

POWER SPOT-CASTLE HILL

FINAL STAGE: THE ISLAND

ORACLE CAVE

McCARTNEY'S CAVE

BURIAL CAIRNS

DEVIL'S CAUSEWAY

STONE CIRCLE

ROTHBURY

BRINKBURN PRIORY

R. COQUET

HOLY WELL

RICHARD AND HIS DOG

HARTBURN

R. WANSBECK

~NOT TO SCALE~

32

WISDOM OF THE ELDERS

S hamans have time on their hands.

They have to, but they don't waste time. When we shared a flat together in Tokyo, my friend Tahir introduced me to the novel idea that it was actually impossible to waste time. Everything has some return, but maybe not exactly what you expect or when you expect it. Even failure can enhance what will eventually work. What many call a waste of time is simply something that failed to come up to expectations. The problem lies with the expectations. Being present, being in the groove, living in a flow state – all these rely on diminishing expectations and simplifying behaviour. That said, you can easily waste a lot of time walking:

1. Fumbling with gates. Opening, dragging difficult ones, relatching.
2. Staring stupidly at gates once they are closed.
3. Checking gates are properly closed once you have closed them.

And add at each stage: the adjusting of the pack and clothing. And: checking the map.

Checking the map every five minutes for two minutes means wasting two hours in a seven-hour day of walking. This is an extreme example, but you get the picture. If you aren't careful to streamline your walking operation, you end up going very slowly indeed.

And crossing rivers is another great time-taker (yet not a time-waster, every river adds something). But you shouldn't hang about, in principle. And, of course, sometimes that principle is wrong.

I was trying to cross a river just past the village of Hartburn. But before I did that I was filling my water-bag to filter the water. It was probably clean enough but years of programming about dead sheep made me filter everything I drank. This river was going to be hard to cross, though, because of a deep section of fast current next to the far bank. I could get close but not close enough.

Then I heard someone coming with a dog, a bouncy red setter. I saw green wellies and the bottom of a tan coat beneath shrouding bushes at the river side. My first thought: 'Oh gawd, some local land-owner to tell me I can't cross here.' But it wasn't, it turned out to be Richard, the only friend I would really make while on this walk up my own country. Oh, I met people, I had chats, some quite long and irrelevant, and others very pleasant and time-passing. I walked with friends of course, but I would make no new ones – except Richard.

In another country I would expect to do just that; in Canada, it was hard *not* to make friends. Because in remote country you get close to people fast. In dangerous country the false barriers are down. You need to cut to the chase.

But back to Richard. He hadn't seen me, dressed as I was in green and crouched by the riverside filling water bottles. His hound came in and sniffed around and I petted him, but still I could tell I hadn't been seen so I broke through the overhanging trees on the bank to say hello.

Richard Cansdale was a vigorous and youthful-looking man who I guessed to be in his seventies. He was a lively talker and interested in my journey. 'I thought you were a deer down there!' was his opening line.

I later learnt his wife had died earlier in the year and he was still adjusting to it. I suspected they had talked a great deal; he had been a schoolteacher and he had a teacher's ability to be interested. As a roving couple, he and his wife had lived and worked in Africa in the 1960s, visiting Lake Chad in 1969 when it still had water in it.

I had wanted to rush on, but Richard persuaded me to walk back, retrace my steps, something I usually never do.

We went back along the river bank, where the river was deep and peat dark, to a hermit's cave or grotto. It had been enlarged to become an eighteenth-century folly, but it was older in origin, much older.

Above the slit of the cave entrance were two large niches (eighteenth century, I'd say) which I imagine once had statues in, now long gone. They looked like eyes and the slit cave was like the nose and mouth. Inside, there was an ecclesiastical-looking stone arch and additions to make the cave more room-like. Hartburn's energetic clergyman, Dr John Sharpe, who was behind all this, encouraged its use as a place for ladies to change before bathing in the deep pools we had just passed.

Richard now revealed something I would never have found on my own: a double line of postholes cut into the stone river bed that marked a truly ancient river crossing, used to aid crossing or support a bridge. Richard pointed across the stream and I thought I was going to have to pretend politely I could see the squarish holes in the rocky river bed. Not at all, they were obvious. And they lined up with an ancient track, a Roman road called Devil's Causeway that extended from Hadrian's Wall. Things that are named after the devil are just unknown, inexplicable, predating modernity. Beauty is never the devil's work but engineering can be.

Richard knew a safe way to cross that deviated a little from the obvious route of the postholes. He was like St Christopher, I felt, helping a wayfarer prevent a soaking. Would he have behaved like this if he had not lived in Africa and known the ways of places other than here? I think we have lost an old openness and old hospitality we once had, and only those who have travelled in inner space or across the world are courageous enough to now display it.

33

CAIRNS, CAVES AND TREES

I stayed in my first 'bunkhouse' last night. A bunkhouse is the new word for a hostel, now that motels and hotels and B&Bs are stupidly expensive and walkers only need a bunk, but might be put off by the requirement of youth in a youth hostel (which no longer applies but, nevertheless, you approach the hostel desk with slight trepidation – I mean, you're fifty and hoping to stay in a place with 'youth' in the title).

Actually Airbnbs in unpopular areas – shitty little rooms with wardrobes made of laminated chipboard, empty except for a single plastic hanger rocking gently in the breeze from the expectant and rapid disappointment of opening said wardrobe – those kind of Airbnbs are still to be had for around £20. But my bunkhouse was only £15 and because no one else was staying I had the entire bunkroom to myself. There were about twelve bunks in there – so if each had been occupied by a snoring, farting, wanking walker then £15 may not have seemed such a bargain. (I bring up wanking as a potential peril as I once stayed in a flashy youth hostel in Nice and one shifty little fellow spent the whole time in a half-pulled-up shabby sleeping bag, pleasuring himself with an unhurried selfishness while he beadily eyed everyone coming and going into the bunkroom. No matter what time of day it was, he'd be tucked away in the gloom on his bottom bunk, whacking off.)

So an empty bunkhouse is a boon.

Plus I can dry off my gear, get a shower, wash my quick-dry vest and Buffalo top, which amazingly always dries overnight. The bunkhouse is attached to a large pub called the Dog and Compass, which sets me thinking. Why would you need this combination of assistance? Perhaps lost, and instead of a St Bernard with a tot of rum, and predating GPS, the moorland rescue dog would bring a handy Silva compass attached to his collar to enable the lost walker to escape. The staff who are all young, wearing black trews and T-shirts with yellow Dog and Compass insignia picked out in yellow; the kind of people who could stay without shame in a youth hostel and are very nice but have absolutely no idea about the origins of the pub name.

The Dog and Compass in Rothbury. Now I really was far north, further north than the southernmost bit of Scotland. People – well, me – forget that Scotland starts on a massive slant. It's close to home at Carlisle but then snakes up and up the further east you go. I was level with most of the lowlands now and I could feel it. North as hell and loving it.

The Dog and Compass served a generous evening meal of bangers and mash. I ate in an airy old-style public bar with a great high ceiling and a long padded bench to sit on. Fellow diners were from Germany and spoke correct but limited English. They looked scared and bourgeois as hell, the kind who prefer to drive camper wagons so their contact with locals is reduced. Nothing about the way they over-perused the fairly crappy menu, to their ordering of 'local ale, please', commended them to me. And next to them, a grey couple who attended to their phones while eating their fish and chips.

Ah, but couldn't I have made the effort? Me, Mr Lonesome, who some days was managing about thirty words of conversation? Honestly, I felt I didn't need to. At long last, some kind of buried command that used to start bleeping 'talk to them, make conversation, make contact' whenever I found myself in similar situations in the past had finally died, or been switched off. I felt content within myself. I had my book, an account by a defector from Al-Qaeda who was recruited by Danish Intelligence (who chose to meet the defector in towns famous for prostitution; yep, Danish Intelligence really needs to think about the implications of promoting police vice officers into spying). The book was good, the food was good; they served my new favourite beer, Moretti. It was all good.

*

Alone in the breakfast room next morning, chewing silently and contemplating a heavy rucksack, I watched, without the usual instant judging, a single man, older than me, also well equipped for walking, come in and sit down. He laid his Tilley hat on his table and made for the cereal and juice stand. I nodded an early morning hello, already intuiting he was the kind who wanted to be left alone. 'Ey up,' he said without conviction. 'Grand day for it.' Then he set to, with a great crunching, on his Special K. There are few places where sound is so amplified as an almost empty breakfast room. It was as noisy as cracked church bells on a still summer morning. It made me self-conscious, so I chewed even more carefully and quietly so he wouldn't have to suffer the jaw-clicking and crunching I was hearing from him. Even with such precautions, you can't help hearing your own munching on cereal also carrying into every corner. The sun was streaming in through the large windows so it was a cheery, if noisy room.

I had crunchy overdone toast and very pleasant fried bread, also very crunchy. Crispy crunchy bacon. So did my fellow walker, after his crunchy cereal. His rucksack, like mine, was down near his feet. As soon as the waitress left after topping up his coffee, he reached down and retrieved a hip flask from the top pocket, the contents of which he poured into his coffee. Power assistance at 8.30 a.m. I'm always surprised by morning drinkers, they are never who you'd expect. I'm sure he didn't clock me clocking him, but as he left, cramming on his Tilley hat, he looked a lot more cheerful. 'Ay up,' he repeated with vim. 'Grand day for it.'

Up through the town, pleased I can find the right alleys to follow, relying on my sense of direction, which has got better over the last seven weeks. But am I fitter? Yes, despite persistent but manageable tendonitis in one Achilles. Up the bluff and through heather to the first standing stones. Mute and incomprehensible as ever, they look down over the riverside town below. The view is tremendous. I talk to a man on a mountain bike out for an early morning blast. Can't remember a thing of what we said except he knew two women on horseback who went by as we talked. An hour later I passed them again, and held a gate open for them, wondering how gracious they would be. Very. So my usual hatred of horse folk had to be shelved . . . until the next time.

For a while I walk along a wide track running alongside a forest, then I cut down to a farmstead and through a gap that looks very easy and reasonable. There is a newly cut track to the farm, harshly cut through the close-cropped turf. It is made of orangey stone, imported. It's darn ugly but I follow it. And then I realise it's taking me off course. I look at my watch, double back as far as I can bear and start following a fence line. If in doubt, follow a marked fence line. And after a while of ploughing upwards through a deep and browning sea of bracken, conscious that it harbours Lyme-disease-carrying ticks (I walk with elbows held ridiculously high) and seeking the patch of bald ground under a gnarled and windblown thorn on the side of a hill, I realise I am completely lost.

I know that sometimes – like finding my way through the alleyways of the town earlier this morning – I have my direction-finding head on. Then I lost it. I got to hoping instead of intuiting. They can feel almost the same but they really are different approaches.

So many ways to get lost: when walking with others, both think the other is the pathfinder; then there's not looking ahead to what the next fifteen minutes should bring; ignoring the context and over-focusing on the path. Then there's the failure to read contours properly. This last is almost excusable because the latest OS 25K maps have *far too much information* on them, including contours that are too close (5m instead of the more sensible 10m) so, unlike the beautifully drawn first and second series 25k maps, it isn't always obvious which way is up and which is down.

When you're lost what do you do? Backtrack to the last known place where you were sure where you were. This is obviously the best plan, but what if the last place was a dishearteningly long distance back? Too far back for you to contemplate? In my case, it would be several miles. I'm not doing that. There must be another way. If the land is visible all around, you look for hills, steeples, and my absolute

favourite: pylons and powerlines. Every single pylon is marked accurately on an OS map, so you can pinpoint your exact spot quite easily.
Oh yeah, GPS does that too, doesn't it? Yes, if you have coverage or if
your batteries aren't flat. Anyway England's landscape is tame enough
without taming it further with technology.

My grandfather's favourite: if in doubt, climb a tall tree. The stunted
thorn won't do, but there's a block of stone, as big as a house, rising
out of the bracken up ahead. That will have a view, for sure.

More ploughing through damp and insect-laden bracken to the
foot of the crag, which has a cave halfway up. It's more of a slit entrance than a cave mouth, but still worth a look en route to the top.
It decides my way up. Should be fine – some big stone lips, eroded
yellow and pockmarked in between, stick out; I can hoist my way up
these.

Amazing how fast you can get quite high up: puzzle out a few moves
and, by jingo, you've a nasty fall's height off the boulder-strewn slope,
which you definitely don't want to land on. It gets harder too, as I get
higher. My nose level with the base of the cave – OK, been there done
that (it is cave, all right, but only good for hiding out, no one lived
here I surmise) – and I move on.

It's hard! I have to concentrate, having first castigated myself for
making a series of moves which will be hard to reverse. Never climb
up what you can't climb down . . . I twist a little to see across the sea
of bracken, which I am now thirty feet above, and spot hills and some
woods in the distance. If I can just hang on long enough to get to the
top . . .

I stick my arms far into a horizontal crack and shudder along side-
ways on them, my feet skidding on micro footholds. This is all very
well but getting out from this position is tricky. I need to reach up
gingerly up and over to the top of the crag. If it slopes or there is
no jug (a large hold) for me to swing out on, I fear I'm doomed. I'll
be stuck like my son used to get stuck in the magnolia tree in our
garden, but with no Daddy to come running out to rescue me . . .

Scrabble, scrabble and my luck is in; a dip so deep it contains a
puddle right near the edge. So hefty, I can swing one-handed on it

and feel safe. Up and over, and on the top I can see for miles. I stand in a crouch, not quite believing I'm secure yet. The residue of fear gives way fast to elation, though.

I really take my time identifying the peaks across the moor. I see that I went wrong way back, before I got to the farm. I should have kept close to the treeline.

So my first task is to find an easy way down – there is one, of course – and wade on across more bracken and boggy looking moor. Which I do.

It is touching; a group of walkers see me foundering through the now boggy, now deep-sprung heathery moor and wait at the forest gate for me; they are worried I may be lost. I wave to them cheerily as I get within hailing distance, making it easier for them to melt away and not have to voice their concerns face to face, only to have them heartily rebutted; *I may have been lost a while ago, but I am certainly not lost now, no sir!*

My path goes past three hilltops with three cairns: not just a regular pile of old stones, pyramid fashion, the kind that adorns most peaks over 2000 feet, but a little enclave or roofless hut; actually an ancient hollow cairn with an entrance made of stones no bigger than hand-sized pebbles. It is recorded as being thousands of years old and yet made of something so easily carted away. Cairns are impressive in their own way. In North Borneo, the Lundaya tribe showed me a huge cromlech on top of a great cairn of river boulders close to the border of Kalimantan. Partly, you have to admire all the labour involved, and partly the fact that if you build a big enough pile of something it *will* remain.

The hill I am climbing is now part of the forest; the trees are well spaced and I can peek through branches to see the expanding view below. Like all views that surprise, it gives a feeling of uplift, sudden joy. Only one more range of hills and I should be able to see the sea.

Further on, I'm reminded it's a day for getting lost and a day for caves. The path is an ancient one, cut through the peaty topsoil into the rooty sand below. Heather blooms over the path, obscuring it; and sometimes the path is no wider than a rabbit run. I am not tuned in because the distracting scenery is sunlit and mysterious; I am in another world. I pass a pond, high up on the ridge of the ancient forested hills. Ah, that's my water source, I think for some reason. Then, having lost the path, I see something up ahead – a snatch of blue behind a low fir tree.

It is half cave, half prepper's hideout, entrance concealed by the fir. Preppers are preparing for the end of the world. I know a couple. And one of my friends sells gear to them on the internet. 'You'd be surprised,' he tells me. 'My best customers are single women with good jobs – doctors and lawyers stocking up on food and fuel for a year in advance . . .' Preppers sometimes put their faith in bunkers they build at home, and sometimes in 'bug-out' shelters like this one. The well prepared have both. It's an all-consuming and fascinating lifestyle predicated on doom and gloom.

The blue that I glimpsed is a waterproof plastic roof tarp, which, in turn, is further disguised by branches. Inside, the little room is neatly swept and equipped for occupancy; there's even a stick broom to keep the earth floor clean. At one end, there is an oil drum stove, stove pipe, a firewood bag and a supplies box. There is a kind of wooden backrest for sitting, which has accumulated some harm-less euro-graffiti by the look of it: a cute munching rabbit and some meaningless initials and names and greetings that don't seem quite English ('hello granda'?).

I know from the map there is another ex-hermit's cave near by, but not here, since I know now I went wrong. Did the modern hermit, preparing for the meltdown of twenty-first-century society, pick this place because of the other cave, the suggestion of it? Or, as I sus-pect, because this place is special? Just down the hill from me is the hermit's real cave and then a mystical fort, which is the last big one before Lindisfarne.

It is all downhill now, steep rabbit-run paths where you constantly have to choose which fork to take. And it's not always the most well-trodden. I am cave-alert but I need not be: the hermit's cave is obvious. It has been hewn from a giant boulder forty feet high, letterbox shaped – well, an upright letterbox the size of a door. It is a door-shaped slot in curving rock, reached by a cut ledge about three metres or so off the ground. Easy to slip on an icy day . . . Inside, the cave is small and the door has obviously been enlarged by cutting. There is enough room to kip and maybe hold court to one other initiate. Otherwise all preaching could be done quite conveniently by sitting on the ledge and talking down to a crowd below. The more I think of it, the more this cave resembles a pulpit. For preaching about the end of the world . . .

The mystical fort or ancient camp above Rothbury was the first I had encountered in all my walking along the Line that made use of a natural rock formation rather than just the shape of a hill. Indeed, the crack descending into its rocky base reminded me somewhat of an ancient oracle. The dug earthworks of the camp enclosed a rocky chamber that led down into the cave entrance, partially blocked. More likely it was a way to get water; perhaps this was the first camp/henge/fort that had its own water supply within it? For it seems odd that all these so-called defensive structures have no water in them; near by, granted, but near is not good enough if you are surrounded and besieged. Of course this is probably because they are not primarily defensive structures. They are symbolic, religious structures with a meaning way beyond our ideas of 'war' and 'defence'.

I look down on the fort/camp from the hill above, under the sway of the giant, languorous beech trees. There is something very strange about these beeches: I am convinced they are enchanted. The trunks are outsize and fabulously convoluted; the ground-brushing branches are immensely long and thick: a class of schoolkids could all sit and rock on one comfortably.

In a dip between the roots swirling out from one trunk's base, I brew up tea and then lie back, looking up at the canopy. At first my interest is purely photographic. I try to get the exposure right to make the capillary-like twigs and branches show up black against the opalescent green of the sunlit leaves. Then the green in all its varying shades begins to take hold of my imagination. I simply stare at the leaves. Each one is a different shade; the range isn't huge but the minute differences intrigue, leave me mesmerised. Then I start to focus on how the leaves connect to the thinnest, almost invisible twigs that lead to the branches and then to the trunks and the Earth itself. The fully functioning whole is intuited as a whole, not a series of parts. And nestling within the roots I am of the Earth too!

Suddenly, I realise the genius of the people who sited the camp here. They knew the ground was special, would grow these giant trees, would entice people for centuries, thousands of years after the camp was built; such knowledge makes the comic barbarism, the Klingon-inspired architecture of such monstrosities as the Burj Khalifa in Dubai and the London Shard seem infantile by comparison. To be able to intuit the right thing to build for the right place – not just some kind of banal architectural aesthetic of 'fitting in with the surroundings' – I am talking a full-blown shamanic awareness of the Truth of a place; now that, I believe, is real sophistication.

In retrospect, I will come to think of this experience as the highpoint of the journey. All the elements come into alignment. I understand what is at stake: the need to trust oneself wholeheartedly yet without obsession. The ability to avoid attractive and easy false certainty and at the same time skirt conventional self-doubt. To tune in to something much quieter and calmer than our usual idea of a 'feeling' or 'intuition'. To be calm enough to register it and not get over excited and lose the thread. It is after all threads I am following, spinning them together, making my way north.

It was appropriate, then, that this, my last night on the trail, should be at another ancient fort, even more remote, on private land and unvisited by anyone for years by the look of it.

But first, on the way there, I had to descend and again walk the lanes of Northumberland, which didn't bother me because they were utterly deserted. Hardly one car in half an hour: something unheard of in the choked South where I started my journey.

In the absolute middle of nowhere (i.e. between villages about two miles apart), I went past a couple of isolated bungalows and could hear the rise-and-fall sound of a chainsaw at work. I couldn't hear the usual snatch and bite of someone hacking at a tree, so I assumed it was a homeowner sawing up logs for winter. But as I rounded the corner, I saw at the end of longish drive, a man in overalls with a flimsy mask on and a helmet, sawing away at a sizeable lump of wood; in fact, it was a veritable tree trunk a good eight foot tall and as broad as a door; and as I focused (i.e., couldn't believe my eyes at first) I saw that it was a life-size wooden sculpture of Yogi Bear . . . and there, next to it, half-wrapped in plastic, was a small one of his sidekick, Boo-Boo.

There are few things more heartening than to see people doing the hobbies they love, and wacko hobbies done for pure love – this had to be one of those – are the most heartening of all. Imagine the snickers and yawns the poor Yogi sculptor must endure. Everyone must be laughing at him except kids under the age of eight, maybe seven. And yet he soldiers on, day after day, chain-sawing away at his damn good likeness, I must admit, of the legendary cartoon bear. What guts, what moral courage! A true Yogi yogi – I salute you!

This sight really spurred me on. Yes, spurred on in trainers now; and after dropping an ibuprofen – which, it has to be said, does work such wonders with foot pain that you have to suspect it is *very* wrong – anyway, on and on to the last fort, which was deep within a plantation owned and run by a local bigwig landowning family.

Not necessarily a bad thing; especially when, as I entered the woods, I noticed a sign saying that though it wasn't a public right of way, people were welcome to use it. Give me old money any day over the newly minted: landed gentry with noblesse oblige over the prick who earned it all himself and then bought a country pile to try to imitate everyone else since the beginning of the Roman occupation of Britain, and who puts up his barbed wire and security buzzers; yes, that bastard. One I knew actually bankrupted his neighbour over an argument involving footpaths through his property. The neighbour, a foolhardy local, was no match for the team of lawyers the nouveau riche biche managed to field. In the end, the poor twit, who only wanted to ride his bike where he had always ridden it (the previous owner being a generous old country squire), lost his house in order to pay the £50,000 bill. And when I asked the big cheese, the man who did this crime, if he had ever even met his neighbour, he said without a flicker of shame that he had not; he had only communicated with him through lawyers. Imagine if, on the first day of the misunderstanding, he had instead taken a crate of wine round to his fellow foolhardy human and talked it out?

So, old money – not to be sniffed at.

It is darkening now and I hurry through the wood. Pheasants squawk up and disappear over the high banks. The path swerves left, a sandy cut with fading Land Rover tracks. I pace it off from the 'Y' junction because I suspect the fort will be invisible, hidden deep in the woods.

I know my pace now very accurately: 654 steps a kilometre and it is exactly – well, pretty much – 200 paces to the turn into the woods. But when I get there, all I see is extraordinarily high bracken interspersed with thorn bushes and stinging nettles. And everywhere rotting logs, holes from unearthed root plates and pointless ditches. No, not pointless: these are the remains of the ramparts and the moat; I am actually at the edge of the fort now. It is an illusion of sorts but the higher ground further on, through more tangled undergrowth, looks less densely vegetated. It is, a bit. There are more felled logs, telegraph-pole-like larches lying in criss-cross, casually lopped fashion. I use one as a seat and hack away at the ground thereabouts to make a crappy but usable campsite. Bumpy, rooty; well, I have my mat, even though it could have been better, should have been better for my last night on the trail. But in another way it is perfect. I am inside an ancient place, I have walked the Great North Line. Almost.

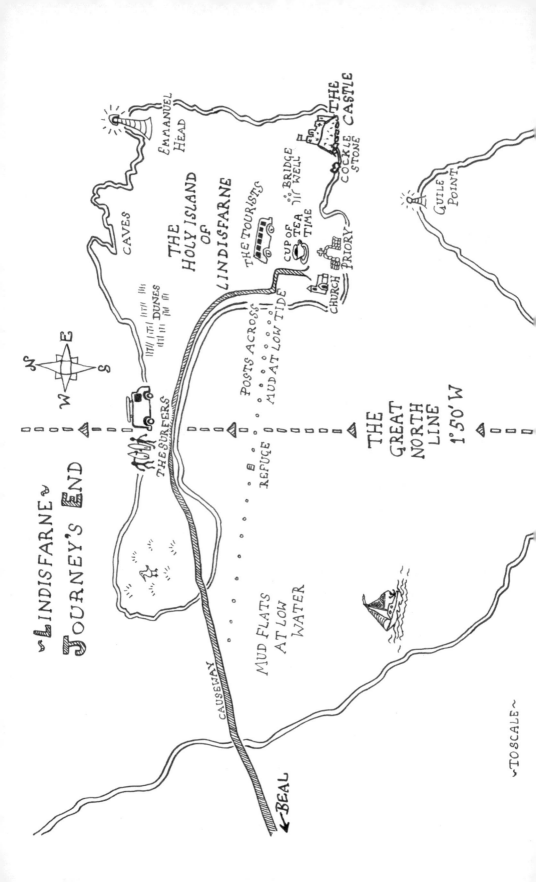

Lindisfarne & Journey's End

THE HOLY ISLAND OF LINDISFARNE

EMMANUEL HEAD

THE COCKLE CASTLE STONE

CAVES

THE TOURISTS

BRIDGE WELL

CUP OF TEA TIME

CHURCH

PRIORY

GUILE POINT

DUNES

THE SURFERS

POSTS ACROSS MUD AT LOW TIDE

REFUGE

THE GREAT NORTH LINE 1°50'W

MUD FLATS AT LOW WATER

CAUSEWAY

←BEAL

~TO SCALE~

34

LINDISFARNE

You can see Lindisfarne for hours before you get there. Hours. I was up before dawn and crashing out of my wood, finding an old logging trail that was easier than the bushwhacking of the day before. My face was itching – I'd been royally savaged by mosquitoes in the night, first time apart from a few odd gnat bitelets on the moors. Oh well, last day, soldier on. Down through the village of Eglingham, up onto another moor, more road and then a ridge – and there's the sea and Lindisfarne.

It appears in silhouette, a long seahorse of an island, its tail the long causeway to the north. The bulk of it displays a mystery castle profile, like the wondrous sight of Mont Saint-Michel or the Lizard peninsula in Cornwall, only lower and more stretched out; no wonder those Vikings came back for more and more.

It encloses a number of bays you can easily see, so the first accidental visit by Viking explorers was probably quite peaceable. I imagine the poor monks may even have entertained their future murderers before the slaughter. Perhaps they even had thoughts of converting these obvious barbarians, who were so admiring of their sacramental gold. Perhaps they showed them the relics of St Cuthbert and the wonderfully illustrated Lindisfarne Gospels in lapis-tinted blue and gold.

But what must have decided the Vikings, with their cowardly, thieving minds, was the incredible fact that this was no peninsula: half the day, it was an island, entirely undefended and with no chance of relief from the mainland (bar the odd rowing boat). It must have been like finding out the alarms were turned off at the bank during the lunch hour . . .

Sneaking back to Vik's Land, somewhere in modern Denmark, the nasty cut-throats plan their raid with skill and cunning. It's a smash-and-grab. Take all the gold, the tapestries; all the booze you haven't drunk already, even if they trip on their wine-soaked beards, running hogsheads down to the long ships. Turn up on two sides of the island at dawn on a high tide; absolutely no chance of escape except for the monks to cower in the dunes. But many monks stand and fight with nothing but sticks and knives, to be cut down in the church, which the invaders finally burn. But probably not on the first raid.

Oh yes, there'd be more raids – and then all along the coast, when, even with the tide out, no one comes to the rescue. From a robber's perspective, nothing could be more perfect. In AD 793, a day of infamy on an island that had underestimated the skulduggery of men who worship war. The direct line from Vikings to Normans to Teutonic Knights to Prussians … It only takes a few determined men who believe strength brings rights rather than obligations.

There is an awful lot of history surrounding Lindisfarne and most of it is to do with the early Church. But before that, we know there were settlers here. Neolithic and even Palaeolithic finds have been made. We know that Lindisfarne was occupied when Doggerland was still in existence, the land that once connected Britain to Europe. Then the spot would have been the first serious hill for miles. Just like Hengistbury Head all those miles south, a definite landmark and steering point. Was it any surprise that the Vikings headed straight for it on one of their first away days? It was *the* landmark that said here is a new land.

So thousands of years earlier, just as the glaciers were retreating, people streamed across from Europe to explore this new land. There were no paths so they went in a straight line. And by some quirk of geography due south, they passed through Thor's Cave and (almost) Hengistbury Head: the only other two 'fixed' points. Everything else could be built to order – and perhaps it was. If our interpretation of the sophistication of prehistoric man is correct, there was nothing strange about their sticking to a central line; it is no stranger than the formation of our own dead straight, but exoteric, power lines.

*

Coming down to the start of the causeway entails a walk across marsh-land and tidal grassland, riddled with saltwater ditches and overhanging turf which make the ditch seem less wide than it is. I vault a few to keep on track, wending a tedious path parallel to the island before I can get across to it. It seems a bugger that the three-mile causeway is at the opposite end to the castle and all the interesting bits.

Seagulls wheeling and calling, I get up onto the road where cars are parked with engines idling. We are all waiting for the all-clear, for when it is safe to cross. The road is still puddled with newly departed tidewater. You can see the water level dropping right in front of your eyes. I think about Morecambe Bay and the scallop fishers who drowned there; on such a flat, open space the water moves almost instantly . . .

The causeway is partly lifted by wooden pilings, a great length of them, and then some iron ones where it forms a bridge in the middle. I scamper across the narrow bridge. Once over, I walk on the mud, watching each footprint fill with water as I step forwards.

Two backpackers keep pace with me on the other side of the road. We both stop to look at the mackerel cloud formation. They crack first and take a photo. Though it might look like I am copying them, I take a picture too. 'It's great sky, isn't it?' the girl says and I grinningly agree.

Alongside the causeway the dunes rise up, over fifty feet high with coarse marram grass and strange little ways through to the sea-shore hidden beyond. This coast is good for waves. I saw their van, a Mercedes Sprinter, the favoured ride of the post-hipster hipster, the kind who wouldn't be seen dead in a Jamie-style VW camper. The door slid back, and, with a lazy grace, a couple in their late thirties finished putting on their wet suits, a process started in the van. Boards on the roof, the woman had that leathery but attractive skin you get from a subtle combination of sun and smoking, before you've smoked for too long. He had the wavy hair and blue eyes of a man in a commercial for surfing.

My God, they were living the dream but just on the cusp, right at the very edge, nearly forty, the point of no return; in mid-life, like surfing, you start going for a wave and there comes a point when it takes you, and then all you can do is hang on tight and do your best and enjoy it for as long as it goes. Until the beach brings an ending of sorts, the sad sink as the board loses momentum and your ankles dip under water. Either that or a catastrophic tumble that leaves you wearing your teeth down on a mouthful of wet sand.

I had friends like this; maybe I'd even been a bit like it before. You think youth or rather youthful inclinations will go on forever. You don't despise the old, you may even value them, but only if they are 'cool' and act younger than their years. The stuffy kind of oldster who stays home and watches TV and keeps out of draughts, you despise. But they are still the elders! They are the ones who won!

I now saw in those neat gardens and polished Honda Jazzes a broad smile of triumph – and surely anyone who has made it that far deserves our praise. But what they know they can't easily pass on. It's tacit knowledge of the deepest kind, and they hardly know they have it. Yet in its acceptance, in our submission to it even, lie the roots of wisdom.

Oh, I love the idea of surfing too. Like in the ads. Some guys even surfed in Norway every day for a year right up near the Arctic Circle. But even they went home one day, to edit their video. Surfing is what you do in your holidays. Like walking?

Or am I just caving into pessimism?

Lindisfarne is a massive tourist spot, just like Stonehenge. Both on the Line, both exerting a massive magnetic pull. Tourists may be scum (oh, of course they are!) but in their unconscious lemming-like behaviour, or elver-like swimming, they nose unconsciously to the source of something. They are here like I am here – for a very good reason.

The Line starts here. Am I really saying, then, that the builders of Sarum and Avebury, the excavators of Thor's Cave and the diggers of Mam Tor all decided to line up with this little island?

Admittedly, it is the only island on or near the central meridian of Britain (2° West). It is the only island on or near the watershed line of England. It would be an obvious choice for anything connected with the notion of 'heart, core, essential'.

But now I am here, all I see after my long trudge over the causeway are tour buses and fields full of parked cars.

I was really in a strange place in my head, almost nervous of making contact of any kind. I ummed and ahhed about which pub or coffee shop in which to get refreshment and 'celebrate'; but hadn't the whole walk been a celebration? I was, as I usually am at the end of a big endeavour, a bit disoriented, rather nonplussed.

Eventually I saw a coffee shop that had plenty of space inside. All the tour buses had debouched their contents. They had found their way into most places and it was annoying, of course, to have to share. A bit like walking round Stratford if you're a Shakespeare fan ('No, I *really* like Shakespeare'). But that wasn't it.

I really didn't mind them and strong in my awareness was the knowledge – deployed often – that I was just a tourist too, even if I had walked over 400 miles or so to be here. Yes, I didn't mind them and I located a long bench and table in the café, where I sat alone at one end with my out-of-place rucksack and poles, all a bit damp as it had been raining. But the other people seemed like aliens, as they often do in such circumstances.

The middle-aged owner was working with her family, I surmised, and they were doing a grand job of rattling through the orders. I sat with my cake and coffee and watched a man of about seventy-five, skinny with grey, longish hair, a mac like the navy blue kind that were once issued to schoolkids as part of a uniform, shoes that were angular and misshapen; Seventies shoes, I thought. But most interesting of all was the fact that his trousers were at least four inches too short. *Way* too short. You could see a good two inches of pale blue-veined flesh above his fawn socks.

I looked to see if his trousers were snagged up in some way. They were not. Was the man mentally ill? Didn't look it. A bit shaky, a bit careful, but pretty ordinary ordering his pot of tea. He was with someone, but who I couldn't see as they were sitting around a corner. And after a lot of staring I went to look but they had gone. A mystery person and a man with ludicrous trousers.

The whole incident was amazingly heartening. It proved you could be completely oblivious to taste and decorum and still live until you were seventy-five. Here was a non-conformist of the highest order, a total freak really, calmly going about his business. I had nothing on this guy. I was Caspar Milquetoaste the Third compared to him.

And really, 'ole shorty' tied off a lot of important ends for this journey. From this frail and almost ludicrous symbol, I found a kind of mini-enlightenment, I saw that identity and the search for it are inextricably linked to the daring capacity to be a non-conformist, an eccentric. It is how you survive. It is one secret of the elders. A great power, one that should be carefully nurtured. I know I might not sound serious. But I am.

Oh yes, the castle. It looked *great*. Like something out of a Viking movie. The battlements really did grow out of the rock, forming a seamless impregnable whole. And there was a winding path up to the castle, which was tempting, but just as with Old Sarum, I didn't pay. Went up to the ticket desk and turned back. Only a tenner, but I didn't want to. Again a ton of dumbass tourists slip-sliding on the cobbles in their inappropriate footwear, but that wasn't exactly it.

This journey was about the Line, not the dots on the Line. The essence of a place may be the baby and not the mother . . . I remembered how all those camps and henges had a 'moon' that was in play with the 'sun' of the main construction. Where was the 'moon' here? The old ruined priory? Nope. (Again, you had to pay to enter.) A 'moon' doesn't have to be free, but when it isn't, some kind of force directs you elsewhere. Not just stinginess: it is as if, once a place has been commoditised, it loses some special dimension; some 'free bonus' that accrues over the centuries.

Which I found in Lindisfarne church, St Mary's. An ordinary parish church, though very likely built on the site of the very first

church on the island. The right spot. It had an almost full visitors'
book, which I signed:

Robert Twigger, from Christchurch, Dorset, by foot all the way.
Summer 2018.

This was a walk in which freedom of a sort was tested. My freedom
to do as I pleased, sleep and walk where I pleased. And freedom also
includes not paying for things that are ours by rights, by the right of
ancient England. The right to roam and the right to kip down in a
different place every night.

The old rights, the old rites.

NOTES

1 Answer: six foot by three foot, a grave space. Tolstoy's 'How Much Land does a Man Need' is a beautiful traditional tale.

2 One that has taken a new turn in the fascinating and erudite *Red Thread* by Charlotte Higgins (Jonathan Cape, 2018).

3 The Norse cosmic tree Yggdrasill is now thought to be a yew, not an ash.

4 A reference to Yogi Bear that will bear fruit later in the book, I promise . . .

5 *The Hundred Tales of Wisdom*, translated and introduced by Idries Shah (ISF, reprinted 2018).

6 David Lewis-Williams, *The Mind in the Cave* (Thames and Hudson, 2002); Jean Clottes, *What is Paleolithic Art?* (University of Chicago Press, 2016).

7 Jeremy Narby, *The Cosmic Serpent* (Weidenfeld & Nicolson, 1999).

8 Nigel decided to attempt the Camino Way in Spain as an attempt to beat his depression. I hoped the walking he had done with me had helped him make that decision. It was a wise decision because he completed the walk and made some new friends along the way. His depression cured, and he ended up at a commune in Spain where he took on the job of marketing their wine, which he does to this day.

9 Courtesy of Michael Symmons Roberts and Paul Farley's great book *Edgelands* (Vintage, 2012).

10 Katy Jordan, *Wells in Depth* (Living Spring Journal, 2000).

11 *Bell's Weekly Messenger* 1860.

12 The latest research into epigenetics shows that learnt characteristics *can* be passed on. See: Brian G. Dias et al., 'Epigenetic mechanisms underlying learning and the inheritance of learned behaviours'. *Trends in Neuroscience.* 38(2), February 2015.

13 Tacitus, *Germania*.

14 Meaning 'rancid', 'distasteful'.

15 John Zada, *In the Valleys of the Noble Beyond* (Grove Atlantic, 2019).

16 John Nicholson, *Poems* (1859).

17 A quote from the movie *Bladerunner*, implies great worldly wisdom.

18 Tiny bits of grit in between pole sections can freeze the pole and make it impossible to collapse.

19 A ring round the penis, though in this context the customer (and wife) wrongly thought it was a ring *through* the penis from which said penis could be hung . . . well hung, you might say.

20 My own clumsy coinage, meaning a tolerance of the units we customarily speak of things in, and a reluctance to assume 'breaking things down into parts' will increase understanding.

21 Inspired by Heisenberg's uncertainty principle: you can know either the position or momentum of a particle but not both.

22 This was actually pointed out by the man in the village, a titbit of insider info, which interesting though it is, I bitterly contest; really, it's the kind of thing corporate types convince themselves is real knowledge when it isn't.

23 William Dixon, the compiler of the oldest collection of bagpipe music in the British Isles, came from Stamfordham.

ACKNOWLEDGEMENTS

Books take their toll. Though some are chuffed to be included, others cavil and some demur; quite are few are simply unaware of how important they have been to the process. A whole caravan of people go to make a book and they include, in no order of significance (since I am sure to miss a few), Ramsay Wood, Gill Whitworth, Anthony McGowan, Patrick Barkham, Miguel I. Vey, Christopher Ross, John Seldon, John West, Rich Lisney, Stephan Otto, William Coles, Margot Coles, Jessica Fox Adrian Turpin, Shaun Bythell, Tahir Shah, Tarquin Hall, Jason Webster, Salud Botella, Rachel Barker, Tony Twigger, Jean Ingram Twigger, Clare Twigger-Ross, Aaron Fuest, Jo Whitford, Alan Samson, Matthew Hamilton, Nigel Hale, Joseph Gillingham, John Zada, David Fitzherbert, Sonali Fitzherbert, Justin Rushbrooke, Nell Butler, John-Paul Flintoff, Jason Goodwin, Patrick Twigger, Catherine Twigger, Al Twigger, Dahlia Twigger, Samia Hosny, the nice people who agreed to walk with me but couldn't be fitted in, and the couple who gave me the lift to Harrogate in the driving rain. *Salut!* Edward Hinnant of Cedar Tree Industry very kindly gave me a free Packa – an excellent item of raingear that covers man and rucksack – that served me well. http://www.thepacka.com

INDEX